PELICAN BOOKS

PUBLIC EXPENDITURE

Professor Andrew Likierman graduated in Philosophy, Politics and Economics from Balliol College, Oxford. He qualified as a management accountant while working for Tootal Ltd. and then became the managing director of the Overseas Division of Qualitex Ltd. He was a member of the Central Policy Review Staff ('Think Tank') and before joining the London Business School in 1979 lectured at Leeds University. He has been an adviser to the House of Commons Treasury and Civil Service Select Committee since 1980 and has advised other Select Committees on public expenditure matters. He is a council member of the Royal Institute of Public Administration and the Chartered Institute of Management Accountants.

ANDREW LIKIERMAN

Public Expenditure

THE PUBLIC SPENDING PROCESS

PENGUIN BOOKS

PENGUIN BOOKS

Published by the Penguin Group
27 Wrights Lane, London w8 5tz, England
Viking Penguin Inc., 40 West 23rd Street, New York, New York 10010, USA
Penguin Books Australia Ltd, Ringwood, Victoria, Australia
Penguin Books Canada Ltd, 2801 John Street, Markham, Ontario, Canada l3r 1b4
Penguin Books (NZ) Ltd, 182–190 Wairau Road, Auckland 10, New Zealand

Penguin Books Ltd. Registered Offices: Harmondsworth, Middlesex, England

First published 1988

Made and printed in Great Britain by
Richard Clay Ltd, Bungay, Suffolk
Filmset in Monophoto Ehrhardt

CONTENTS

vi   *Public Expenditure*

PREFACE

When first trying to learn about the public expenditure process I looked in vain for something which explained how it all worked. Later, when asked by others for a source, I was only able to point to a collection of official documents and other writings. Some of these were highly technical, others covered only parts of the subject. So eventually I decided to bring material from many sources together, hoping that others would have less of a struggle than I did.

Having completed the book, it is much clearer why there was originally nothing of the kind I was looking for. Some parts of the subject are technically complex. It involves at least some knowledge of economics, politics and accountancy. You, the reader, may be an economics undergraduate wanting to know something about the politics of public spending, a politics 'A'-level student with no knowledge of economics, or a student of accountancy with a first degree in astronomy. You may even be someone who picked the book up on a whim, wondering where all your taxes went. But did you leave school at sixteen, or do you have a doctorate in British politics?

Since I don't know who you are, this book has to be a compromise. It assumes, wherever possible, a minimal knowledge of the subject. But some parts – the definition of public expenditure in Chapter 1, the formal parliamentary procedures in Chapter 7 and the details of audit in Chapter 8 – have a good deal of technical detail for those who need to know about detail. Just glance at them if you don't, because above all the idea is to give an overview.

For this reason the book cannot hope to do justice to certain parts of the process, such as the more technical economic aspects and the evolving role of management. I hope, nevertheless, that it will be a useful source for those at school, university, or studying for professional examinations. I hope it will also be useful to those working in the public sector

who want an introduction to how and why decisions about their resources
are made. Finally, I hope it will provide a guide for those who are simply
interested in a better understanding of a key area of policy-making and
decision-taking in the United Kingdom.

This, of course, is why public expenditure itself is so important. We
all benefit from it. Our schools and universities, our hospitals and roads,
our defence and our police are part of it. We all contribute to it, directly
through taxes on income or indirectly through taxes on some of what we
buy. This importance means that public expenditure is very much a
'living' subject. So policy is made all the time and arrangements are
subject to constant review. While this is exciting and interesting, it also
means that you will need to keep up to date with developments.

Like any other specialist subject, public expenditure is full of jargon
and initials. Terms are explained where they first appear and there is a
technical glossary for reference. Some acronyms – VAT, BBC – will be
familiar. Others – PAC, RSG, NAO – may be quite new territory.
Acronyms are set out in each chapter where they appear and a full list is
given at the end of the book.

I am particularly grateful to those who gave their help and advice in
writing this book. Funding and general support of my work in this area
has been provided by the Chartered Association of Certified Accountants. Help with research work was provided by Ernst and Whinney.
Officials from a number of government departments, especially the
Treasury, most kindly and courteously answered many detailed questions. Acknowledgements for permission to reproduce passages are due
to Basil Blackwell (*Getting and Spending* by Leo Pliatzky); Andre Deutsch
(Joel Barnett's *Inside the Treasury*); the Controller of HMSO for several
sources; Methuen (*Policy-Making in a Three-Party System* by Ian
Marsh); the Public Finance Foundation (*Public Domain 1987*); and Sidgwick & Jackson (*Ministers and Mandarins* by J. Bruce-Gardyne). A
number of individuals gave invaluable help with various parts of the
text. Above all, I am indebted to Susan Bloomfield and Kenneth Kehoe
for their careful and helpful background research. I would also like to
thank Pauline Creasey, David Higson and Jane Partington for help on
various parts of the text and for the friendly assistance of a number of
colleagues, particularly Norman Flynn, Sue Richards and Ellie Scrivens.
I am most grateful for the comments of Priscilla Baines, David Dewar,
Clive Holtham, Geoffrey Hulme, Peter Jackson, Clifford Judd, Malcolm
Levitt, Bill McKay and John Whiteoak on parts of earlier drafts. Took

Card and Stephanie Macauley most patiently helped to type and edit successive redrafts of the manuscript. Finally, I am indebted to Meira my wife for all her encouragement to get the book finished, and to Andrew Franklin of Penguin without whose amiable bullying the book would still be something I would like to have done 'one day'.

London, 1987 A.L.

NOTE IN PROOF

As the book was in proof, the government announced that it proposed to accept the recommendations of the Treasury and Civil Service Select Committee and discontinue publication of the Public Expenditure White Paper. Summary information on public expenditure plans now in Volume 1 would be published in an expanded Autumn Statement from November 1988. Volume 2 of the Public Expenditure White Paper would be split into departmental booklets from January 1989. The remaining information in Volume 1 would be published separately in a form still to be decided.

These arrangements will last until 1991, when the departmental booklets would be published as departmental reports in March each year. The reports would contain a link to the Supply Estimates.

Alterations to various aspects of Parliamentary activity stem from these proposals. There would be no Treasury and Civil Service Select Committee report on the Public Expenditure White Paper and no February public expenditure debate on the floor of the House of Commons. So the debate on the Autumn Statement would become the main opportunity for the House as a whole to deal with overall public expenditure policy. What further debate on public expenditure matters would take place was still to be decided.

The above changes are subject to the results of consultations, so readers interested in these aspects of public expenditure will need to check on which arrangements were finally confirmed. It is also worth noting that detailed decisions were pending on several other important areas at the time of going to press, notably the precise form of the Community Charge.

I

INTRODUCTION: THE FINANCING, CALCULATION AND GROWTH OF PUBLIC EXPENDITURE

Public money is like holy water. Everyone helps himself to it. (Italian proverb)

The first part of this chapter explains where the money to finance public expenditure comes from. The second part deals with how it is defined and calculated. Finally, there is an analysis of how public spending has grown and some of the theories about why that growth has taken place.

Where the money comes from

In this world nothing can be said to be certain, except death and taxes. (Benjamin Franklin)

It may be that death and taxation are inevitable. But at least death only comes once. (Anon.)

Some of the money to finance public spending can come from the sale of goods and services by a variety of public bodies. Some can come from cash raised by local government through local taxes and charges for services, such as rent for housing. Some can come from borrowing. Some can even come from the sale of nationalized industries or public housing. But the bulk of the money has to come from taxation raised by central government, and today's complex pattern of taxation reflects many different influences in the century or so since the significant growth of public expenditure first had to be financed.

The need to raise revenue has of course been the foremost consideration among these influences but, in meeting this need, those devising the taxes have had to be aware of a number of key principles, including:

- efficiency in collection. Some taxes (for example, those on capital gains) are very expensive for the government to collect. Others, such as Value Added Tax (VAT), put a heavy administrative burden on the taxpayer.

- the importance of incentives for certain kinds of activity, and the reduction of the disincentive effect of taxes on a person's willingness to earn more. Indirect taxes, such as duties levied on petrol and tobacco, are generally considered to have less of a disincentive effect on the desire to work than income tax.

- fairness. The principle that the tax system should be seen to be fair and equitable to the country's citizens has always been regarded as important. It is widely accepted that people who are better-off should pay more tax, though there is less agreement about how far the system should be deliberately used to redistribute income in society as a whole.

While the form of the present system has been highly influenced by such principles, other factors have also been very important. The effects of a tax on the economy is one of these. Taxes have often been used as a regulator on the level of economic activity and an increase in taxes may be used to reduce spending, or a decrease to increase it. There are also external constraints (the European Economic Community's attempts at tax harmonization) and purely party political priorities to consider. Nor can the increasing sophistication of taxpayers in finding ways to minimize their tax bills be forgotten.

The mechanics of raising central government taxes is centred on the Finance Bill, which has to be considered by Parliament each year. Without the passing of this bill the government cannot raise the necessary cash to finance public expenditure. The bill includes the proposals for changes in taxation put forward in the Budget each spring by the Chancellor of the Exchequer, though the details of those proposals may be modified when the bill is considered by Parliament. In 1986, for example, there was a successful campaign by British companies with a certain kind of shares quoted in the United States to modify the changes proposed in the Finance Bill. As Chapter 6 explains, the procedure for raising taxes proceeds largely independently of the procedure for getting parliamentary authorization to spend the money.

Pence in every £1[1]

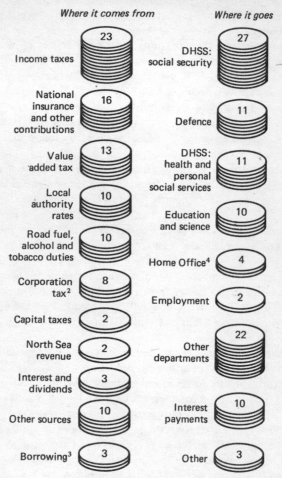

Where it comes from

Income taxes	23
National insurance and other contributions	16
Value added tax	13
Local authority rates	10
Road fuel, alcohol and tobacco duties	10
Corporation tax[2]	8
Capital taxes	2
North Sea revenue	2
Interest and dividends	3
Other sources	10
Borrowing[3]	3

Where it goes

DHSS: social security	27
Defence	11
DHSS: health and personal social services	11
Education and science	10
Home Office[4]	4
Employment	2
Other departments	22
Interest payments	10
Other	3

Figure 1.1   *Overall balance: raising and spending the money*

Source: Financial Statement and Budget Report 1987–88, Table 1.2

Figure 1.1 shows the overall balance of where the money comes from and how it is spent, combining what is raised and spent by central and local government. The percentages normally vary slightly each year as spending priorities change and as there are variations in the way taxes are levied. There are rarely dramatic year-by-year shifts in expenditure, not

least because the sums are so large that although there may be major
changes over a number of years, it is difficult to spend a great deal more
or less very quickly.

On the income side, the variations can be much greater in the short
term. A new tax may be introduced or an existing one abolished, such as
happened in 1973 when VAT was introduced. There may also be major
increases or decreases in rates of tax – the rate of VAT was doubled in
1979. Finally, there may be shifts in income from existing taxes through
big changes in revenue as a result of political and economic pressures, as
when North Sea oil revenues dropped dramatically following the fall in
world oil prices in 1986.

The figures in Figure 1.1 may come as a surprise to those who believe
that most public revenue comes from income tax. As the chart shows,
this tax constitutes only a quarter of public revenue and there are a
large variety of direct and indirect methods of raising the required sums.
Many are not clearly as visible as income tax, since they are included in
the cost of goods and services. The 10 per cent of 'other sources' includes
income from nearly twenty types of tax, including those on inheritance
and capital gains. Other features in the figure worth noting are the small
proportion of tax which comes from corporation tax on companies, and
the relative importance of income collected by local authorities and of
national insurance contributions collected from both employees and
employers.

Two items which do not appear in Figure 1.1 are tax expenditures and
income which is netted off against expenditure.

Tax expenditures are losses in government revenue which arise from
various tax reliefs and allowances. The best-known form of tax expenditure is probably relief on mortgage interest payments by house-
owners. This alone currently reduces the interest from income tax by
about £4 billion each year, but such reliefs do not appear in any conven-
tional analysis of income and expenditure. The logic of this treatment is
at least open to question when subsidies to public sector tenants count as
public expenditure.

Netted-off income includes income raised by central government
through charges for its activities – the charges for passports, for example.
It also includes the income of nationalized industries. To take the case of
the Post Office: this means that income from sales of stamps, etc. is
offset against its expenditure, and only the amount (if any) which the
Post Office requires from the government to finance its activities as a
whole is recorded as public expenditure. More contentiously, the pro-

ceeds from the sale of nationalized industries, government shareholdings and other public assets are also netted off against government expenditure as a whole. The arguments surrounding this way of presenting public expenditure are set out below.

Defining and analysing public expenditure

> But the age of chivalry is gone. That of sophisters, economists and calculators has succeeded. (Edmund Burke, *Reflections on the Revolution in France*)

Public expenditure can be defined and analysed in a large number of different ways and the technicalities can be complicated. (So if in doubt, don't get stuck on this section. Skip and come back to it if necessary.) It can be analysed:

- by function – setting out the purpose of the spending. Housing or defence would be classified in this way, and more than one government department might be responsible for administering a single function. This kind of analysis is useful for those interested in policy, particularly whether more or less is being spent on an important area, often referred to as a programme.

- by department responsible for the expenditure. The activities of the major government departments are outlined in Chapter 2 and the analysis of these activities is the basis of the main information documents published by the government. It is also the basis of planning, control and accountability.

- by economic category. The key categories are expenditure on goods and services (for example a contract to a firm to build a section of motorway); transfers by government to the personal sector (such as social security payments); transfers by government to the corporate sector (such as grants to companies); departmental running costs (administration expenses); other public sector pay, and payments overseas. It is important for the planning of economic policy to be able to link spending plans to economic categories.

- by spending authority. This identifies the type of public organization responsible for spending – whether it is central government, local government, a nationalized industry, etc. – and also identifies the amounts voted by Parliament. It is mainly of use to those working on and analysing the public spending planning and control system.

- by territory. Public funds may be spent in England, Wales, Scotland or Northern Ireland, and, as Chapter 6 explains, some functions are administered for the country as a whole, others are not. The territorial analysis provides information for those who are particularly interested in the affairs of the individual parts of the United Kingdom.

A number of different methods can also be used to define the total. The United Kingdom national income statistics, used for economic analysis, do not use a measure which is called public expenditure. Instead, the measures reflect the division of the economy into general government and the public sector. The connections are:

> Central government
> *plus* local authorities
> = general government

> General government
> *plus* public corporations
> = the public sector

> The public sector
> *plus* the private sector
> = the domestic economy.

General government expenditure is the basis of Figure 1.1 and includes, as shown, interest on government debt – that is, government borrowings still to be paid off. Another measure used by the government is *public expenditure excluding special sales of assets*. The use of this measure is an attempt to make comparisons over time more meaningful by excluding the one-off effects of income generated by privatizing industries and selling public assets to the private sector. This measure in particular is used in calculating *public expenditure as a percentage of GDP* when discussing whether the role of government in the economy is increasing or decreasing. (GDP, Gross Domestic Product, together with GNP, Gross National Product, are often used as approximations to the measure of national income.)

But the measure most commonly used to measure the total of public spending in the administrative planning and control process is the *planning total*. There are four major differences between the planning total and general government expenditure. The former excludes interest

Table 1.1   Reconciling the different measures of public expenditure: projections for 1989–90

	£ billion
1. Public expenditure planning total, excluding privatization proceeds	167
adjustment for privatization proceeds	(5)
= 2. Public expenditure planning total	162
less List 3 public corporations capital expenditure	neg.[1]
Market and overseas borrowing by nationalized industries and List 1 public corporations	(1)[2]
= 3. General government component of the planning total	163
add General government gross debt interest	19
Other items, including capital consumption, VAT refunded, fines and penalties imposed by magistrates' courts	7
= 4. General government expenditure in national accounts	189

1. neg. = less than £500 million.
2. Negative borrowing (i.e. repayments).
Source: Public Expenditure White Paper, 1987 (mainly Table 2.19)

on government debt; it includes borrowing by public corporations; it offsets certain income (fines imposed by magistrates' courts, for example) against expenditure, while the national accounts treat it as income; finally, it excludes what is technically known as the imputed value of capital consumption on non-trading activities. This measures the using-up of public assets such as hospitals, schools and roads.

The relationship between these measures and their relative sizes is shown in Table 1.1.

The process of revising the definition of public expenditure goes on all the time. As a recent Public Expenditure White Paper explained:

The scope and definition of public expenditure may be altered from one White Paper to the next for various reasons: perhaps to reflect more closely the extent to which a service makes a call on taxation or government borrowing; perhaps because a recurrent item is taken into account for the first time, or because an activity previously undertaken by the government is taken over by the private sector (or vice versa).[1]

These category changes have on occasion been very significant indeed. Until 1977, nationalized industry spending on capital items was treated as public expenditure. This was then changed for most industries to cover what they had to borrow from government. Two years later, interest on government debt was excluded from the planning total. The number of changes is also very significant. In the period 1977 to 1983 there were no fewer than twenty-six changes in definition and coverage. Some were very minor, while others – as in the two cases quoted above – were enough to make a major difference to the percentage of GDP apparently accounted for by public spending.

Changes of this kind can make problems for those who try to analyse trends over time. Sir Leo Pliatzky, a former Treasury official in charge of public expenditure, wrote in a book describing his professional life:

It will be clear from the story so far that different definitions of public expenditure have been used over the years and that the choice of definition is anything but an academic question. It determines what comes within the government's expenditure limits, and we have seen how time after time spending Ministers and Departments have fought to get round the limits by arguing that particular items should not count as public expenditure.[2]

There has also been concern about whether some changes are used to improve the look of the figures rather than being purely technical matters. The reason for excluding debt interest, which amounts to around 10 per cent of the planning total, was given five years later in the House of Commons by the Chief Secretary to the Treasury as being that it 'is too volatile to form part of the control total', a reason not advanced for any other form of expenditure.

The treatment of the proceeds of privatization is another interesting example of controversy surrounding presentation. As already outlined, these proceeds come from the sale of nationalized industries such as British Telecom and British Gas, of government shareholdings in companies such as BP, and of local authority housing. In the late 1980s the proceeds have amounted to 3 to 4 per cent of the planning total, an amount which has been treated as a reduction of expenditure, not as income. It has been argued that such treatment is wrong and that the United Kingdom is almost alone internationally in using this treatment. The House of Commons Treasury and Civil Service Select Committee has argued for treatment as income, or that the amounts should be put into a special category. As the Chairman of the Committee, Terence Higgins, put it:

'We are also deeply worried about there seeming to be systematic distortions in the planning total. My Right Hon. friend the Chancellor referred to two –

debt interest and asset sales. The Treasury and Civil Service Select Committee's view has been, and remains, in conflict with that of the Chancellor. It is not sensible to say that proceeds from privatization should be treated as a reduction in public expenditure. They could conceivably be treated as revenue or, as the Select Committee would prefer, as a means of financing the public sector borrowing requirement – otherwise, they give a false impression of the extent to which the Chancellor has succeeded in controlling public expenditure.'[3]

However, the Chancellor of the Exchequer, Nigel Lawson, was unconvinced:

'The Select Committee also recommends that asset sales should not be treated as negative expenditure . . . The Select Committee recognizes that that is well-trodden ground and the government's position has been made clear on a number of occasions. Purchases of assets add to public expenditure, so it is entirely consistent for sales of assets to reduce it.'[4]

Whatever the basis of the calculation, the present treatment has given a convenient reduction in the public expenditure total and in the proportion of public expenditure to GDP.

There is one final item which does not appear as public expenditure and over which there has been contention. This is the treatment of guarantees given by the government on behalf of private sector bodies. It has been argued that in terms of the economic effects, there is little difference between government borrowing and government-guaranteed borrowing for these organizations. The current conventions exclude such guarantees from the total because no actual borrowing is involved.

A flavour of the way in which governments have found useful means of selective presentation is given by Joel Barnett, a former Chief Secretary to the Treasury. In his memoirs he describes the work of his Cabinet colleague, Harold Lever. (For those unfamiliar with the acronym PSBR, this stands for Public Sector Borrowing Requirement. It is the amount the government needs to borrow to cover the difference between income and expenditure.)

When Denis Healey wanted to reduce the PSBR painlessly he would ask Harold if he could come up with what he called any 'ripping wheezes' to achieve his objective. He did so to the tune of many hundreds of millions of pounds by, for example, persuading first the clearing banks and later the Trustee Savings Bank to re-finance export credit and shipbuilding so achieving two gains by reducing both public expenditure and the PSBR. Similarly he persuaded the Building Societies to take some of the burden of financing local authority mortgages, with the same magical result.

Another example, on a smaller scale and therefore known as a 'Leverette', occurred when I had been involved in one of my regular battles with Peter Shore, the Secretary of State for the Environment, in trying to get a cut in housing capital expenditure. Part of Peter's budget was finance for Housing Associations. This had been found through the National Loan Fund, and counted as both public expenditure and PSBR. Harold's 'ripping wheeze' was to form a private limited company, the Housing Corporation Finance Company Ltd, as an associated company of the Housing Corporation through which government grants were channelled. The difference was that the company borrowed from banks and it did not count as either public expenditure or PSBR, even though it was effectively guaranteed by the government.[5]

A more recent example of the fine dividing line in the definition of what is counted came in the wake of the privatization of British Airways. Before privatization, £352 million of outstanding commercial borrowings and lease obligations were guaranteed by the Treasury. Both borrowings and interest counted as part of the PSBR. After privatization the same guarantee operated, but the sums were no longer part of the PSBR.

Another area where the calculation of public expenditure raises difficult issues is the distinction between capital and current expenditure. In the private sector, capital is distinguished from current expenditure by the fact that capital expenditure is on fixed assets which are expected to last for more than a single accounting period. In the private sector, this distinction is crucial in determining whether the cost of buying, say, a machine-tool or a motor-car should be treated as a cost in the year in which it was bought, or whether the cost should be spread over its expected period of use by the organization.

In the public sector, the position is much more complex and convention does not always follow what might appear to be logical. Current expenditure covers the vast majority of public spending to provide goods and services, but – unlike the private sector – there is no allowance for capital consumption, the using-up of assets. By international convention, almost all defence expenditure is treated as current. Capital expenditure covers the purchase and construction of land, buildings, machinery, etc., but this is calculated after crediting any sales of assets, including local authority housing, but not the proceeds of the sale of complete undertakings (such as the Royal Ordnance factories), to the private sector.

The complexities set out above mean that although the trend in capital expenditure is some indication of the level of public investment, the distinction between capital and current in the public sector is probably more important in political than in economic terms. 'Cuts in capital spending' or 'Boost to capital spending' make good political debating material, but it would be wrong to suppose that all capital expenditure was good and an investment in the future, any more than it might be thought that all current expenditure was bad. For example, spending on research and development is classified as current expenditure, while the building of new prisons and unemployment benefit offices is counted as capital.

In looking at the differences between public and private sectors in relation not only to capital and current expenditure, but also to more general issues of accounting for public expenditure, there have been those who have said that the public sector in general and central government in particular should adopt accounting conventions more like those prevailing in private sector practice. This would mean using some form of what is known as the accrual basis of accounting rather than the cash basis currently in use. The difference between the two is best illustrated in relation to fixed assets. With accrual accounting, the cost of a public sector fixed asset (say, a road) would be counted as being spread over its life. With cash accounting, the whole cost is counted when the money to build the road is spent. Almost all the accounting in the public sector is on a cash basis. However, trading organizations such as British Coal and London Regional Transport follow practice based on commercial principles and charge depreciation on their fixed assets.

Virtually all the rest of the public sector use the cash basis and charge the whole cost of buying or building such assets immediately. Those who would like to carry commercial practice much further have said that such a basis does not give a clear enough indication of the capital consumption. They have argued that by providing an annual depreciation figure for fixed assets, the private sector shows a more accurate assessment of their use over time. Spreading the cost of such assets over their useful lives would, it is said, give a more accurate picture of how public assets are used and also help to show how much might be needed to replace them. It is also argued that it would be desirable to value public sector assets, since at the moment there is insufficient information about the stock of assets used by the public sector.

Those who argue for retaining the present system contend that the purpose of public sector accounts is different from those for the private sector. Accounts in the public sector are primarily about stewardship. Private sector accounts have a variety of purposes, of which stewardship is only one. So the fact that one of the purposes of calculating the value of fixed assets in the private sector is to compare this with the profitability achieved by these assets is not relevant in the non-trading part of the public sector. Those who are sceptical about introducing private sector practice also point to the enormous difficulties in calculating the amounts involved. It is argued that the attempt to calculate depreciation for bridges, jet fighters or prisons is of little practical use. While in the private sector a profit has to be calculated which links income and expenditure for a given period (expenditure including the use of an asset for that period), there is no such need to produce a profit figure for the non-trading parts of the public sector. In terms of the context of public sector accounts, there is no question that the existing cash system fits in well with the present government and parliamentary control systems.

One final aspect of calculating the trends in public spending has been the subject of continuing controversy: the treatment of changing prices. As Chapter 3 will show, the impact of this debate has had a crucial effect on the way public spending is now planned. From the mid 1960s to the mid 1970s, the calculation and planning basis was in volume terms, that is, plans were for a certain quantity of goods and services to be provided. If the cost of these goods and services rose at a higher rate than the rate planned, additional cash was provided to buy them. From the mid 1970s the planning system was progressively changed to a cash basis, with public expenditure plans providing for a certain amount to be spent assuming a certain rate of inflation. This meant that if inflation was higher than planned, the volume of goods and services bought would have to be reduced. If lower, the value could be increased. A compromise method, cost planning, was discussed in the early 1980s but not implemented. Cost planning would have adjusted cash expenditure using a general price index relevant to the economy as a whole, such as the GDP deflator (an index used to distinguish between alterations in the money value of GDP caused by price changes and those caused by changes in physical output).

The difference between cash, cost and volume can be illustrated through the example of books for a university library. Under cash planning, £1 million might be allocated for such books. It might be assumed that this would purchase 100,000 volumes. If the average cost of books rose or fell, fewer or more books could be bought. Under cost planning, 100,000 books would be budgeted for at £10 per book. The £1 million budget might assume inflation of 10 per cent. If general inflation rose by 20 per cent, cost planning would allow for a correspondingly higher budget, but it would buy a different number of books if the price of books went up at a different rate to general inflation. Under volume planning, 100,000 books would be budgeted for and these could be purchased, whatever the rate of price increase.

An indication of the significant differences in the way these figures demonstrate trends is given in Table 1.2. It can be seen that the growth in local authority current expenditure for Wales was over 80 per cent in cash terms, only 2 per cent in cost terms, and involved a small reduction in volume terms. So depending on the method of calculation used, it could be said that the expenditure had gone up a great deal, hardly at all, or had actually fallen. Such differences show how assertions about whether expenditure is going up or not need to be treated with great care, particularly since there are alternatives to using the GDP deflator to adjust the figures, and each of these will give different results.

There are a number of arguments which have been put forward for and against all three systems. For volume planning it has been said that it ensures that the amount of goods and services which are expected to be bought are indeed purchased. Another argument in its favour is that trend figures in volume terms allow comparisons in what is being bought to be made over time. Such comparisons cannot be provided if there is only a succession of figures in cash terms, since the figures are distorted by inflation. On the other hand, volume planning leaves the planning system very vulnerable to unexpected increases in the cost of

Table 1.2   Cash, volume and cost: an illustrative example

	Local authority current expenditure		
	1978–79 £m	1984–85[1] £m	% change
WALES			
Cash terms	698.4	1,274.2	+82.4
Cost terms [2]	698.4	713.2	+ 2.1
Volume terms [3]	1,225.5	1,220.2	− 0.4

1. Plans.
2. Cash deflated by GDP deflator.
3. Cash deflated by changes in local authority pay and prices.

Source: D. Heald, *The Control of Public Expenditure*, Manchester Statistical Society, 1984

the public sector, which means that more money has to be provided than the taxation and borrowing plans in the Budget had allowed for. It also provides less of an incentive to control costs and improve efficiency than cash planning. In essence, the argument is between giving greater priority to control or to the fulfilment of expenditure plans irrespective of cost. By the end of the 1970s the government's priority was control, so volume planning was abandoned.

Cash planning has the opposite advantages and disadvantages to those of volume planning. The total amount being spent is controlled at the expense of sacrificing the quantity of goods and services if inflation exceeds the planned rate, thereby distorting public expenditure priorities. Furthermore, unless the assumptions behind changes in the cash total are given, it is virtually impossible in cash planning to know the reasons behind those changes. The House of Commons Social Services Select Committee managed to get a breakdown of these assumptions in relation to various parts of Health and Personal Social Services, together with relatively sophisticated explanations, from the early 1980s. For example,[6] current expenditure for one year was broken down as follows:

	%
Cash increase	7.5
of which	
Allowance for pay and price movements	6.5
Growth of resources	0.9
Efficiency Savings	0.5
leaving	
Growth in services	1.4

In other words, the assumption was that almost all the increase in cash would be required to cover pay and price increases in the coming year, leaving just less than 1 per cent available as 'new money', supplemented by 0.5 per cent from efficiency savings.

Another factor which is important in these calculations is the Relative Price Effect (RPE). Inflation does not affect all prices to the same extent, and if the prices of goods and services bought by government rise, for example, faster than those for goods and services in the economy as a whole – the RPE – it could be that any apparent growth is due largely to relative price factors. In the early to mid 1980s, for example, the costs of defence rose about 1 per cent a year more than general inflation, while housing costs rose about 0.5 per cent a year less. Figures for the relative price movement for road construction are shown in Table 1.3.

Table 1.3 Changes in road construction compared with GDP deflator

	First quarter 1980 = 100						
	1981	1982	1983	1984	1985	1986[2]	1987[3]
Roads output price index[1]	123	113	115	115	117	120	122
GDP deflator	115	125	133	138	145	153	160

1. First quarter index values. This index takes into account the different types of scheme in progress, movements in tender prices and variations in cost. It shows the trend in prices paid for roads and this reflects increased efficiency in the uses of materials.
2. Provisional estimates.
3. Forecasts.

Source: Public Expenditure White Paper, 1987.

From this table it is clear that the RPE was highly favourable over the period – more road could be bought with the same amount of money.

Figures broken down in this way are rare. The government has stated that the use of volume figures diminishes the impact of cash planning, and that planning strictly in cash forces managers to respond to higher than expected rates of increase in the costs of what they buy. Conversely, if the increases are lower than expected, they have the opportunity to buy more.

Unfortunately there are also problems in calculating the RPE. Public spending measures are concerned with inputs – what is bought. But output is even more interesting as a measure – that is, what the expenditure achieves. This is very difficult indeed to measure. What, for example, is the output of an army? Understandably, there is no measure of output in the national accounts other than the sum of all the inputs. As a result, no allowances are made for increases in public sector productivity. So there is a continuing tendency to show an unfavourable RPE where this may not be justified, as there is clear evidence that productivity in many public services is rising.

It is worth noting that the system of cost planning has a number of the advantages of volume planning. By allowing for general inflation, it enables the volume plans to be maintained as long as there is no RPE. (If there is, volume will be squeezed if the RPE is unfavourable, or could be expanded if it is favourable.) But it also has many of the same disadvantages as volume planning, particularly the difficulty of being able to control exactly what the cash outlay will be in a given year. And if there is an RPE, the volume will still be uncertain.

In its financial planning documents, notably the Public Expenditure White Paper, the government publishes cash figures in detail and also some cost figures. For reasons already given, very few volume figures are included though supporting information makes it possible to calculate at least some of the volume assumptions.

The growth of public spending

> Though the profusion of government must undoubtedly have retarded the natural progress of England towards wealth and improvement it has not been able to stop it. (Adam Smith, *The Wealth of Nations*)

> The Civil Service does not make profits and losses. Ergo we measure success by the size of our staff and our budget. By definition a big department is more successful than a small one. (*Yes Minister*, BBC)

While there is no doubt whatever that public spending has grown, calculating exactly by how much it has grown is not at all straightforward. To start with, as was made clear above, there is the issue of what definition to use. Furthermore, in measuring growth any economic comparison over time is difficult; the further back in time, the less reliable the figures. Comparisons are made more difficult because of frequent changes in the definitions of what is measured and the need to take account of changes in the value of money. Unless this last factor is taken into account, it becomes very difficult to understand whether major increases reflect price changes, increases in the volume of goods and services bought or a combination of the two. But if price changes *are* taken into account, there is the problem of how to adjust for changing price levels and the RPE.

Even adjusted for changing prices, moreover, the growth means little in isolation and needs to be put in the context of growth in the economy as a whole. Public expenditure rising at 5 per cent a year when the economy grows at 10 per cent would not cause much anxiety. But if the economy was growing at only 2 per cent, there would certainly be those who would worry about the increasing proportion of GDP taken by public spending.

Despite all the problems outlined above, it is in practice possible to make a reasonable attempt to trace the growth trend of government

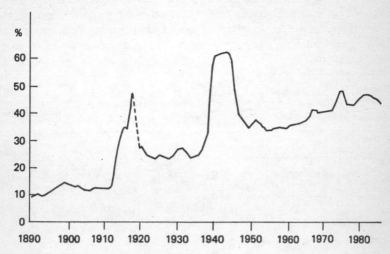

Figure 1.2   *Growth of ratio of United Kingdom government expenditure to GDP,*
1890–1986
Source: *Economic Trends*, October 1987.

expenditure as a percentage of national income, measured in this case by
GNP, over an extended period. Figure 1.2 does so for various dates in
the last 100 years, using general government expenditure as a measure.

In the preceding century expenditure actually fell as a proportion of
national income, though the fall was interrupted by bursts of government
defence activity for the Napoleonic Wars at the beginning of the century
and the Crimean War in the middle. The major rise really only occurred
at the beginning of the twentieth century and the increase was even
faster than the growth of national income.

The growth figures for public expenditure as a whole mask the fact
that there have been very different rates of growth for different programmes. Expenditure tables from a hundred years ago show Britain
playing a full world role, with separate headings for the Abyssinian War
(£18,000 over two years), the Ashanti War, the Russo-Turkish War, war

in South Africa, and the Afghan War. Table 1.4 shows how spending on three areas of great importance in the nineteenth century – administration, interest on the national debt, and defence – have declined as a proportion of a total which covers a much wider range of services. In part the relative decline reflects growth elsewhere, but it is also worth noting that inflation has been a major help to governments in eroding the inflation-adjusted value of the national debt and therefore the interest which has been payable.

Table 1.4   The changing composition of government expenditure in the United Kingdom, 1790–1976

	% of total expenditure				
	Administration	National debt	Defence	Social	Economic and environment
1790	17	39	26	9	9
1840	16	42	23	9	9
1890	22	15	28	20	15
1910	14	7	27	32	20
1932	7	25	10	45	14
1951	6	11	25	43	15
1961	7	10	20	47	16
1976	5	9	11	55	20

Source: Open University Module D323.

The two areas of expenditure which have grown enormously in importance are social services (health, housing and education provision and social security payments, including unemployment benefit), and economic and environmental services (industrial and regional subsidies, roads and sewers, employment creation, etc.).

To put the growth of public spending in the United Kingdom in context, the growth is in line with that in other developed countries. International comparisons of this kind are politically sensitive and are often used to make political points rather than to illustrate differences. Table 1.5 shows the pattern for the seven major developed countries in recent years, adjusted to a comparable statistical basis. It is worth noting that tax revenues have not necessarily increased in line with the increase in expenditures for all these countries. While there were only six countries out of twenty-three with budget deficits in the early 1960s, twenty years later all but two were in deficit.

It is important to try to understand the reasons for the growth, because of the arguments advanced by powerful economic and political groups with the aim of justifying changes in policy. There are those with political concerns about the proportion of the economy under control of the state. Some want a higher proportion, others want to reduce it. In economic terms there are those who are interested in the impact of the size of the public sector on the rest of the economy, especially the need to finance state spending.

Many different theories have been advanced to explain what has happened and why, some based on empirical evidence, others on ideological or political theories. Of the empirically based theories two of the best known are Wagner's 'law' of increasing government activity and the displacement theory of Peacock and Wiseman.

Wagner, a German economist, set out his 'law' at the end of the nineteenth century.[7] It was based on observation of a number of Western European economies and stated that government expenditure would inevitably increase at a faster rate than national output. There were, he contended, several reasons for this. First, the protective and social control

Table 1.5 Growth of public expenditure in some other countries

	General government expenditure (% of GDP at current prices)		
	1966	1975	1985
United States	28.5	34.6	36.7
Japan	19.1	27.3	32.7
Germany	36.7	48.9	47.2
France	38.5	43.5	52.4
United Kingdom	35.3	46.3	47.8[1]
Italy	34.3	43.2	58.4
Canada	29.5	40.1	47.0
Total	30.2	37.7	39.6[2]

1. 1984.
2. Excluding UK.

Note: The table is based on statistics for general government expenditure, not public expenditure. This measure poses the fewest problems in definition and measurement, though there are still problems with international comparisons since certain items are classified in different ways. Taking the case of help to families with children, this is given as a tax allowance in the United States but as a cash payment in West Germany. In the United States they are therefore treated as reductions in tax revenue, in West Germany as public spending.

Source: OECD *Economic Outlook*, op. cit.

activities of government would have to increase as the fragmentation of social and economic life through economic development led to greater social friction. Second, the scale of investment would increase with economic development and Wagner believed that public corporations would handle large amounts of capital more effectively than would private corporations. Finally, he suggested that technical progress encourage the development of monopolies, increasing the need for government control.

A more recent variation of Wagner's ideas has suggested that, with increasing income, societies will tend to spend an increasing proportion of that increase on 'luxury' goods and services of the kind which are provided by the state – education and health, for example.

Peacock and Wiseman, writing in the 1960s,[8] developed a very differ-

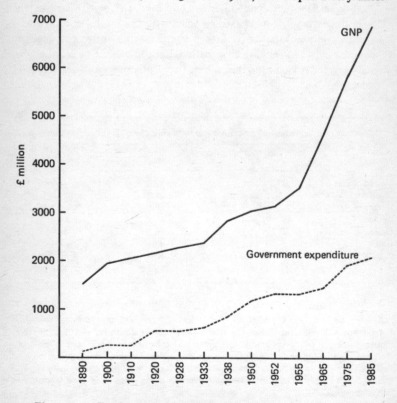

Figure 1.3   *Total government expenditure at 1900 prices, 1890–1985*

ent view, identifying not the factors which increased the demand for government services but the ability of the government to supply them. Using observations about the United Kingdom economy, they contended that the growth of government expenditure had been very uneven and that it had been pushed upwards in the twentieth century by social upheavals, notably the two World Wars. They suggested that such 'upward displacement' takes place because during social upheavals there is an increase in the tax burden which society finds tolerable. The tolerable burden of taxation is increased during periods of social upheaval because such periods have two 'effects'. The 'imposition effect' means that it is possible for government to impose new methods of taxation which would previously have been considered unacceptable. The new revenue allows the government to spend on programmes which it considers desirable but for which it lacked funds before the upheaval. The 'inspection effect' means that there is a tendency for government to identify additional social problems during periods of upheaval such as major wars. As a result, there is the expectation that government will continue to provide additional public services to deal with the 'newly discovered' problems.

Both theories have been questioned on a number of grounds. Wagner's evidence was developed after observations at a particular time and in a particular area. Some of his assumptions have not transposed well in time or place. What is more, the 'law' only deals with the demand for goods and services. It says nothing about the willingness of government to supply extra services or their ability to do so in the light of the fact that resources are almost always constrained.

The implicit assumption of Peacock and Wiseman that the government are interested in spending more has also been questioned. They suggest that governments are elected if they promise to increase spending, since there is a distinction in the voter's mind between voting for more public expenditure and any resulting increase in the tax which he pays. But it now appears that some governments do not want to spend more and that voters are aware of this. Evidence of continued growth in public spending since the Second World War (see Figure 1.3) has also cast doubt on the permanence of the displacement effect, though different definitions of government expenditure help to account for some of the differences in interpretation.

There have been a large number of other theories to explain the reasons for the growth in public expenditure. The work of the American economist Baumol[9] is the basis for one of these. The theory divided the economy into two sectors: a progressive sector in which there are steady gains in productivity and a non-progressive sector in which there are not. Wages in the economy as a whole, it was argued, rise at a similar rate throughout the economy, led by productivity growth in the progressive sector. Others subsequently took Baumol's distinction to be one between the private and government sectors, though Baumol himself did not. They argued that government expenditure in the non-progressive sector has a tendency to rise, even though it does not achieve the productivity gains of the pro-gressive (private) sector.

The Baumol-related model has been criticized on the grounds that it excludes transfer payments, that is, payments for which no goods or services are received in return such as social security benefits. These have been a major source of the growth of government expenditure. A further criticism has been that the model makes a number of simplifying assumptions about the division between two sectors, the way in which wage increases take place and the ability to pay for government services. It should also be noted again that since outputs, under national account-ing conventions, are measured in terms of inputs, it is not possible to measure any productivity gains by government. This does not mean, however, that there are none. Thus it seems inappropriate to assume that the government sector and the non-progressive sector are the same.

Turning to explicitly ideological and political theories, there is a wide variety of explanations of public expenditure growth. At one end of the spectrum there is public choice literature which explains growth in terms of decision-making processes. Buchanan and Tullock,[10] for example, claimed that since benefits from public spending are concentrated on particular economic groups but tax costs are spread more widely, voter coalitions will tend to form in order to press for additional provision for their own group. The net effect will be increased expenditure since the benefits to any group will be greater than the tax costs, leading to a constant pressure for increases. Against this, it has been pointed out that there is evidence of successful pressure groups of taxpayers who have achieved cuts in the growth of public spending by restraining govern-ments' ability to increase taxation.

Other factors which have been brought forward to explain the growth have included:

- the need of politicians to buy votes by spending public money;

- the desire of bureaucracies to expand their influence and power by increasing the range of government activities;

- the work of commercial pressure groups seeking to increase their sales to the state;

- demographic trends which have increased the proportion of those requiring public spending (notably the old);

- the 'demonstration effect' of other countries feeling obliged to match services available in other countries;

- the 'ratchet effect' of expenditure continuing in order to improve the *quality* of a service, when the original reasons for having the service at all no longer apply;

- linked to the ratchet effect, the tendency to maintain an increase in government spending during a recession after that recession ends;

- faulty control mechanisms.

At the other end of the spectrum, there are complete ideological frameworks to explain the growth of public spending. It is not possible to do justice to these frameworks in an introductory book. But to illustrate the difference in approach to the explanations put forward and in view of its impact on thinking in other countries, it is worth noting the Marxist approach. This attributes the increase to inherent contradictions within capitalism. The argument is that there is a long-run tendency for the rate of profit to decline, resulting in a slow-down in capital accumulation, which is the motivating force of capitalism. Unemployment therefore increases, requiring an increase in government expenditure to provide the basis for an increase in capital accumulation. Under this theory, the rise in government expenditure is seen as inevitable with the decline of capitalism.

The difference in approach between the various theories about the growth of public spending illustrates why those who look for an answer may not always be asking the same question. Most explanations of the growth of public expenditure mix economics, political science and sociology in various combinations. None has been accepted as completely satisfactory – indeed it is not likely that any could be. It will be particularly interesting to see whether the various theories are robust enough to explain any success in reducing public spending over an extended period.

2

WHAT THE MONEY IS SPENT ON

> For forms of government let fools contest,
> Whate'er is best administer'd is best.
> (Alexander Pope, *An Essay on Man*)

> A state comes into existence because no individual is self-sufficing.
> We all have many needs.
>
> (Plato, *Republic*)

Most of this book discusses public expenditure as a whole, but what exactly is the money spent on? As Chapter 1 indicated, there are various ways in which government spending can be calculated. An economic analysis shows that about

- one third is spent on the running costs of departments and other public sector pay;

- 40 per cent is spent on transfer payments to individuals (i.e. social security payments) or companies (i.e. grants);

- a quarter is spent on buying goods and services (aircraft, roads, consultancy services, etc.).

An analysis by spending authority shows that around

- three-quarters of all expenditure is by central government;

- a quarter is by local authorities.

Public corporations, such as the water industry, the Post Office and British Coal, account for only a very small proportion of the total, currently around 2 per cent.

But the analysis which gives the best 'feel' for how public money is spent is an examination of each of the twenty or so government departments responsible for spending the money. Parliament and government also use departments as the unit of control. Not that all departments necessarily cover the whole of the United Kingdom. While some do (defence, for example), responsibility for others, such as education and local government, is split between England, Scotland, Wales

Table 2.1 Public expenditure by department

	(amount and % of public expenditure)	
	£ billion	% (rounded)
The Biggest Spender		
Department of Health and Social Security (of which social security = £49.3 billion)	70.1	44
The Big Spenders		
Ministry of Defence	19.4	12
Department of Education and Science	17.8	11
The Smaller Spenders		
Department of the Environment	7.0	4
Home Office and Lord Chancellor's Departments	6.7	4
Department of Transport	5.1	3
Department of Employment	4.3	3
Chancellor of the Exchequer's Departments	2.4	1
Foreign and Commonwealth Office/Overseas Aid	2.2	1
Department of Trade and Industry/ECGD [1]	1.0	1
Ministry of Agriculture, Fisheries and Food	2.5	1
Office of Arts and Libraries	0.9	1
Other Departments	1.9	1
Department of Energy	(0.2)	—
Territorial departments		
Scotland	8.2	5
Wales	3.4	2
Northern Ireland	5.2	3
Other		
European communities	1.1	1
Privatization proceeds	(5.0)	(3)
Reserve	7.5	5
Total	161.5	100

1. Export Credits Guarantee Department.

Source: Public Expenditure White Paper, 1987 (projections for 1989–90), adapted.

and Northern Ireland. Care also needs to be taken in analysing trends over time, since responsibility for particular functions can shift from one department to another. Departmental divisions themselves are subject to change as decisions are made about the most suitable organization of Whitehall and of ministerial responsibilities.

Table 2.1 gives the relative sizes of departmental spending programmes. The figures are taken from the planning total and therefore exclude interest payments and other items, as Chapter 1 explained. The table shows clearly how three departments alone account for two-thirds of government spending – one of these, the Department of Health and Social Security, for more than 40 per cent of the total on its own. This represents over eighty times more than the smallest, the Office of Arts and Libraries. Small as it is, this deportment still accounts for hundreds of millions of pounds, an indication of the sheer magnitude of public expenditure.

The rest of this chapter describes government expenditure in terms of the Biggest Spender, the Big Spenders and Smaller Spenders. There are additional sections to show how spending on local government and nationalized industries is included in the total. (Acronyms are included for most departments to show the usual form of abbreviation used in central government, as well as to avoid repetition of lengthy names.)

In looking at the relative size of departmental expenditure, it is worth bearing in mind that size does not mean political priority. As Richard Rose has commented:

> There is a tendency to be fascinated by big numbers, especially when the numbers have £ signs in front of them. Ministers are conscious of the purposes of programmes before their cost, and there is no exact correspondence between what ministries spend money upon, and what they deem important politically.[1]

The Biggest Spender

DEPARTMENT OF HEALTH AND SOCIAL SECURITY (DHSS)

The scale of DHSS expenditure dwarfs that of all other government departments. As Table 2.1 shows, the sheer size is formidable. Its budget is similar to the Gross National Product of Sweden or Switzerland and, if defence is excluded, as much as all the other public expenditure programmes put together.

DHSS responsibilities can be divided into two major sub-sections: Health and Personal Social Services (HPSS) and social security.

HPSS, which include the whole of the National Health Service (NHS), take a quarter of departmental spending. The aim is no less than 'to provide treatment and/or care to extend life and to maintain or enhance its quality for individuals with the best use of available resources'. The largest component of spending is the cost of maintaining the hospital and community health services, which in themselves amount to two-thirds of the HPSS funds. Over half the rest goes to family practitioners, and the remainder is spent mainly on social services.

Although the HPSS are major spenders on capital equipment, a high proportion of the expenditure goes towards paying the 800,000 employees of the NHS.

By far the largest proportion of departmental funds goes towards the social security system – indeed about 30 per cent of all public expenditure goes on social security. The general aim of the programme is

to provide an efficient and responsive system of financial help, at levels determined by Ministers and Parliament and paying due regard to wider social and economic policies.[2]

About 10 million people currently receive retirement pensions or widows' benefits through the system. About half the cost is met by contributions; the rest is funded by general taxation.

Forty per cent of the huge expenditure on social security is for pensions and widows' benefits. Supplementary benefit is the next largest component of expenditure, at 17 per cent. Relatively smaller amounts go on sickness and disability benefits (12 per cent), family benefits and housing benefits (each 4 per cent). It is worth remembering, however, that 'relatively smaller' in a programme of this size still means around half a billion pounds for every one per cent of the programme.

Whereas many departments spend relatively small amounts on administration, the DHSS has a large staff to deal with claims; this accounts for nearly 8 per cent of the total budget.

The Big Spenders

MINISTRY OF DEFENCE (MOD)

The MOD has as its objective to 'ensure the security of the nation, and to keep it free to pursue, by just and peaceful means, its legitimate interests and activities both at home and abroad'.[2]

To do so, it has a budget amounting to over 12 per cent of public expenditure, much of it earmarked for meeting NATO, and not just United Kingdom, commitments. The defence budget amounts to a significant burden. The United Kingdom's defence expenditure as a proportion of national income, at about 5 per cent, is higher than those of almost all its European allies.

The main area of expenditure is the purchase of equipment, accounting for about half the total. Three-quarters of this goes towards production and repair, a quarter towards research and development. Of the other half, pay is the main item of expenditure, with the armed forces and other military personnel accounting for a quarter of the defence budget, civilians for about 10 per cent.

A breakdown of defence expenditure by service reveals that the air force general purpose forces take about 20 per cent of total defence expenditure. A smaller proportion – 16 per cent – goes on the army's European-theatre ground forces and other combat forces, and 14 per cent on the naval general purpose combat force.

DEPARTMENT OF EDUCATION AND SCIENCE (DES)

With aims which include to 'raise standards at all levels of ability; to increase parental choice; and to secure the best possible return from the resources which are invested in the education service',[2] the DES is another of the major spending departments, accounting for over 10 per cent of public expenditure; but unlike the other major spenders, the DES has not seen a constant and steady increase in its budget in real terms during the 1980s.

The department itself only directly administers one sixth of education expenditure. Almost all the rest is spent by local authorities. Spending is divided amongst five main areas – schools, higher education, student awards, non-advanced further education and research councils. Schools claim by far the largest share (60 per cent), more than half of which is used for teachers' salaries. Higher education spends another 18 per cent of the DES total. Most of this goes towards providing and maintaining the 600,000 or so university and polytechnic places for United Kingdom students. Mandatory student awards account for about 5 per cent, and non-advanced further education (vocational courses, such as City and Guilds courses) another 7 per cent. Finally, the science budget accounts for approximately 4 per cent of the DES allocation. Most of this amount is used to support five research councils, which in turn allocate the funds for which they are responsible according to the advice of the Advisory Board for the Research Councils.

The remaining 6 per cent of DES spending supports other services and covers central departmental expenditure.

The Smaller Spenders

DEPARTMENT OF THE ENVIRONMENT (DoE)

The DoE performs two main functions. The first is to carry out the government's housing policy. The second is support of local environmental services.

DoE functions cover a host of other areas and include: administration of the registration of births, marriages and deaths; provision of and support for water research and supervision of the water industry; the Urban Development Corporations and the urban programme; support for new towns, such as Milton Keynes (though the new towns are scheduled to be sold to the private sector); and support of the national heritage, historic buildings and monuments.

Many of these functions are carried out by other bodies, mainly local authorities, though a large variety of other organizations are also involved.

HOME OFFICE AND LORD CHANCELLOR'S DEPARTMENT

These two departments are responsible for the criminal justice system and the prevention, detection and punishment of crime.

The funding of the police force accounts for over half the funds spent, with most of this going on police pay. The penal system is the next major area of expenditure and, while running costs of the prison service are significant, a greater proportion than is usual in government departments goes on capital expenditure. The increase in prison building as a result of the increase in detected crime has represented a major use of funds in recent years. The two other main areas of expense are the administration of justice and the Fire Service. Civil Defence, immigration and passport control absorb relatively little funding.

DEPARTMENT OF TRANSPORT (DTp)

The DTp is responsible for the efficiency and effectiveness of the infrastructure for all forms of national transport services. About half the department's funds go into the development and maintenance of a national road network. Most of the rest of the department's budget is split between two main programmes:

- local transport and buses, which includes spending on London Regional Transport – London buses and the Underground;

- subsidies for British Rail, called the Public Service Obligation, to support uneconomic services.

Two relatively small items of expenditure are Swansea's Driver and Vehicle Licensing Directorate, and port, shipping and civil aviation services.

DEPARTMENT OF EMPLOYMENT (DE)

With the rise in unemployment levels in the 1970s and 1980s from well below a million to around three million, there has been a major increase in the workload and spending of the DE, which also covers the Manpower Services Commission (MSC), the Health and Safety Commission and the Advisory, Conciliation and Arbitration Service (ACAS). In a period in which most departments have been cutting their workforce, the department is unusual in having significantly increased the number of people who work for it.

The department has objectives which include: [2]

- promoting enterprise and job creation;

- supporting programmes to help unemployed people into work;

- helping the labour market to work efficiently, effectively and fairly;

- improving training arrangements;

- helping to improve industrial relations;

- helping to maintain and improve health and safety at work.

The DE's training function is by far the largest user of its funds, especially on those programmes run by the MSC, such as the Youth Training Scheme, and various adult training schemes. In total these programmes account for more than one third of DE funds. Another third goes to organizations in various forms of employment aid. The rest goes in efforts to meet other objectives including those set out above.

MINISTRY OF AGRICULTURE, FISHERIES AND FOOD (MAFF)

The aims of MAFF are a blend of measures to help farmers and to make them more competitive, and also to help the consumer. United Kingdom membership of the European Community is central to the department's role, and means that its expenditure differs in an important respect from that of other departments. Control over policy, and therefore expenditure, lies outside the United Kingdom, and the department's expenditure is largely determined by the Community's common agricultural policy.

Nearly two thirds of the department's funds are allocated to financing the common agricultural policy and are spent on European Community programmes, some of which may be spent outside the United Kingdom. By far the largest item of expenditure is the support of market prices according to Community decisions. The rest is spent on United Kingdom domestic agriculture, fisheries and food. The other three major areas of expenditure are:

- support for less-favoured agricultural areas and other specific grants;

- drainage, and flood and coast protection;

- departmental research, advisory services and administration.

Departments of the Chancellor of the Exchequer

The Chancellor of the Exchequer is responsible for a number of central government bodies, of which the one with the largest expenditure, accounting for half the total, is the Inland Revenue. This administers personal and corporate taxation and a complex series of tax reliefs. Another tax-gathering department, Customs and Excise, accounts for a further 20 per cent of the total. Its main duties involve the collection of Value Added Tax (VAT), car tax, and excise duties levied on oil and petrol products, tobacco and alcohol. The costs of the Inland Revenue and Customs and Excise together amount to about 1 per cent of the total of tax collected.

The Treasury, a key policy department whose role is described more fully in Chapter 3, is far smaller than either the Inland Revenue or Customs and Excise. Apart from general financial administration, the Treasury has responsibility for the United Kingdom coinage and the government's Central Computer and Telecommunications Agency.

Finally, there are a variety of even smaller departments, including the Department of National Savings, the Registrar of Friendly Societies, the Government Actuary and Her Majesty's Stationery Office.

Foreign and Commonwealth Office (FCO)

While it is one of the most prominent of government departments in its media exposure, in terms of its percentage share of public spending the FCO is near the bottom of the expenditure league table. Its responsibilities cover two main areas. The diplomatic wing takes one third of the budget; overseas aid, administered through the Overseas Development Administration (ODA), takes two thirds.

The main objectives of the diplomatic wing are the security and protection of British interests. A large proportion of this expenditure goes towards the costs of maintaining some 3,000 United Kingdom staff in their overseas posts. The BBC overseas service is also funded by the FCO.

As for the ODA, the vast majority of the funds go directly into the aid programme and relatively little into administration. As a proportion of national income, Britain's contribution comes to about one third of one per cent, about the average for developed countries but less than United Nations guidelines for such countries.

'Other departments'

There are a number of other items and public bodies which do not fit under any other heading and which are grouped together for planning and control purposes.

By far the largest item is public service pensions, which is classified separately. It is therefore not charged directly to the organizations which originally employed the pensioners, who in any case may have served more than one department. The rest cover a collection of departments and other bodies, most of which are important and influential parts of the administrative structure, but which in public expenditure terms are very small fry compared with the major spending departments. These include:

- the Cabinet Office, which coordinates Cabinet business and includes the staff of the Central Statistical Office and the Office of the Minister for the Civil Service;
- the Director of Public Prosecutions and the Crown Prosecution Service;
- the expenditure of the House of Commons and the House of Lords;
- the National Audit Office (described in detail in Chapter 8);
- the Ordnance Survey;
- the Property Services Agency, which administers much government property. Since the cost is then recharged to departments, there is no net spending.

Department of Trade and Industry (DTI)

The DTI has as its responsibility the support and encouragement of United Kingdom commerce, trade and industry at home and abroad. It has a relatively small budget following major cuts in the 1980s.

Research and development is one area in which it is a significant spender, and projects range from the provision of financial support for the Patent Office to contributions to the European Space Agency. The aircraft and aero-engine general research and development programme, in which it collaborates with the Ministry of Defence, is another major area of expense.

The second largest allocation of DTI funds is the financial assistance devoted to regional and general industrial support, which has been cut back very heavily in recent years.

Of the other areas of spending, the most significant is on support for international trade, including financial support for exports through the

Export Credit Guarantee Department (ECGD). The support is managed by the British Overseas Trade Board, which generally assists export promotion and helps to secure overseas contracts. Finally there are the DTI's administrative functions, including regulation and consumer protection, and support for specific industries, notably aerospace, shipbuilding and steel. Such support has been another area of major cutbacks in the 1980s.

Office of Arts and Libraries

This is a government department accounting for less than half a per cent of total expenditure. The department is responsible for supporting the performing and visual arts, maintaining national museums and galleries, developing collections of items of literary interest, archives and for preserving objects of importance to the national heritage. About half the funds are spent on libraries; the rest is divided almost equally between museums and galleries, and arts and the heritage.

Department of Energy (DEn)

The work of the department covers the whole of the energy field, including the management of relations between the publicly owned energy industries and the government. As Table 2.1 shows, expenditure on the department was projected to be negative, a feat which is explicable because the nationalized energy industries which come under the department's administrative wing have been raising an increasing proportion of their revenue from customers. As a result, industries have in many cases been able to repay government debt. Since these inflows are 'credited' to the department, it means that the department has become a net contributor to government funds. However, privatization of industries, while providing a one-off cash inflow, reduces future cash contributions.

The other activities of the department include support for research and development, particularly in the nuclear field, and the control of the United Kingdom's oil and gas discoveries.

Territorial departments

About 10 per cent of total public expenditure is administered by the Scottish, Welsh and Northern Ireland Offices. This is far less than their proportion of the population of the United Kingdom and reflects the fact that responsibility for several major public expenditure programmes is centralized.

For a combination of historic and political reasons discussed in Chapter 3, the Northern Ireland programme covers more items than are covered by those for Scotland and Wales. The main difference is that Social Security payments are identified separately for Northern Ireland, and amount to about 30 per cent of the total. Three other areas of Northern Ireland expenditure take relatively more resources than Scotland and Wales. Law, order and protective services is one, though even this does not include the cost of the armed forces stationed in Northern Ireland. Education, arts and libraries is another, reflecting different administrative responsibilities. Finally, the allocation of support for industry, trade and employment is higher, arising out of a history of the highest levels of unemployment of any part of the United Kingdom.

Details of how allocations are made, which areas of expenditure are covered and how responsibility for some programmes is passed down to the three Offices are given in Chapter 3.

European communities

The European communities have a budget which is dominated by agriculture but which also has funds allocated for regional development and social matters. Member states pay contributions towards the budget and in Britain's case such contributions greatly exceed receipts. Indeed, contributions regularly run at a rate roughly double those of receipts. This imbalance has been narrowed by a series of negotiated refunds and abatements which have significantly cut the net contribution. The figure shown in Table 2.1 is the net amount after crediting those amounts.

Privatization proceeds

This figure grew steadily in the 1980s and has included proceeds from selling whole nationalized industries, such as British Gas and National Freight; shareholdings in companies such as BP; and assets, such as land and buildings formerly owned by the Property Services Agency.

Reserve

In each year's plans the government sets aside an amount to meet unforeseen spending requirements. These can arise for a variety of reasons. There may be policy changes which demand more spending – to boost employment, for example. There may be unexpected events, such as emergency aid for a natural disaster or an unexpected downturn in the fortunes of one of the nationalized industries. Or there may be unexpectedly increased demands for services which are demand-led – that is, available by right – such as social security.

Local authorities and public corporations

Included in the departmental totals are amounts spent by local authorities and those which relate to the funding of public corporations.

Table 2.2 Spending by local authorities and on public corporations within departmental totals

	% spent by/on	
	Local authorities	Public corporations
Defence	—	—
Foreign and Commonwealth Office	—	neg.
Ministry of Agriculture, Fisheries and Food	8	neg.
Department of Trade and Industry	neg.	10
Department of Energy	—	contrib.
Department of Employment	3	neg.
Department of Transport	51	22
Department of the Environment	73	2
Home Office	74	—
Department of Education and Science	84	—
Office of Arts and Libraries	60	—
Department of Health and Social Security		
Social security	8	—
HPSS	15	neg.
Scotland	52	4
Wales	50	3
Northern Ireland	14	8
Chancellor of the Exchequer's Departments	—	neg.
Other Departments	—	—
Planning total	27	11

neg. = less than 1 per cent.
contrib. = net contributor to department.

Source: Public Expenditure White Paper, 1987 (1987–88 figures).

Table 2.3   External financing limits (EFLs)
for some nationalized industries:
1987–88 forecast

	£ million
British Rail	751
British Coal	727
London Regional Transport	275
South of Scotland Electricity Board	84
British Steel Corporation	66
Water (England and Wales)	35
British Shipbuilders	49
British Waterways Board	45
Civil Aviation Authority	15
North of Scotland Hydro-Electric Board	(1)
National Girobank	(3)
Post Office	(54)
Electricity (England and Wales)	(1,305)

Note: As given in 1987. The aims and objectives set out in this chapter may well vary over time.

Source: Public Expenditure White Paper, 1987.

Table 2.2. shows that this applies to the majority of departments, with some having a half or more of their budgets spent by local authorities. The percentages in Table 2.2. vary over time, particularly for public corporations, but the importance of the local authority dimension for departments such as Education and Science and the Home Office is unlikely to change very much over the years.

Local authorities in Great Britain (i.e. excluding Northern Ireland) are responsible for about a quarter of public expenditure. Not all this money comes from central government. Their income comes from a number of sources – rates, rents for council housing, charges for services such as leisure facilities, etc. – which finance around 40 per cent of the total. An analysis of their expenditure and the sources of their finance is given in Chapter 6.

Even before the major privatizations in the early 1980s, which included such household names as British Airways, British Gas and British Telecom, *public corporations* had not been major users of government funds for many years. With a combination of the ability to charge for their services and the possibility of eliminating loss-making capacity, there has always been far more freedom of manoeuvre for governments to limit their spending in this area than in other parts of the public sector.

But while the total amount of money for nationalized industries as a whole has been relatively small, there have been major differences within the total, as Table 2.3. illustrates for some of the major industries. Cash injections have been required, either because, like British Coal, British Steel and British Shipbuilders, they were making losses or because, like British Rail and London Regional Transport, they were involved in major capital expenditure programmes which they could not fund from their own earnings.

3

DETERMINING PUBLIC EXPENDITURE PRIORITIES

The largest determining factor of the size and content of this year's budget is last year's budget. (Aron Wildavsky, The Politics of the Budgetary Process)

Planning is not only of great importance in deciding public expenditure priorities. It is also crucial to decisions about how much revenue to raise and the required level of borrowing to finance any deficit. The sequence of decisions set out in this and later chapters appears to show that in the United Kingdom the level of expenditure is decided first. Taxation is then raised to finance that expenditure. But in practice it is not realistic to decide on spending plans without reference to whether they can be financed. Decisions on the total of public spending each year will be strongly influenced by the implications for taxation (including the scope for tax reductions) and borrowing.

The present system of planning for public expenditure had its origins in the Plowden Committee's report published in 1961. As a result of the committee's recommendations, the Public Expenditure Survey Committee (PESC) was set up. (Rather confusingly, both the process of planning and the committee itself are sometimes called PESC. Within the government, however, it is now known by those involved as 'the Survey'.)

The Survey is the focus for the planning of public expenditure, covering not just central government's own activities but the whole of the public sector. Sir Leo Pliatzky points to its central role:

If you are a Department wanting money for an expenditure proposal, and if you have got provision for your proposal 'in PESC' – that is, somewhere in the survey tables, possibly subsumed as a small component item in a much larger

40 · *Public Expenditure*

aggregate – you are on the way to success. If your proposal is 'not in PESC', you have a hard time ahead of you.[1]

The main landmarks in the annual planning cycle are shown in Table 3.1.

It can be seen that the cycle begins well before the beginning of the financial year, which runs from 1 April. Under the Survey system as it was first developed, expenditure was planned for five years ahead. But after it had become clear, with experience in the 1970s, that the final years of the planning cycle were too far away to be realistic, the number of years was reduced first to four and then to three. Even with three, the final year of the plan has an air of unreality about it. Everyone knows that a great deal can happen to alter priorities before that year becomes the basis for the current year's planning. Nevertheless, the process at least means that there will have been two attempts to provide outline projections for the coming financial year before it becomes the focus of attention. It will certainly not be a question of starting from scratch.

The process of adding an additional year (unrealistic or not) to the cycle is to use the previous year's figures, altered by any changes made

Table 3.1   The Planning timetable [1]

January (15 [2])	Post-mortem on previous Survey
February (14)	
March (13)	Treasury issues guidelines
April (12)	Baselines agreed
May (11)	Departments submit material on output, performance and value for money
June (10)	Bids submitted by departments. Treasury analyses bids
July (9)	Chief Secretary's proposals to Cabinet for overall Survey totals. Cabinet decides totals
August (8)	
September (7)	Bilaterals start
October (6)	(or early November) Cabinet decisions on departmental totals
November (5)	*Autumn Statement* published
December (4)	Departments submit Estimates bids to Treasury
January (3)	*Public Expenditure White Paper* published (see p. ix)
February (2)	Treasury Ministers approve Estimates
March (1)	Budget
	Financial Statement and Budget Report published
	Supply Estimates published

1. Timing may vary.
2. Numbers represent months before beginning of financial year being planned.

on technical or policy grounds which have been agreed, and to increase or decrease them by a standard percentage approved by Ministers. This standard percentage will normally be the expected inflation rate for the coming year.

The planning round itself gets under way when PESC, chaired by the Treasury, first meets to coordinate the planning process. Following a post-mortem on the previous year's work the committee decides on the timetable for the current round, which topics should be given particular attention and what kind of information is required. The Treasury then sends its assumptions about the economic developments affecting public expenditure to spending departments. In the light of these assumptions, departments have to submit details of changes of programmes to the Treasury. In fact departments will already have started to work on building up the information for new proposals well before the beginning of the Survey discussions. The process is rather like the Forth Bridge: no sooner does one cycle finish than the next one starts.

In submitting new proposals, each department will have a 'baseline' for their cash plans. This will be the figures previously published in the Public Expenditure White Paper (the annual document setting out plans in detail – but see page ix) adjusted for the Budget and any policy changes. The baseline applies not only to the total of the cash plans, but to each sub-programme. Variations from the baseline show up as bids or statements of reduced requirements as the planning process unfolds.

What happens then varies from department to department. Little precise evidence is collected on a systematic basis. Indeed, since departments are in a bargaining position it is not in their interest to disclose details of how they think or what they do. But from what information is available, it appears that in most cases alterations are made by relatively minor adjustments to the amounts set aside in the previous year. However, there is increasing evidence of pressure for departments to use more of a 'zero-based budgeting' approach, with programmes being reassessed from first principles and with nothing taken for granted. As the Chief Secretary to the Treasury, the Cabinet Minister responsible for public expenditure (at that time John MacGregor) explained to the House of Commons:

'Although the government do not operate a formal zero-based budgeting system of the kind that has been tried abroad, we do ensure that a number of areas of policy are fundamentally reviewed each year. These reviews will ask: is this programme essential, does it have to be carried out in the public sector, have its objectives kept pace with changing circumstances and can these objectives be achieved more economically?' [2]

The reasons why certain items are favoured over others will vary, department by department and item by item. They will also be the result of taking several sets of influences into account. A major influence will obviously be changing requirements for the department to fulfil its aims and objectives. To help in this process, material gathered on output and performance will be used. Or it may be that the department is seeking to move the focus of its activities. Some areas may simply be deemed more politically attractive than others, based on the Minister's own views. Certain items may be favoured as a result of comparing them with others (see Appendix A for how investment appraisal is carried out). There will certainly be pressures and constraints from influential bodies, including other departments and the Treasury.

But even if they wished to do so, it would be a mistake to think that departments had complete freedom of manoeuvre to decide their plans for the coming year. About two thirds of all public expenditure consists of programmes, such as social security benefit, which are determined by entitlement or demand. Another 20 per cent consists of long-term commitments, such as payments to finance European Community expenditure, notably the common agricultural policy. This leaves only 10 to 15 per cent which is open to short-term variation. Most of this expenditure can only be varied quickly at the margin, though in the long term, of course, all expenditure can be varied by altering entitlement to benefits and long-term commitments.

What happens to departmental bids varies from government to government in overall terms and from year to year in detail. During the 1980s, the requirements for additional bids were progressively tightened until they had to include not only bids for additions to programmes but also any reduced requirements for funds, options for reductions and possible offsetting savings to match the bids. Allowances were not automatically made for inflation and departments generally had to show that any increased costs could not be absorbed by increased efficiency.

Once discussions on bids between Treasury officials and officials from spending departments have been completed, the results are coordinated by PESC into a report to the Chief Secretary to the Treasury. It is this report which forms the basis of the Chief Secretary's proposals to Cabinet for their meeting at the end of July which decides the level of total public expenditure for the next three years. In making their decision, the Cabinet uses an assessment of economic prospects from the Chancellor of the Exchequer.

Following the July Cabinet decision on the planned total for the coming year, a series of discussions (known as 'bilaterals') between departmental Ministers and the Chief Secretary to the Treasury follow in the early autumn. Bilaterals are designed to ensure that if the total of all departmental bids is higher than the agreed total for public expenditure and the Reserve, they are reduced to maintain the total. But over the years it has become increasingly difficult for bilaterals to achieve their task; while some bids have been reduced to what is judged to be an acceptable level (though what is 'acceptable' is not disclosed before or after), over the last few years agreement has not been possible on an increasing number.

Bilaterals can only achieve a limited amount, as Peter Rees, John MacGregor's predecessor as Chief Secretary to the Treasury, commented:

... negotiation takes place against a background of manifesto commitments, of individual decisions over previous years, of known government priorities and of ... long-term expenditure trends ... the process of determination is subject to inputs from many sources. The more sensitive the political issue, the less likely it is that it will be determined, even in the first instance, by just two Ministers. [3]

These problems are then passed to the 'Star Chamber'. This is a special Cabinet committee with a membership of senior Ministers which hears the case presented by the Chief Secretary to the Treasury and by Ministers from spending departments which have not agreed their allocations. The composition of the Star Chamber normally consists, for obvious reasons, of Ministers without departmental spending responsibilities and those who have already settled their departmental totals. So membership varies from year to year. The methods by which the Star Chamber reaches its decisions are not disclosed, though the process is undoubtedly political rather than scientific.

Even in the Star Chamber, agreement may not be possible on the required cuts. If this is so, their findings are then submitted to the full Cabinet. Not that this will necessarily mean that dissatisfied Ministers will get more money. If such tactics were seen to be regularly successful, the Star Chamber would become redundant and Ministers unwilling to accept reductions would go straight to Cabinet. Following final decisions on disputed bids. this Cabinet meeting is able to approve the departmental totals in time for publication of results in the Chancellor of the Exchequer's Autumn Statement in November.

Throughout the period of discussion, details of some parts of the negotiations may come out in the Press. Departments are shown as coming out fighting – 'Ministers in extra £4 billion spending clash', 'Ministers vie to satisfy appetite for spending'; while the Treasury is portrayed as powerful but beleaguered – 'Cash battles come out in the open', 'Treasury to cut spending bids', 'Keeper of the public purse faces a rough Cabinet ride'. Which of the stories are planted and which are pure speculation is hard to judge, but it is very likely that the Press is used, through inspired leaks, as one of the battlegrounds on which departments try to improve their chances of success.

An interesting experiment into how the process described so far might work was provided in a simulation organized by the Public Finance Foundation. The published record [4] provides all the detailed figures and since the Chairman was a former Cabinet Minister, Edmund Dell, it can be assumed to be in touch with reality.

To give the flavour of the bargaining process, an irreverent and rather idiosyncratic insider's view by a former Treasury Minister, Jock Bruce-Gardyne, is worth quoting at length. We take up the story when departmental bids are being brought together before submission to the Cabinet in July.

Thus begins a stately minuet that lasts from around the end of June to mid November. The Treasury mandarins take their partners from the spending departments, and find themselves confronted with 'bids' for indispensable increments in their budgets for the following year, and the years thereafter, running into billions of pounds apiece. They know, and their partners know they know, that these 'bids' will contain judicious padding intended to protect their real core ambitions from the Treasury's dread axe. The first round of attrition takes place immediately, and by the time the Cabinet foregathers several billion pounds of padding will already have been bargained away.

At this stage it is mostly shadow-boxing, but both sides owe it to their *amour propre* to play up and play the game. The first result, logged at the Public Spending Cabinet, is almost drearily predictable. The Chancellor reminds his colleague that in the previous autumn they agreed a global figure, and individual departmental budgets coinciding with it, amounting to X hundred billion pounds for the following year. Unfortunately it now transpires that they are apparently hell-bent on spending X plus £4bn, or plus £6bn, or plus £10bn, as the case might be. This is wholly unacceptable, and threatens the whole fabric of society, not to mention the balance of payments, sterling, and inflation. So after a couple of hours of heart-searching he persuades his colleagues to re-endorse the original targets of the previous year and the last Budget Day.

That is the easy part. For both the Chancellor and his colleagues know quite well that this is no more than a collective Midsummer resolution. To be sure the Chancellor will take it down and seek to use it in evidence against them as the real battle moves towards its climax in the autumn. They know it is a conditional – a very conditional – agreement. When we really get down to the figures, they say to themselves, well primed by their mandarins, he will have to concede that my case for extra pennies is quite unanswerable. Furthermore my preparedness to make concessions to the Treasury will depend on the corresponding preparedness of my colleagues. If the Treasury allows them to get away with murder, then they are certainly not going to stop me getting away with petty larceny.

When the autumn comes,

... regardless of the colour of the government, the Treasury knows it has few allies as the annual public spending round begins in earnest, when the Ministers depart with Parliament for their chosen watering-holes. That section of the Treasury concerned with public spending, and their counterparts around White-hall, embark upon a much-loved and familiar season of horse-trading through the dog days. By the time the Ministers return, the battlefield has narrowed. Usually by around one third. It is time for the Chief Secretary to embark on his 'bilaterals'. One by one the Ministers from the spending departments, sustained by vigilant minders from their departments, are called in for individual haggles. These are supplemented by person-to-person arm-twisting between the politicians on the same lines as the arm-twisting within the Treasury which takes place over the drafting of the Finance Bill. The parties are programmed: if they make concessions beyond the chosen limits of their mandarins, Whitehall marks them down as men of straw.

With all this jousting going on it is inevitable that the Chief Secretary and his colleagues invariably emerge with a large gap remaining to be bridged between the Treasury's ambitions and those of the big spenders. In good years it may be £1bn, or even less. In bad years it may be £5bn or more.

But the end is in sight.

By this late stage both Treasury and the spending departments are starting to throw dancing girls to the wolves. The officials have had ample time to judge the clout (it is usually described as 'political clout', but it is more often, even at this late hour, 'mandarin clout' in reality) behind the items in contention. The Chief Secretary will be advised to go quietly on some, the spending Ministers on others, and a rough dovetail will have been contrived at official level.

The Star Chamber assembles ... The Treasury puts the case for the prosecution of the outstanding would-be overspenders, and they put the case for their defence.

The Star Chamber does its best to arbitrate. But everyone knows that there is a
right of appeal – to full Cabinet. Everyone also knows that he or she will get short
shrift for digging in on what is deemed to be a peripheral issue; and everyone has to
make an individual judgement about the relative sympathy of Star Chamber and
full Cabinet to a particular cause. Not that Ministers will necessarily accept the
verdict of Star Chamber because they think they would be bound to lose in
Cabinet. They may decide that they owe it to their careers to be seen to stand
by their standard to the bitter end. Or again, their mandarins may decide so
for them.

The Treasury has more complex sums to do. As the Star Chamber completes
its work it will see that it is still £½bn or, if it has been unskilled or unlucky, £1½
bn, wide of the global figure reconfirmed in Cabinet before the summer holidays.
It faces three choices. It can settle for what it has got. It can go for what it is
missing in Cabinet – and run the risk of being routed in whole or in part, and
worse, being seen to have been routed. For spending departments, and particularly spending Ministers, are not renowned for magnanimity in victory. Or it
can creatively account.

The choice it makes will depend on its judgement of the Chancellor, Chief
Secretary, and Prime Minister it is saddled with at any given time.[5]

Joel Barnett gives the flavour of the detailed bargaining process in
bilaterals (or in the first case 'trilaterals'), with a description of how £87
million available might be divided between the Department of Health
and Social Security (then headed by David Ennals) and the Department
of Education and Science (then with Shirley Williams as the Minister
responsible):

My 'trilateral' meeting with David Ennals and Shirley Williams was a fiasco.
It was one long harangue to persuade me to agree to increase the £57 million to
£100 million. I tried to get David and Shirley to discuss what I politely told
them was our Cabinet remit, which was how to spend £57 million. They could
see no objection to taking another £43 million out of the Contingency Reserve.
They had a better point than they realized, as I could have juggled the figures to
fit in with their wishes. But their approach to the whole issue, and me, was
turning me into an even harder 'hard man'. If we wanted to spend another £50
million, they were going about it in just about the worst possible way. We parted
after a rather more acrimonious meeting than I normally have with colleagues. I
could only be thankful that all my previous meetings had been bilaterals, and I
had never looked forward to those.

Naturally, we went back to Cabinet. There, the three-cornered argument
began again. But it was brought to a merciful end by the Prime Minister, who,
winking at me across the table, interrupted my argument to say I should find

another £12 million, making £69 million, of which £50 million would go to David Ennals . . . and £19 million to Shirley . . .

In another Cabinet the bargaining procedure was much the same:

On Thursday 11 November . . . Cabinet at last agreed the Expenditure White Paper. It was a not untypical example of how such decisions are made. I got £180 million out of the £200 million for which I had asked, when I would have been quite happy to settle for £100 million. On defence, I had asked for £50 million, and was helped enormously by Fred Mulley, the Secretary of State. Fred spoke at such great length that the Prime Minister left the Cabinet room for some time – I assume for the toilet – and was still speaking when he returned. Jim then put pressure on Fred and I got £30 million, rather more than I expected. The other interesting case was Overseas Aid. Until then, there had been no cut. I reluctantly suggested £35 million, which led to a struggle, with Tony Crosland seeking to keep this one programme free from cuts, but we eventually agreed on £10 million. It turned out that John Morris, Secretary of State for Wales, was the luckiest Minister in that we did not reach his programme until late in the proceedings. I asked for £30 million, but because we were already so near our target, Jim asked John for an offer. He said £5 million, and to his astonishment, had it promptly accepted. I had no doubt that he was ready to be pushed to £20 million. I later had one last try, suggesting that we make no cut in Overseas Aid and substitute a further £5 million cut from Wales, but the Prime Minister brushed it aside – it was nearly 1 p.m.

On another occasion, John Morris was less fortunate. He was asking for more for an important programme. He had a good case, and I was ready to make a concession, but again it was nearly 1 p.m., and the Prime Minister would not listen to any more bids. Cabinet democracy works in strange and mysterious ways.[6]

The territorial dimension

One part of the planning process which is of great importance to the parts of the United Kingdom other than England are the special provisions for Scotland, Wales and Northern Ireland. These special provisions reflect their jealously guarded degrees of independence.

The difference from English arrangements which is most immediately apparent is that all other parts of the United Kingdom have their own government departments, headed by Cabinet Ministers. Not all services are covered by the territorial departments. Responsibilities for defence and overseas aid, for example, are covered by arrangements for the whole of the United Kingdom.

SCOTLAND AND WALES

Although most of the arrangements for Scotland and Wales are similar, there are also differences between them. Thus certain Home Office services – Police, Fire, Civil Defence – are under the control of the Secretary of State for Scotland. The same services in England and Wales are treated as a single administrative unit. This reflects the fact that historically Scotland has always enjoyed a greater degree of autonomy in its legal as well as some other systems.

The main programmes covered by the Scottish and Welsh Offices are:

Education (not higher and further education in Wales; not the universities in Scotland)
Health
Housing (including Housing Benefit)
Social services
Transport (excluding certain nationalized industries)
Economic development
Agriculture, fisheries and food (Wales only)
Home Office services (Scotland only).

Since 1978, changes in spending on those Scottish and Welsh programmes comparable to those for England have automatically been made according to what is sometimes known as the 'Barnett formula', named after the Chief Secretary to the Treasury of the day whose account of his period of office is quoted several times in this book. The present formula provides that Scotland should receive ten eighty-fifths and Wales five eighty-fifths of any change in a programme which is comparable to that in England and covered by the formula. The proportion for Scotland is ten ninetieths where the programme is linked to England and Wales together. These relationships reflect relative populations; in 1977, 9.57 per cent of the population of Great Britain lived in Scotland and 5.1 per cent in Wales.

The Barnett formula covers about 95 per cent of the funds under the control of the Scottish and Welsh Offices. The rest is subject to the same public expenditure planning discussions as any other programme. Once the allocations covered by the Scottish and Welsh blocks have been made, the Secretaries of State have some discretion to enable a switch of expenditure between programmes within their own blocks, subject only to Treasury approval. This discretion does not cover a number of major programmes determined by policies covering the United Kingdom as a whole; policy on universities, for example, is made nationally and cannot be varied for each part of the United Kingdom.

In practice, of the funds allocated annually to the Scottish Office nearly 90 per cent are controlled and spent by local authorities and other public bodies. This still leaves the Secretary of State with direct responsibility for expenditure of a number of public bodies, such as the Scottish Development Agency and the Highlands and Islands Development Board.

On the whole, Scotland and Wales have received relatively generous funding as a result of the allocation system in recent years, though studies of their needs in relation to England have indicated that this relative generosity is justified. While not all public expenditure can be identified separately, there are amounts which are identifiable for each part of Great Britain. Expenditure per head in Scotland on this basis is more than 20 per cent above the United Kingdom average; in Wales, it is about 10 per cent above.

NORTHERN IRELAND

Northern Ireland, too, has its separate public expenditure programme and its own Cabinet Minister. But the political and financial relationship between Northern Ireland and the rest of the United Kingdom is much more complex than for Scotland or Wales.

History is a major factor in explaining the differences and the origins of the current arrangements, which were established in 1921 at the time when the Irish Free State became independent. More recently, however, arrangements have been determined by political factors, particularly the failure to produce a successor to Northern Ireland's own elected legislative assembly. This had enjoyed a considerable degree of autonomy since 1921, but the system broke down in 1972 under the pressure of political turmoil and civil unrest.

For planning purposes, about two thirds of Northern Ireland's public expenditure is linked to similar functions in Great Britain through a formula based on their share of the total United Kingdom population. Virtually all the rest is social security, which is based on demand. But this does not mean that there is no scope for varying the uses to which the allocation is put. The Secretary of State for Northern Ireland is exceptionally allowed to make bids when he believes there are special circumstances for him to do so. The Treasury has the corresponding option to propose a reduction in the allocation–based formula if it considers this would be over-generous.

Once the allocation has been made, however, it forms a block which can be allocated within Northern Ireland with a great deal of discretion by the Secretary of State – subject, of course, to the overall direction of government policy and factors such as wage settlements largely determined by settlements in Great Britain. The block includes the Northern Ireland Office and the Northern Ireland departments, as well as their associated bodies such as the Health and Education Boards and the Housing Executive. What happens, in effect, is a mini-Survey by the Northern Ireland departments. This takes place in parallel with the Survey being carried out in Whitehall. So the exact total available is not known until late in the process when the departmental totals are agreed by Cabinet in late October or early November.

The mini-Survey takes place in very much the same way as the 'senior' version, with Northern Ireland departments submitting bids to the Department of Finance and Personnel. This department is the equivalent of the Treasury in Northern Ireland and carries out a coordinating role similar to that of the Treasury. Allocations from the block are up to the Secretary of State, not the department, of course, and an illustration of the way in which his discretion has been exercised is shown by the relatively generous provision of housing finance in Northern Ireland compared to the rest of the United Kingdom.

There is another curious and interesting financial relic of Northern Ireland's stormy history: the Northern Ireland Consolidated Fund. The Fund's 'income' comes from a variety of sources, the most important of which is a calculated sum representing what is thought to be Northern Ireland's share of United Kingdom taxes. The bulk (but not all) of Northern Ireland's public expenditure is debited to the Fund. In other words, an integral part of the United Kingdom is treated as if it was a separate financial entity. This arrangement reflects the earlier separate legislative assembly and continues because it would be too politically contentious to do away with it.

The Treasury and public expenditure

The Treasury are always complaining. Even in Heaven they would
be worried about excessive imports. (Anon.)

Even before the development of constitutional monarchy, when kings ruled with virtually no check on their powers, there were officials to look after the financial side of government. The office of Lord Treasurer dates from Norman times and no doubt there was always someone to look after money matters even before that. But financial administration began to take today's shape mainly in the seventeenth and eighteenth centuries. The Treasury as a department and the office of the Chancellor of the Exchequer both date from these times.

Reflecting the national importance of financial affairs, the titular head of the Treasury is the Prime Minister with the title 'First Lord of the Treasury'. In the realm of constitutional fantasy, the Treasury is technically managed by the Board of Commissioners, which consists of the Prime Minister, the Chancellor of the Exchequer and the five Lords Commissioners. But this is not a working Board and it last met in earnest in 1921, though for sentimental reasons it gathered more recently to bid farewell to the department's Permanent Secretary on his retirement.

In practice the responsibility for the Treasury is very much that of the Chancellor of the Exchequer (more usually referred to simply as 'the Chancellor'). He is supported by a number of Ministers, of whom the most senior is the Chief Secretary to the Treasury. The fact that this post too carries Cabinet rank indicates the importance of the Treasury in a much more tangible way than the Prime Minister's title. It also indicates the importance attached to public expenditure policy and control, matters which are the principal concern of the Chief Secretary – the usual abbreviation of the title.

There are a number of other Ministers in the department. The Financial Secretary to the Treasury has responsibilities which include parliamentary financial business as well as overseeing the Inland Revenue. The Economic Secretary to the Treasury has a more diverse portfolio. It includes monetary policy, the regulation of the financial system and overseeing a variety of bodies, including the Royal Mint and the Department of National Savings. Finally, there is a Minister of State who deals with public sector pay and pensions, and European Community financial matters, as well as looking after another group of departments including Customs and Excise, the Central Office of Information and Her Majesty's Stationery Office.

In addition, a whole group of government members, known as the Whips Office, are technically categorized as part of the Treasury ministerial team. They are responsible for the smooth passage of government parliamentary business. Their direct connection with the Treasury extends only to their titles, though they sign certain documents on behalf of the Treasury. The Chief Whip is called the Parliamentary Secretary to the Treasury; others being Lords Commissioners to the Treasury.

Financial matters affect all activities in the public sector and the Treasury is administratively, politically, and indeed physically, at the centre of government decision-taking for them all. It is regarded as the most senior Civil Service department although it is one of the smallest. Its officials are regarded, and regard themselves, as a Whitehall elite.

The Treasury's power is reinforced by the fact that it is responsible for presenting expenditure proposals to Parliament and that no legislation which requires public expenditure can go before the House of Commons without the support of a Treasury Minister. Nor can a proposal from a department which requires additional expenditure be put to the Cabinet without first being discussed with the Treasury.

While the Treasury's organization is complex, as Figure 3.1 shows, the direct responsibility for public expenditure is more straightforward (Figure 3.2).

Officials in the public expenditure sector are involved in discussions at all stages of the annual expenditure cycle. They brief the Chief Secretary for the many discussions with Cabinet colleagues and other Ministers. They play a major role in discussions with officials from other departments.

Their involvement starts when plans are being prepared by departments well before the beginning of the Survey round. Officials give early, informal indications to departments of the likely constraints which they will face. They are then responsible for chairing PESC and coordinating bids to be submitted to the Cabinet in July. The Chief Secretary leads the Cabinet discussions at this meeting on the overall expenditure totals. Assuming that the total of individual bids exceeds the overall public expenditure total which is agreed, the Chief Secretary and officials are involved in an intense period of activity between September and late October through the bilaterals, Star Chamber (if necessary) and finally the Cabinet.

Towards the end of this process, the public expenditure sector is responsible for the annual investment and financing review which fixes the amounts required to finance the nationalized industries, but does not intervene in day-to-day policy matters. However, officials do become involved in certain matters such as changes in financing plans (particularly if more money is required), discussions about subsidy policy (for example on British Rail rural services), major capital expenditure project approvals (such as new power stations or shipyard modernization)

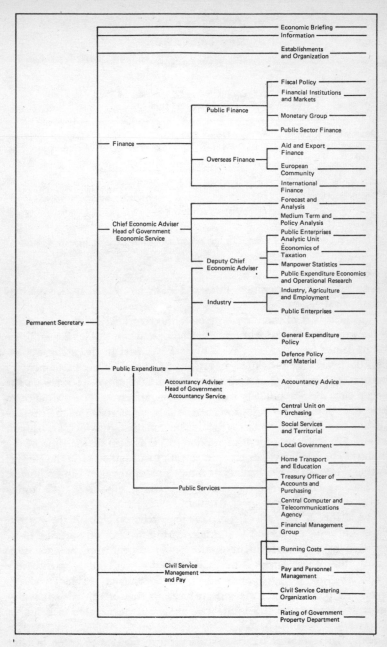

Figure 3.1   *HM Treasury organization chart, December 1987*

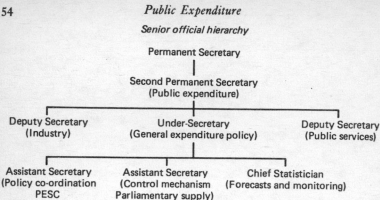

Figure 3.2 *Public expenditure organization in the Treasury senior official hierarchy*

or general policy discussions. They also play a key role in any discussions about privatization.

The next part of their work involves the coordination of the material to be published in the Autumn Statement and the Public Expenditure White Paper (see also page ix). Officials take part in discussions about how the figures are presented, in briefing Ministers for the parliamentary debates and in House of Commons Select Committee hearings on the documents. Senior officials will themselves appear to give evidence to Select Committees. In addition there will be supervision of the preparation of the Supply Estimates (the documents through which Parliament makes cash available) for presentation to Parliament at the time of the Budget. The whole cycle is completed with involvement after the Budget in the process of parliamentary scrutiny and approval of the Estimates, culminating in the Appropriation Act, which authorizes the funds required, in late July or early August.

While this is the end of the planning cycle, officials of the general expenditure policy part of the public expenditure sector continue to be involved in the management of the public expenditure process until nearly three years later. Table 3.2 sets out where and approximately when key Survey figures appear in main documents. Table 3.3 shows where the relevant figures appear which are part of the parliamentary process. More about the individual published documents is given in Chapter 7.

Although several of their activities refer to matters to come in later

Table 3.2   Where Survey figures appear in main documents

Example: 1988–89 public expenditure

January 1986	First projection published	Public Expenditure White Paper
January 1987	Updated projection published	Public Expenditure White Paper
July 1987	Cabinet decision on total expenditure	Press announcement
November 1987	Agreed departmental planned totals	Autumn Statement
January 1988	Detailed figures	Public Expenditure White Paper
March 1988	Total amended by any Budget changes	Financial Statement and Budget Report
November 1988	Estimates of out-turn by department	Autumn Statement
January 1989	Revised estimates of out-turn by department	Public Expenditure White Paper (see p. ix)
March 1989	Revised estimate of total expenditure	Financial Statement and Budget Report
November 1989	Out-turn figures	Autumn Statement
January 1990	Detailed out-turn figures	Public Expenditure White Paper (see page ix)

Notes: The timing of each document may vary, as may the content and format of each document.

The final out-turn figures may be subject to further changes after the year-end.

Parliamentary documents and in-year monitoring are excluded.

chapters, it is worth completing an overview of the rest of the Treasury's work.

Monitoring and control is a major activity during the financial year. This includes supervision of the presentation to Parliament of requests for additional funds. Departments who need to cover excesses of expenditure or shortfalls in receipts will have to ask the Treasury to submit Supplementary Estimates to Parliament. The sheer scale of the amounts involved in relation to the staff available means that there is a limit to what officials can examine; but because monitoring is on the basis of variations from plan, the task is less daunting than might at first appear. The control mechanisms are discussed in detail in Chapter 4.

Even when departmental funds have been approved by Parliament, the Treasury still keeps an element of formal control through its responsibility for the Consolidated Fund. When funds are required, departments have to draw them from the Consolidated Fund through the Treasury, who require the Comptroller and Auditor-General's agreement – see Chapter 8) that they have been approved by Parliament. Only

Table 3.3 Where the voted expenditure appears in parliamentary documents

Example: 1988–89 public expenditure		
March 1988	Estimates for year	Supply Estimates
June 1988	Initial changes	Revised and Summer Supplementary Estimates
November 1988	Half-year out-turn figures and second set of changes	Winter Supplementary Estimates
February/March 1989	Third set of changes and estimated out-turn (by vote)	Spring Supply Estimates
Autumn 1989	Final out-turn for past year	Appropriation Accounts

when the Treasury is satisfied about the timing of the request will funds be issued. Although in theory this scrutiny could apply to every item of government expenditure, because of the lack of time and manpower only large amounts are considered in this way. So the process is more 'good housekeeping' than an element in a substantive control process.

The responsible officials within the public expenditure sector are also involved in granting permission if departments wish to use savings on one or more subheads (the smallest category in Parliamentary control) to meet excess expenditure on another subhead or subheads within the same Vote (the individual unit of expenditure approved by Parliament). The Treasury acts on behalf of Parliament in examining such proposals, and the assumption is that the cash will not be used to finance wholly new services or to bring about politically contentious increases in services which Parliament would expect to consider separately.

The Treasury's role is further strengthened through the exercise of its responsibility to appoint an Accounting Officer for each Vote granted by Parliament – normally the senior civil servant in the department concerned. The officer is responsible for signing the accounts relating to that Vote (the Appropriation Accounts) which are audited by the National Audit Office (NAO). These accounts, with any reports on them, are laid before the House of Commons and published a few months after the end of the financial year, as Chapter 8 explains. Thus the Treasury has detailed knowledge of the use made of funds during the year, especially in comparing actual expenditure with plans. It is also responsible for departmental implementation of any recommendations made by the NAO or PAC as a result of the reports.

The other parts of the Treasury are less directly concerned with public spending, although since government economic policy does not fit into neatly separate compartments, in practice each part has policy links with the others. Pay, for example, is a crucial element in public expenditure as a whole and is dealt with in the division 'Civil Service Management and Pay', while for the Budget the public expenditure sector is represented on the Budget Committee which considers revenue-raising proposals for several months before the Budget is presented to Parliament. Otherwise most aspects of economic policy have public expenditure implications and the public expenditure sector can expect to be involved in discussions about them.

Less directly, the division looking after public finance is responsible for government borrowing to fund the difference between receipts and expenditure. There is close collaboration with the Bank of England in doing so. Borrowing by other public bodies, notably local authorities and public corporations, also takes place, and can either be from the market or from central government. Policy on what these bodies are allowed to do is subject to the constraints of overall macro-economic policy. This too is supervised by the Treasury, which also sets interest rates for bodies such as the Public Works Loans Board which lends on to public bodies.

The Chief Economic Adviser is particularly involved with public expenditure in providing the forecasts which are the basis of the planning process. There are three forecasting rounds a year:

- the winter forecast in January/February, in time for the Budget;
- the summer forecast;
- the autumn forecast in time for the Autumn Statement.

A staff of economists and statisticians use models of considerable sophistication (if not always complete accuracy) to provide short-term and medium-term forecasts. Short-term forecasts are for two years ahead and are used as a basis for immediate economic policy decisions and Budget policy. Medium-term forecasts are for up to five years ahead and give a more general view of the economy. Public expenditure is obviously an important element in these forecasts.

The part of the Treasury which has the least to do with public expenditure is the Overseas Finance division. While international events clearly influence public expenditure planning decisions, the areas where the sector plays a direct role is confined to the international elements of the Budget and as part of the coordination of the country's role in the European Community, especially the contentious area of the United Kingdom's share of the Community budget.

Despite its pivotal role in public expenditure matters, indeed in government policy as a whole, the Treasury is one of the smallest government departments, employing around 1,400 people of whom many are support staff, messengers and so on. The relatively few people involved means that officials engaged in policy work have to be highly capable. As Michael Posner, an adviser with extensive experience of government, put it in *But Chancellor*, a radio series which gave one of the very few insights available into the department:

'The Treasury has always been the power-house. Harold Lever once said that moving to the Treasury from another department was like coming to the Savoy from a two-star hotel out in the provinces. I wouldn't want to be unfair to other departments, I've worked in several outside the Treasury and I love them and they're very important, but the Treasury has always contained very clever people, at least as clever as one meets at High Table in an average Oxbridge college. They're well read, they're accomplished, they're intelligent, they're knowledgeable, they're powerful − it's an immensely exciting environment.'[7]

The department is not, however, without its critics. It has been said that the background of its officials is too narrow; in particular, the disproportionately high number from Oxbridge and public school backgrounds is often criticized. Others have said more, accusing them of being blinkered in their outlook, elitist, arrogant, ignorant of industrial and commercial realities and out of touch with the mainstream of the social and economic life of the country. Sir Frank Cooper, at the time the Permanent Secretary at the head of another department, less offensively described it thus:

'The people who work there are very clever. Intellectually they are extremely able, outstandingly so, there's no doubt about that. But they live in an isolated world and a different world from the rest of humanity. And until you change this, you're never really going to get an effective Treasury.'[8]

The Treasury would contest these accusations. Officials point out that the graduates they choose are the most able and that the training they give is designed for the role their staff will play in future years.

Criticism of the Treasury also comes from those who accuse it of being anti-public spending. Indeed this is perhaps the most common view of the department both within government (notably by spending departments with axes to grind) and by outsiders. It has been said − borrowing a phrase from Oscar Wilde's definition of a cynic − that they know the cost of everything and the value of nothing. But as

Stephen Godber, a Treasury official, explained, there is no Treasury policy on individual spending areas:

'I don't think the Treasury necessarily has a housing policy. It will have a housing aspect of a general public expenditure policy, and if there are general policy objectives, such as keeping the level of public expenditure down or trying to shift the balance between capital and current expenditure, then that will influence the attitude that one takes to policy issues that come up in housing. But I don't think it has a free-standing housing policy as such.'[9]

On a wider front, Treasury power over decision-making in general is often resented. Tony Benn, for long a ministerial critic of the power of the Treasury, said:

'It has a lot of international links and is the pipe through which a lot of powerful forces in the world express themselves to the Chancellor rather than directly to the Cabinet. It has its own policy. I suppose you could argue that the economic failure of Britain since the war could be attributed primarily to the Treasury because they've always been in power.'[10]

This begs the question of whether the Treasury actually does make policy – an assertion the Treasury would deny. In many cases it could be argued that it is simply being blamed, like the messenger, for bringing the bad news. Certainly the Treasury's job as the central guardian of government financial and economic policy is to fit claims on public funds into the resources available to finance them. Since the resources are never enough, officials spend a good deal of their time having to resist the appeals of spending pressure groups, whether these are government departments, other public bodies, Members of Parliament or organized lobbies for various kinds of interests. This makes the Treasury a useful scapegoat for those who want to increase the overall amount of spending or their own share of it. It is not uncommon for government departments to blame the Treasury when talking to outside bodies who are putting pressure on them to increase expenditure. But in the last resort if individual Ministers do not limit their own expenditure the Treasury is bound to be the agency responsible for doing it for them.

Cuts

Frankly, I'd like to see the government get out of war altogether and leave the whole field to private industry. (Joseph Heller, *Catch 22*)

While cutting back the aspirations of Ministers and their departments is a normal part of Treasury business, cutting total public expenditure may be a matter of political and economic policy. Governments may wish to cut. They may have to cut. They may have to but not wish to, or wish to but not have to.

There are a number of motives for cutting public expenditure on particular programmes. One is based on the philosophical viewpoint that the state plays too great a role, so public expenditure is itself undesirable. Reducing it is therefore worthwhile as an end in itself. Another is that while expenditure is not undesirable, cuts in some programmes are necessary because the money is not available to pay for them through taxation or borrowing.

The pressure to cut in the 1970s and 1980s, not only in the United Kingdom but in many other countries, has been the result of a combination of both motives. Not that it has always been easy to distinguish between them. Cuts are rarely popular to those directly affected and, since democratic governments are generally against alienating whole sections of the community, the tendency is to present cuts as something else as a way of softening the blow.

Most of the reasons for the desire to cut public expenditure as a whole are connected to the belief that if possible the state should not take and then spend too much of the nation's income. As John MacGregor explained to Parliament:

... restraint of public spending goes even wider than improving the way our economy works, critical though that is. It is at the heart of the kind of society which this government are seeking to build. A society based on choice, on freedom and on responsibility. A society in which people keep more of what they earn to spend or save as they decide, and a society in which industrial and commercial companies are left with greater capacity of their own to invest, and to earn a good return. [11]

At the level of the individual programme, the reasons are usually linked to beliefs about the role of the state in relation to those programmes. Thus the state is reckoned by some to be a poor substitute for the private sector in almost any field, having a tendency to inefficiency in general and over-staffing in particular.

The arguments for cutting expenditure as a matter of necessity rather than ideology are easy to explain – the money is not available to pay for what is otherwise considered desirable. 'Not available' does not automatically mean that the money could not be raised if required, but rather that it is considered better not to raise it. The reasons are generally linked to economic policies, such as the importance of reducing the disincentive effects of taxation. The result may be that some programmes are cut to allow a rise in other programmes which take a higher priority. 'Guns or butter' used to be a familiar way of putting the dilemma, though in recent years the *cause* of a squeeze in the defence budget has more often been a rise in unemployment, requiring an increase in social security payments. It may be that it is not a question of choices between programmes, but that there is outside pressure for public spending as a whole to be pruned. Such a situation occurred in 1976 as a result of pressure exerted by the International Monetary Fund when the UK was obliged to ask for a loan as a result of its economic difficulties.

Announcing cuts is not the same as actually achieving them, either in total or for individual programmes. As the House of Commons Treasury and Civil Service Select Committee commented, the aim in the 1980s appeared to shift from

... 'a reduction in public expenditure' to 'hold total spending broadly level in real terms' to a determination to 'see to it that total public spending, even without taking account of privatization proceeds, continues to decline as a percentage of GNP'.[12]

Nor is cutting plans for spending the same as cutting spending. One reason is put forward by Christopher Hood and Maurice Wright:

... determining whether the result of cuts will really be a public sector slimmed down to the more effective pursuit of government's tasks is what might be called the 'fungibility factor'. This unlovely but necessary term refers to the ability of organizations in receipt of grants to defeat the objectives of the grantor – that is, responding to grant changes by reshuffling elements of their budget not under the grantor's control.[13]

There is no guarantee that there will even be reshuffling. Joel Barnett explained that

... like so many other 'cuts' these were very much dependent on assumptions that might or might not materialize. It particularly applied, as in this case, where the actual expenditure was not under the direct control of central government but in the hands of local authorities. On mortgage lending, we had some control over the total spent, but on council house rents all we could do was to fix the Rate Support Grant [RSG] on an assumption about the increase there should be in rents. Many councils ignored our proposals and either did not increase the rents at all or raised them by a smaller amount. So our assumption on savings ('cuts in subsidies') might not materialize – but we would not know about that until much later. Meanwhile, we could take credit for a 'cut' in public expenditure. It was, like so many 'cuts', a changed assumption leading to a changed estimate which was more or less dubious. Even so, we and outside commentators would imbue a public expenditure total of over £50 billion with a spurious accuracy, as if we were planning to within the nearest £1 million.[14]

There is a similar problem with individual programmes. For example, it has taken many years to achieve a substantial reduction in the amount given to nationalized industries as a whole. The problem, year after year, was that unexpected factors – poor weather, a strike, a downturn in demand – persisted in pushing up the amounts required by the industries.

A different manifestation of 'cuts without cuts' is to announce a cut in the year-on-year rate of increase in expenditure rather than the programme itself. Thus the rate of increase of expenditure on defence was 'cut' in the mid 1980s from the high level of growth in the earlier part of the decade. Yet another way is to increase the charges for services, so that net expenditure is reduced. Increasing charges to water consumers in the 1980s meant not only that consumers financed the current investment programme, but also that the industry was able to make a useful contribution to the Exchequer by repaying its debt. Finally, 'cuts without cuts' can seem to be achieved for the announced total of public expenditure through altering the basis of calculation. Two examples already given in Chapter 1 were to take debt interest out of the planning total and to transfer public services into the private sector.

The other side of the coin is to make cuts without it being clear that anything is happening. Allowing an inadequate amount for expected inflation or for a known increase in demand, or assuming unrealistically high productivity gains, are ways of cutting the volume of resources devoted to a particular programme – or even public spending as a whole – without being seen to be cutting. The amount set aside for public sector pay, for example, was consistently below the actual settlements in the early 1980s, though whether this was intentional or not is impossible to prove. A more subtle variation of providing an inadequate provision for inflation is to allow an amount which is linked to general inflation, but does not take into account the unfavourable relative price effect. Defence has consistently argued that the resources it has been allocated buy less than the cash figures indicate. Finally, altering the rules of entitlement to benefit is a way in which even demand-led programmes can be cut.

These factors can give rise to disputes about whether there have been cuts or not. In the case of the National Health Service, there have been many assertions in the 1980s that the NHS as a whole was under-funded and in danger of collapse. Against this it was pointed out that the level of real resources going into the NHS was greater than ever before and there were vigorous denials that there had been cuts at all.

On the basis of the facts, both sides undoubtedly had a case. On the one hand, the amount of money devoted to the NHS was indeed increasing. On the other, the resources available to meet the needs of those seeking health care was declining. This apparent paradox could be explained in terms of several factors, two of which were particularly important. First, the proportion of older people in the community was rising and this group makes a greater call on health services than that of other age groups. Second, the quality and price of drugs rose faster than general inflation. The combination of these and other factors meant a major increase in resources was required to maintain existing standards.

Setting other targets which result in spending reductions without specifically demanding them is another way of exercising pressure for cuts in volume. A freeze on appointments, manpower reduction targets or unrealistically high required rates of return on new investment are some of the possibilities here.

A way of making it easier to achieve cuts lies in the introduction of measures to encourage greater efficiency and value for money. Not that all such measures should be cynically regarded as cost-cutting in disguise. Undoubtedly they are important in helping to provide the maximum impact for a given amount of public expenditure. But what-ever the reason for their introduction, the measures described in Chapter 5 certainly helped to create a favourable climate for implementing cost-cutting measures in the 1980s.

Nevertheless, there have certainly been an increasing number of in-stances when straightforward cuts have been announced and pushed through. The major reduction in the housing programme and in grants provided by the Department of Trade and Industry in the early 1980s showed that it could indeed be done. In the case of housing, the reduction was of a third over five years, and in the case of industrial and regional support grants, spending was nearly halved.

The fact that these two programmes could be cut back to such an extent shows the type of expenditure most easily cut. It is generally

those programmes with a substantial discretionary element. Most difficult have been those which consist primarily of employment costs. Joel
Barnett noted gloomily:

> In the public sector, capital expenditure will have been deferred, deferred and
> deferred again. In this, I am as guilty as any of my successors, and as has been
> explained in this book, the only plea in mitigation is that it was politically easier
> to cut capital rather than current expenditure. It is not an edifying excuse to set
> against the daily, more visible, signs of a public sector deprived of desperately
> needed resources to replace run-down capital assets. [15]

The House of Commons Treasury and Civil Service Select Committee
made the same point in one of their reports. In response to government
assurances that capital expenditure was being safeguarded, they stated
that

> ... to some degree capital expenditure is declining because it is easier to control
> than current spending. Some confirmation of that view may be read into the
> Chief Secretary's comment that 'I would like to see it (capital spending) increased
> but then that means one has to have greater constraints on areas of current
> spending.' [16]

In looking for cuts, successive United Kingdom governments have in
general discriminated between programmes rather than taking an across-
the-board cut on a percentage basis – a technique common in the private
sector. While percentage cuts would have the apparent advantage of
sharing the misery equally, they do not distinguish between the important
and the unimportant. Such cuts would in any case be difficult to put
into effect because of the existence of so many demand-led programmes.

Whatever the ways in which cuts are implemented, the message has to
be put across in the right way. In a review of expenditure-cutting programmes across Europe, Daniel Tarschys commented:

> Packages must be launched with energy and *élan*. A recent cutback program in
> Sweden was called 'the autumn offensive'. The string of statutory reforms
> proposed in connection with the 1982 budget of the Federal Republic of
> Germany were boldly presented as 'Operation 82'.
>
> Why are proposals so frequently thrown together into a bundle and presented
> at the same time? There seem to be several motives behind this. One is the aim
> of 'critical mass' – if the government is out to show its muscle the sheer number
> of measures may help make the desired impact. Another and frequently more
> important motive is the need for political balance. Most packages emerge from

deals between coalition partners or between the government and other political and/or economic forces. By connecting a number of disparate proposals, the negative effects of some measures to certain concerned groups will be neutralized by other policy changes in a more favourable direction. In the well-balanced package there is good news and bad news for everyone, and even if the bad news dominates, the ambiguity of the package helps mollify resistance.

The rituals accompanying economic–political packages follow a reliable pattern. The sponsors of new measures advertise them as vigorous and offensive remedies to acute economic problems imported from abroad. Opposition parties, however, prefer to characterize them as the ultimate proof of the government's incompetence and the logical sequel of its past misdemeanours. The favourite welcoming line of other bystanders is 'too little, too late'.[17]

How should public spending priorities be decided?

Everybody is always in favour of general economy and particular expenditure. (Lord Avon, Conservative Prime Minister)

'A Minister has three functions.
1 He is an Advocate. He makes the department's actions seem plausible to Parliament and the public.
2 He is our Man in Westminster . . .
3 He is our breadwinner. His duty is to fight in Cabinet for the money *we* need to do *our* job.'

(*Yes Minister*, BBC)

The Survey is the focus for medium-term planning of total public expenditure and for allocation of the total between different programmes. To put the process in context, however, it is certainly not the only time when such matters are discussed. As John MacGregor put it:

There is, of course, no ideal system for setting priorities, and if we had an academically or theoretically perfect system it would not work. There are many decisions, some small, some major, to be taken through the year. It just does not all happen in the basic public expenditure round. Outside events and changing economic assumptions can have a material effect on plans. Ministers have to make judgements individually, bilaterally and collectively on a range of issues, and have to take into account the many pressures upon them, not least from Hon. Members in this House, and to judge what is sensible and acceptable. It is not just in the annual PES round that priorities are set and decisions are made.[2]

Nevertheless, the Survey is certainly the time when the chips on

priorities are down. It will already be clear that there is plenty of jus-
tification for the Chief Secretary's comment that there is no straightforward mechanism for allocating the total between programmes. The
process is in practice a series of negotiations on the bids put forward by
departments. In order to get their programmes approved, departments
have to cross a number of thresholds, with more and more senior bodies
involved, if they wish (and are allowed) to press their case further.
Treasury officials and Treasury Ministers will in any case be involved.
The Star Chamber and the Cabinet as a whole could be.

Although a system of progressively more difficult thresholds may
seem logical, it tends to turn the annual Survey into what is in effect a
highly stylized game. Departments have every incentive to start the
bidding process at as high a level as possible and to hold out for as long
as possible in the negotiating procedure. In this way they are likely to get
the maximum for the department and, as important, to be seen to be
tough negotiators. Regardless of whether the political advantage is to be
seen to be cutting expenditure or increasing it in total, Ministers and
officials in any department know that they have a common cause in doing
better – i.e. getting more – than other departments, and that they lose
face if they are seen as agreeing too easily to cuts in their programme.

A retired civil servant and former Permanent Secretary to the Treasury, Sir Douglas Wass, gave an earthy version of the final stages:

> It is, however, when it comes to dividing the agreed total between the different
> programmes that the concept of rationality begins to come under strain. Decisions
> in this area are governed by two well-entrenched, if rather arbitrary principles.
> Number one: 'as things are, so broadly they remain'; and number two: 'he who
> has the muscle gets the money'.[18]

An even more important consequence of the system is that by putting
the emphasis on departmental totals, there is hardly any consideration of
priorities between departments. Decisions about departmental priorities
are made when the initial plans are drawn up within departments,
although some idea of overall priorities will be useful to them in deciding
what to concede during the Survey. The DHSS discusses whether to
put money into heart surgery or family doctors, the Department of
Transport whether to build motorways or upgrade existing roads. But
there is really no opportunity to discuss the choice between heart surgery
and better roads.

The concentration on departmental totals has been reinforced by an
additional threshold erected in 1986 to curb departmental bids. Under

this procedure, a Minister wishing to bid for extra spending *has* to specify possible departmental savings which would offset the increases being sought. To add pressure against making bids, the Minister has to sign the bid personally, with a copy to the Chief Secretary and the Prime Minister.

The lack of an overall look at priorities is nothing new. Peter Hennessy quotes the Secretary to the Cabinet in 1950, then Sir Norman Brook:

It is curious that in modern times the Cabinet, though it has always insisted on considering particular proposals for developments of policy and their costs, has never thought it necessary to review the development of expenditure under the Civil Estimates as a whole.

It is remarkable that the present government have never reflected upon the great increase in public expenditure, and the substantial change in its pattern, which has come about during the past five years in consequence of their policies in the field of the social services.[19]

More recently the House of Commons Treasury and Civil Service Select Committee, among others, has suggested that the absence of a mechanism for deciding between priorities is a serious weakness in the public expenditure planning system. In a series of reports in the early 1980s, they took revealing evidence from Treasury Ministers and officials on such mechanisms. Although in evidence it was said that interdepartmental comparisons of priorities were made, it appeared that discussions on relative priorities were *ad hoc* and informal. In 1984 they recommended

. . . a reappraisal of the machinery for determining public expenditure priorities, as reflected in the Autumn Statement, with particular reference to the need to improve the allocation across departments and a more open discussion of the best machinery for achieving this.[20]

But they did not come up with a solution.

Who, then, could take on the crucial task of looking at public expenditure priorities as a whole? It might be thought that the Treasury, being at the centre of the whole negotiating process, might do so. But it would be difficult to find supporters of such an idea, even within the Treasury. As Nicholas Monck, a Treasury official, said in *But Chancellor*:

'You [the Treasury] don't actually have the power to say we're going to get a desirable total by a combination of expanding some things which clearly have a good economic case and knocking out this other rubbish; you have in practice to take a cut wherever you can get it.'[21]

Another candidate for the task could be a type of Star Chamber. Joel Barnett certainly saw it in this way in the late 1970s:

I complained about our way of considering priorities, whether it be on how to allocate increases or cuts. I had previously written to the Prime Minister suggesting a new approach, which was a variation on something that had been tried in the last Labour government, but had not been given a proper chance to work. My suggestion was basically to set up a small, but very senior, committee of non-spending Ministers, to sit through all major programmes, and then put proposals to Cabinet. They should examine programmes in depth, and seriously consider major changes so that Cabinet could take decisions that would not simply be on the margin.[22]

Simon Jenkins [23] suggested using the existing Star Chamber, though strengthening it with a secretariat and convening it earlier to alert the Cabinet of problems so that it could take a more considered view of priorities. Sir Douglas Wass suggested something similar,[18] backed up by a central analytic review staff watching over the Survey, and producing its own report suggesting solutions to the problems of choice which were raised. He also suggested there should be a more analytic approach before issues came up, with a greater emphasis on a zero-based budgeting approach and policy reviews.

Edmund Dell took a different line, arguing in favour of recognizing that collective responsibility was on the decline and putting forward an enhanced role for the Prime Minister:

... decisions on the level and distribution of public expenditure would be taken by the Prime Minister and Chancellor of the Exchequer jointly, after taking account of the political and economic considerations involved, and of the views of their colleagues. The problem of allocation would probably be a great deal more difficult than decision as to the total. That makes it more desirable rather than less that the decisions should be as rational as possible, and as little as possible determined by power-bargaining and threats of resignation.[24]

Then there is the Cabinet, which after all can review expenditure plans as a whole and alter them if it wishes. While at the moment the Cabinet acts as a final court of appeal, it could decide priorities in a series of meetings, if necessary throughout the year. It has also been suggested that Parliament should have more say in determining priorities.

Some have dismissed all these suggestions as unrealistic. Nigel Lawson explained to the House of Commons without apology that

'Whatever the group of Ministers or Departments involved and whatever the forum or setting, there can be no magic mechanism for setting priorities within and between programmes. However detailed the factual basis provided by the officials and however sophisticated the analysis of output and performance for the programme concerned, in the end there has to be a political judgement and a political decision.

. . .

'In government there is no utilitarian calculus that permits numerical comparison of the respective benefits of, say, the extra military aircraft as against more disaster relief or more equipment for the research councils. There is, of course, extensive analysis and appraisal, but at the end there is a political judgement to be made which in practice is necessarily determined as much by constraints as by priorities.'[25]

Peter Rees refused to go along with the modish enthusiasm for things Japanese:

'I understand that the Japanese Cabinet goes into continuous session, which often lasts for two days, to determine these issues. Whether that suits the Japanese temperament and system is not for me to say. I am not certain whether the outcome in British terms would be more successful than that which we have achieved.'[26]

And in putting forward their own ideas, commentators have been less than enthusiastic about the alternatives. Thus Edmund Dell commented on the proposals of Sir Douglas Wass:

I suppose that it would be possible to conceive of a more certain road to chaos, but I cannot for the moment think what it is ... a recipe for a mixture of fudging, mudging and intolerable delay well beyond what the doctrine of collective responsibility already produces.[27]

There are also the problems of sheer mechanics. The pressure of Cabinet business, the number and dominance of spending Ministers mean that it is ill-suited to make complex interdepartmental comparisons. Most issues are settled before they get to the Star Chamber. The parliamentary timetable is not well aligned with the Survey process.

All these problems *could* be overcome if the government had the collective will to do so. But there is no such will and, looking at the balance of advantage and disadvantage of each proposal, it is easy to see why it is more comfortable to proceed on the current basis of ambiguity and political bargaining. It is not that it is satisfactory; rather that it is the least objectionable of the possibilities to the major players in the game, for whom ambiguity means a welcome freedom of manoeuvre.

4

CONTROL IN CENTRAL GOVERNMENT

Annual income twenty pounds, annual expenditure nineteen, nineteen and six, result happiness. Annual income twenty pounds, annual expenditure twenty pounds ought and six, result misery.
(Charles Dickens, *David Copperfield*)

Just as individuals or organizations need to control how much money they spend, so the government needs to control public expenditure. Without a system to do so, the danger is that plans will not be implemented and that spending priorities will be distorted, as programmes absorb more or less resources than they were allocated. There is also the danger that the government will run out of the money raised through taxation and planned borrowing. If they do, emergency measures will be necessary to cut expenditure or borrow additional amounts, causing problems for the government's economic strategy and bringing into question its ability to plan and manage the economy. There are also highly undesirable consequences if expenditure is overestimated in the plans. This will mean that some programmes will have been held back in the planning process on the basis of the false assumption that the money was not available to finance them. So the planning issues set out in Chapter 3 are closely linked with the control issues set out in this chapter.

It may seem that it is mere rhetoric for newspapers and politicians to proclaim regularly that government spending is 'out of control'. After all, the fabric of ordered government hardly seems under threat. But the term 'out of control' is almost always used in commenting that the government is spending too much, rather than worries about the process of ensuring that what is spent corresponds to what was planned. Three reasons were advanced by Michael Fallon, a Conservative Member of Parliament, in commenting on the failures of control:

'First, public expenditure continues to be dominated by public sector pay. We all know that pay and pensions in the public service take a huge slice of public expenditure ... either we impose more central control over the pay arrangements of public service workers, teachers, police, and so on, or we delegate that function to responsible local bodies that can truly reflect the realities of regional labour markets. The middle way – such as we have seen recently with teachers' remuneration and other public sector groups – simply leaves public spending as a whole at the mercy of indirect pressures that Ministers cannot control.

'The second reason why we have not succeeded in controlling public expenditure is that so much of it is constructed on the basis of political entitlement rather than continuing need. There are sectional interests ... One is the demand for mortgage interest relief on second, third, fourth and fifth mortgages taken out by families. Another is the payment of three-quarters of the amount spent on child benefit to people in receipt of no other payment, and thus the payment of a fairly meagre sum to those who need it ... As well as the sectional interests, there are important geographical interests. Most dramatically, there is the consistent and continuing over-provision in Scottish spending.

'. . . Thirdly, public spending is still dominated by the demand-led pressures that have been all too familiar from the early years of the government – agriculture and social security.'[1]

This chapter deals with the relationship between planned and actual expenditure, not the essentially political question of whether what is planned is more or less than the country can afford or than some of its citizens want to spend. It deals only with the way central government, through the Treasury, exercises control over public expenditure as a whole. Control over local authorities, health authorities, nationalized industries and other bodies is covered in Chapter 6.

Before going into the details of control, it is worth remembering – since there is often much talk about the need for the government to exercise firm control over public expenditure – that only some of such expenditure is fully within the control of government (one of the points made by Michael Fallon to his fellow Members of Parliament). There are also unexpected factors which regularly contribute to uncertainty, and there are policy reasons why spending on some items cannot be fully 'under control':

- The size of many programmes, including most of the enormous social security and NHS budgets, is determined by the right to take up certain services.

- Pay settlements have a major impact on public spending and have rarely turned out to be at the planned level, not least because the planned level has often been regarded as the basis for starting, not finishing, negotiations.

- Prices of public sector goods and services are frequently unpredictable, including, for example, those for imported goods which depend on exchange rates.

- There has been regular overspending by other bodies which are responsible for public money, notably local authorities and nationalized industries.

- Capital spending on construction has been difficult to predict because of the uncertainties of the timing of expenditure and project costs.

So in the short term government cannot be completely 'in control' of its expenditure in the sense that it can define precisely what is spent or keep exactly within the planned total. True, a limited number of steps can be taken to improve control and lessen the government's vulnerability, and these are outlined below. In the longer term the story is quite different. Policies can be changed, and rights to take up services can be increased, reduced or even taken away altogether. Legislation can be passed to alter the content of any spending programme. In the longer term the only limit is the politically possible.

Controlling public expenditure as a whole

> Social security . . . is a huge, demand-led programme that is often, if not always, overshot, difficult to forecast and impossible to control. (Peter Rees, former Chief Secretary to the Treasury)

The present control system has its origins much more in successive responses to crises than in a carefully thought through and coherent plan. Above all, it was the acceleration in the rate of inflation in the mid 1970s that provided the conditions in which a comprehensive system of control became essential. Figure 4.1 shows the magnitude of that acceleration, which meant that public expenditure could not be controlled in volume terms when prices were not only rising, but rising at rates which fluctuated dramatically and unpredictably from one year to another. Such volume plans, which bore less and less relation to cash outlays, became known derisively as 'funny money'. The tendency of public sector prices to fluctuate at different rates from those of the economy as a whole (the RPE) made matters even worse. As Heclo and Wildavsky commented, 'PESC grew into a procedure that contributed to all the other troubles by making it difficult to know what was happening', since 'PESC has never provided a way of translating numbers from planning to detailed control figures within departmental programmes'.[2]

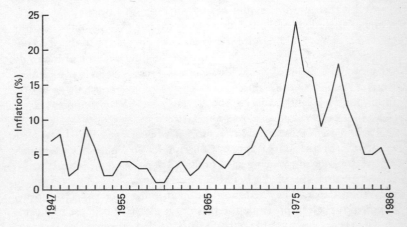

Figure 4.1　*How the rate of inflation has varied, 1947–86*

Source: Central Statistical Office

Criticism that public spending was 'out of control' in this period did indeed refer to fears that the government could no longer control the relationship between planned and actual expenditure. The situation was made worse by primitive internal control systems and the problems of controlling the expenditure of devolved bodies, especially local authorities and nationalized industries.

In setting out the basis for change, the government emphasized additional concerns about cost control: 'The volume system did not supply any pressure to reduce the costs, since the volume of programmes was protected against rising costs.'[3] There was also criticism that cost increases could simply be passed on and help to feed inflationary pressures.

In fact, as the Armstrong Report pointed out, the system was not one of 'pure' volume:

The exercise of control, however, was in practice an uneasy mixture of volume and of cash. This was unavoidable not only because there are always elements of expenditure which can in practice be controlled only in money terms but more especially because the problem of identifying expenditure at constant survey prices meant that this was difficult to monitor, and therefore to control, in these terms across the board.[4]

The first moves to try and introduce a better system were made in 1974. The basis of these moves was the belief that expenditure should be controlled through the amount of cash allocated to a programme, not in terms of the goods and services to be provided. At first only building land and some building programmes, including local authority construction, were made subject to a limit on the total amount which could be spent in a financial year. The next year the system was extended when a cash limit was announced for the most important source of funds for local authorities – the government's Rate Support Grant (RSG).

Then in 1976 these *ad hoc* measures were developed into a complete framework by the White Paper 'Cash Limits on Public Expenditure'. The reasons for introducing cash limits – the net amount of cash which can be spent on specified services during a financial year – were given in the White Paper. They reflected the main causes for concern already outlined, though in principle the reasons would have been as applicable with a lower or less variable rate of inflation. The reasons given included the following:

- 'to ensure that resources taken by the public sector are sensibly related to the total resources available to the economy as a whole';

- 'to control the amount exactly spent in the current financial year so that it fits into the plan set out in the annual budget';

- 'because the budget estimate (when expressed in volume terms) did not operate as a direct control on the amount of cash spent';

- because 'when inflation gathered pace and especially as the price of goods and services increases at very different rates' the budget estimates 'become even more inadequate as an indicator of the amount of cash that would be needed during the year';

- to give greater financial discipline;

- 'to contribute to countering inflation by making it clear to both spending authorities and to suppliers that the government's purchases of goods and services will have to be cut back if prices rise too high'.[5]

In an atmosphere of great uncertainty, arising from the period of high inflation, these reasons were accepted and the changes were generally welcomed. Most public authorities preferred the idea that they should have a clear idea of the amount they could spend in any financial year and indeed many had previously expressed concern that the old system did not give them sufficiently clear guidelines. Nevertheless, the change to a cash basis of control was only partial. About two thirds of the total was cash-limited, a proportion which has changed little since the system was introduced. This is because the few extensions of cash limits have been offset by significant increases in expenditure on some items which cannot effectively be cash-limited because they are available on demand. Social security payments are by far the largest of these, but there is a wide variety of other benefits to individuals which are also based on entitlement, including pensions, housing benefits and child allowances. Table 4.1 shows the percentage of departmental expenditure voted by Parliament which is cash-limited. It can be seen that the proportion varies greatly between departments depending on the nature of their responsibilities.

Table 4.1   Percentage of voted departmental expenditure cash-limited [1]

90%–100%	Arts and Libraries Employment Defence DoE – other environmental services
70%–90%	Chancellor of the Exchequer's departments Education and Science Foreign and Commonwealth Office Health and Personal Social Services Scotland Wales
50%–70%	Transport
30%–50%	Agriculture, Fisheries and Food Northern Ireland Trade and Industry
10%–30%	Energy Home Office Other departments
less than 10%	Social security DoE housing

1. 1986–87.

From 1976 to 1982 cash limits operated in parallel with the planning system, which continued to be expressed in volume terms. This meant that Ministers took decisions about the volume of goods and services which they wanted, and then superimposed cash limits which could if necessary override the volume decisions for the year ahead. Sir Leo Pliatzky, the Treasury Second Permanent Secretary responsible at the time, explains why:

I would dearly have liked to get away from constant prices and have the new survey carried out in current prices, that is, in terms of the prices expected to be current in future years when the time came – in other words, to substitute cash programmes for volume programmes throughout the survey period. This was the way in which the Germans did their forward planning, but they could rely on an inflation rate not exceeding 5 per cent a year. If we were to do our cash projections on the assumption of 5 per cent or 10 per cent inflation, and if prices actually went up by 15 per cent a year, it was not to be expected that the government would cut the physical size of programmes year by year to fit the cash projections. It was one thing to enforce cash limits fixed for a single year; it would be a different matter to fix cash limits for several years ahead and stick to them even if it meant massive cuts in volume programmes. But if the initial current price projections had to be adjusted as we moved along in time, these 'current price' programmes would become a sort of bastard constant price programme – an especially funny kind of funny money – and it was doubtful whether we should be any better off. So the conclusion was that we had to stick to volume programmes for the survey, at any rate for the time being and until inflation was more predictable and under control.[6]

From 1982 onwards, however, Pliatzky's wishes were granted and cash was used as the basis for planning from the start. This made it possible to make the system wholly consistent on a cash basis, including consistency between spending and revenue projections. It was also very much easier for everyone to understand what was happening.

To ensure that the old system did not carry on alongside the new, and to ensure that departments understood that they had to live within their means, any references to volume were discouraged. If what was bought cost more than had been estimated, there was to be no assumption that they would be entitled to extra resources. In evidence to the House of Commons Treasury and Civil Service Select Committee, the Treasury explained that:

If there is this very powerful force one has to do two things. Firstly, one has to make choices. If it is a force for higher spending in the same way as demography, it is something one has to take account of and, if one is having to spend more because the relative price effect is adverse, one may have to spend less on something else. The second conclusion is that one does not necessarily take the relative price effect as being given; one sets up arrangements so that the managers of various programmes have an incentive to resist that relative price effect and keep it to a minimum. Under the old system of volume planning that was not done, the relative price effect was, whatever it was, acquiesced in. Now under the arrangements of cash limits and cash planning there is some incentive to resist that.[7]

A variation of the same cash control system was also applied to nationalized industries in the form of external financing limits (EFLs). These are limits on the amount provided by government or borrowed from the money market, whether or not the loans are formally guaranteed by the government. EFLs operate in much the same way as cash limits, though with some variations, such as the inclusion of the capitalized value of leased assets in the EFL to stop the industries getting round the limits by leasing rather than buying.

One aspect of the move to planning and control in purely cash terms was regarded with dismay by several House of Commons Select Committees. They were concerned that if only the cash figures were provided, it would not be possible to identify changes in the volume of goods and services being purchased. So additional volume-based information was requested. Apart from the Social Services Select Committee, few were successful in obtaining it.

The government resisted these requests because it did not want to dilute the impact of the cash planning system and weaken cash disciplines by allowing departments to plead that the volume of services had to be maintained. It was also argued that the figures themselves would not be very meaningful. But there are those, including Sir Leo Pliatzky after leaving the Treasury, who have said that it is important in any complete planning and control system to have at least some information about volume assumptions:

> My own feeling is that, though volumes have been officially outlawed, they have gone underground rather than fled the country ... While I certainly do not advocate turning the clock back to the original PESC system, I feel that there will have to be some accommodation between cash control and volume programming.[8]

In due course, perhaps when the Treasury is more relaxed about the operation of cash controls, more information may be made available.

Certainly the cash-based system appears well established and has

demonstrated too many advantages for a return to what many would see
as the bad old days of 'funny money'. But it could be threatened. It was
fortunate that the system was established at a time of a combination of
successful pay norms, falling inflation, cuts in capital expenditure to
safeguard current spending and more flexibility than is generally acknowledged. Indeed the system has played a part in acting as an additional
restraint in pay settlements by making clear the consequences of settlements which are above those assumed, but without being a formal 'pay
policy'. Terry Ward has pointed out that the restraint may be more far-
reaching:

... a cash limits system represents a useful device for a government which
wishes to restrain public expenditure growth whilst avoiding political debate
about the implications of this. Even though expenditure plans might have been
agreed in advance, the fulfilment of these plans becomes necessarily conditional
upon cash limits not being infringed. More generally, if there is an in-
compatibility between the planned development of public services and cash
limits, then the presumption is that services have to adjust.[9]

But the very factors which helped the system in its early years could
go into reverse. With accumulating backlogs on many capital programmes, considerable spending will be necessary in due course. More
fundamentally, some combination of rising inflation, pay settlements
continuously ahead of assumptions, substantial revisions to plans and/or
overspending combined with lack of effective sanctions could put the
whole system under intolerable strain. The 1976 White Paper acknowledged this by pointing out that 'the government would have to take
stock of the position in the light of all the circumstances of the
time'.[5]

During the 1980s there have been a number of modifications to the
system originally introduced, including the alignment of cash limits
with Parliamentary Supply Estimates to eliminate the confusion arising
from having two separate but parallel control systems in that area.
Provisions were also introduced for greater flexibility at the year-end
to allow some underspending to be carried forward to the next financial year. The effect of these changes is dealt with in greater detail
below.

Supplementing the move to cash as the basis for planning and control,
other types of controls over central government expenditure were also
introduced. Targets for reductions in manpower were imposed in the
early 1980s as a means of reducing the size of the Civil Service, and

shortly after this control was further reinforced by a system of 'running cost controls'. Running costs – the costs of central administration in government departments and other public bodies – account for just under 10 per cent of the planning total. The objective here was to identify departmental administrative costs as part of the total being controlled, so that a limit within the cash limit could be imposed as a means of putting on yet more pressure to reduce administrative costs. The logic was that departments would not be able to protect such costs by reducing expenditure on other items within a cash limit, thereby keeping within the total for the cash limit as a whole. Shortly after running cost controls were introduced, it was clear that manpower targets were no longer necessary. So they were dropped.

How the control system works

The system for monitoring public expenditure as a whole and government expenditure in particular is known by the acronym FIS (Financial Information System). FIS is run on the Treasury's computers and can provide both regular and *ad hoc* reports as well as forecast out-turns (how much was actually spent) for the financial year as a whole. Much of the information is fed in from similar computerized systems run on most departmental computers.

The control system provides information in the first place for the government's own expenditure monitoring staff whose job is to provide Ministers with the information to see whether actual public expenditure is staying within plans and to allow action to be taken if problems arise during the course of the year. The system covers the whole field of public expenditure, though naturally it is likely to be most accurate and up-to-date in the field of the government's own expenditure from Votes. It provides the information for Exchequer expenditure to date. It also provides the revised estimates of what it is likely to be for the full year, some of which are reported to Parliament.

The control unit for Parliament is the Vote, as Chapter 7 explains. Votes (which vary enormously in size) are also used as the basis of the relevant parts of the government's cash limits system. For the purposes of monitoring and control, departments draw up a quarterly profile of their expected expenditure for the coming year and agree these with the Treasury. Separate profiles can be drawn up for distinct blocks of expenditure within Votes where there may not be a uniform expenditure pattern or where there is a need to monitor separate components of a Vote. Drawing up a profile is easier for items which are reasonably predictable, such as central administrative functions where no major changes are expected in the coming year. It is much more difficult for items affected by unpredictable factors – for example, road-building programmes affected by unseasonable weather or defence contracts affected by technological uncertainties.

Much information for monitoring against departmental expenditure profiles comes from the APEX (analysis of public expenditure) records of payments from and receipts to the Consolidated Fund – the government's bank account – kept by the Paymaster General's Office. Information on these payments is provided to the Treasury and departments every month. In addition, departments have to send the Treasury their estimated expenditure for the half-year and any revisions to their budgets they believe will be necessary for the year as a whole.

Monthly monitoring by the Treasury is based on the comparison of APEX figures with the profiles submitted by departments, adapted where necessary. This does not always provide a very accurate comparison, but at least it alerts the Treasury and departments to any potential problems at an early stage so that remedial action can be taken after further investigation. The information for these exercises will not only be used to identify areas for remedial action. It will also be helpful in updating forecasts for the year for the Autumn Statement in November. Departmental forecasts will be used to provide the estimated out-turns for the year for the Parliamentary Supply Estimates published with the Budget and for the calculations which go into planning that Budget.

Estimates of the monthly out-turn supply expenditure are published each month by the Treasury in a Press Notice, and figures for the first six months are published with the Winter Supplementary Estimates and presented to Parliament in November.

The principles governing how large a cash limit should be were set out in the White Paper which announced the arrival of the cash limits system. The 1976 White Paper stated that a cash limit should be 'large enough to provide spending authorities with scope for finding the most economical and effective way of carrying out their programmes within the limits, whilst at the same time ensuring effective financial control'.[5]

With the alignment of cash limits and Parliamentary Supply Estimates, as mentioned above, the size of most Votes is now defined by the relevant cash limit. There are, however, a few cash limits which cover expenditure beyond that voted by Parliament. One example covers some of the Bank of England's administrative costs. Another covers capital expenditure by local authorities on police, courts and probation.

In principle, the decision about how large a cash limit block should be is a question of balancing three requirements: effective control, a realistic amount of flexibility and the need to carry out tasks as efficiently as possible. If the cash limit blocks are too small, those who spend the money will not be able to operate as flexibly as they might wish in order to complete a given task. On the other hand if they are too large, control will not be sufficiently tight. There is an additional danger from operating with cash limit blocks which are too small; if this means that, through completely unforeseen circumstances, there is overspending on too many blocks, the system as a whole might fall into disrepute as confidence is eroded in its effectiveness.

Recognizing these considerations, one of the few compromises in the system between tight control through separate cash limit blocks and the need for flexibility has been made for the Ministry of Defence. The Ministry's cash limit blocks are treated as one for control purposes. Overspending on one of their cash limit blocks can be offset against underspending on another, subject to parliamentary approval for switching between Votes.

Another means of ensuring that the system reflects changes in circumstances is to change cash limits during the course of the year. Here, too, it is a question of balance, as Pliatzky explains in describing how the relevant passage in the 1976 White Paper was formulated:

A crucial passage came in the penultimate paragraph which dealt with the circumstances in which individual cash limits might have to be reviewed. This part of the White Paper text could not be settled at the Cabinet meeting which approved the rest of the White Paper and had to be negotiated outside the meeting. Spending Ministers naturally wanted as many loopholes as possible, and in any event it would not have been possible, at the start of the experiment, to say that in no circumstances would cash limits be revised. But if it were believed that they could be exceeded with impunity in the expectation of a higher cash limit, we should be no better off and there would be no point in the new system. The eventual formulation was that 'spending Departments will not be able to rely, as they have in the past, on supplementary provision if this would take their total provision for the year beyond the cash limits'.[10]

In setting the cash limits, of course, the intention is that they should not normally be changed. Nevertheless, there are two main reasons why changes may be necessary – changes which may be up as well as down.

The first is that a policy change has been made in the middle of the financial year, say to provide more overseas aid in response to famine in a developing country. The second is that circumstances may have changed and as a matter of policy it is decided to accommodate the change. The hypothetical example quoted earlier, of a rise or fall in the value of sterling which alters the price of imported defence equipment against plan, is one such instance. It is worth emphasizing that if there is no action, a fall in the value of sterling which increases the cost of equipment would mean that less equipment could be purchased in order to keep within the limit. An alternative is that the limit could be raised sufficiently to accommodate some of the changes, but not enough to compensate for them. In most cases, however, changes in policy or in outside circumstances will have to be accommodated within the original limits set.

Examples of circumstances in which cash limits have been increased (picked arbitrarily from past years) include:

- funds needed to convert an old RAF station into a prison as a result of a surge in the prison population;

- more money required for building projects to boost activity in the construction industry;

- a need to increase the strategic food reserves;

- the widened scope of employment measures;

- additional resources required for the National Heritage Memorial Fund.

Reductions in allocations to cash limits occasionally take place. This can happen when, for example, expenditure is reclassified and switched to another block, or when it is decided not to go ahead with the expenditure originally planned, or when offsetting savings are provided against overspending.

The details of the parliamentary implications of changes in plans are given in Chapter 7, but in summary, all the changes in cash limits made in a year are announced to Parliament through answers to written parliamentary questions. These changes are then listed together in a White Paper in July, which gives the provisional out-turn for the year up to the end of the financial year ending in March and the final out-turn for the year before.

Changes in cash limit blocks or Votes do not normally affect the total of public expenditure. As Chapter 2 explained, each year a Reserve is set aside to meet unforeseen calls on government funds. Increases in expenditure, whether or not they are cash-limited or voted, are normally charged to the Reserve. There is no guarantee that the amount set aside in the Reserve at the beginning of the year will be large enough to meet all the calls on it, and if it is not, the planning total will be exceeded. A jaundiced view of what he (wrongly) described as the 'contingencies fund' was given by Jock Bruce-Gardyne:

In practice the fund is also called in aid for the expected. Thus the Treasury, having secured acceptance through Whitehall of a cash-limited increase in provision for departmental payrolls – an increase which reflects its aspirations for the ensuing pay-round rather than its expectations – will seek to insist that where the eventual pay settlement exceeds the provision, the excess must be recovered through additional economies, whether in manpower or in services provided. But it knows full well it will not succeed in every case. In some politically emotive instances – the nurses, for example, or the police – ministers will feel obliged to honour a pay settlement which substantially exceeds the cash-limited provision without seeking to claw it back through economies. The excess will then be carried on the contingencies fund although it can hardly be regarded as an unforeseen contingency. The great thing, though, is that unless so many claims are made upon it in the course of a year that the fund is exhausted, the agreed total of public spending will still not be exceeded, since the contingencies fund issue is included in that total.[11]

While the supposition behind the creation of a Reserve is that there are almost certainly going to be unexpected calls on public expenditure, there is no similar amount of unallocated provision voted by Parliament, which will only approve funds for specific purposes. So use of the Reserve by government departments will almost inevitably mean a request to Parliament to vote an additional amount through a Supplementary Estimate. If this involves an increase in a particular cash-limited block, an announcement on that also has to be made to Parliament.

Because control is exercised on a year-by-year basis, there is often a problem with certain kinds of items in keeping expenditure exactly to the plan for a particular financial year. Obvious examples are major capital projects, such as hospital buildings. Very large payments can easily fall either side of the beginning or end of the financial year, with consequences for the relationship between planned and actual expenditure in two financial years. As a result, those who manage the programmes may be tempted to take decisions which could be counterproductive and uneconomic. Slowing down construction of a project, such as a road, to keep within the limits for a particular year, even though the country as a whole would benefit from its early completion, is one example. Another is buying new office equipment which is not really needed for another year to 'use up' underspending on a budget in the current year.

In practice, however, departments have become highly skilled at adjusting payments at the end of the financial year to achieve just the 'right' result. Sometimes, however, even the most skilled departments can run into trouble if things go 'too right', as the House of Commons Select Committee on Procedure (Finance) commented:

> At present Departments give undue emphasis to cash limits, especially in the context of capital expenditure. The effect of this is graphically illustrated by the Ministry of Defence witness who noted certain problems relating to some of his Department's projects in 1980 and 1981. These 'problems' were not, as might have been expected, delays, but rather the reverse: the contractors 'came nearer to the planned performance than we were expecting', thus threatening the cash limits for that financial year.[12]

Everyone knows that this kind of game is played. It is indeed little different in private sector organizations. As a result, there are now limited arrangements to allow the carry-forward of unspent amounts on capital programmes of this kind to avoid just such 'using up' of entitlements to spend for fear of losing the entitlement and having to re-apply. The Treasury has been reluctant to allow the scheme to be extended too far, both for control reasons and because of the added uncertainty which flexibility causes in managing the Reserve. The case for still more flexibility will continue to be argued. The advantages – less pressure to distort expenditure at the year-end, more efficient use of resources planned on a longer time-scale, etc. – have to be weighed against the dangers of weakening financial discipline and the difficulties for macroeconomic planning.

Overspending

One of the main objectives in the control mechanism is to avoid overspending. There are various kinds of action that can be taken to avoid it for public expenditure as a whole, or at least to reduce the chances of it happening.

Uncertainties on the *quantity* of what is supplied can be reduced by getting rid of items of expenditure which are not within the government's control, cutting them in size, privatizing them, or reducing the level of commitment to spend. Examples from recent years include abolishing certain grants to industry; cash-limiting certain employment measures whose size was previously determined by demand; and deciding against automatic increases in the United Kingdom defence commitment to NATO. Improved management can also help to cut the chances of overspending on major projects caused by constantly adding to the basic design of the project.

Price uncertainties can be reduced by realistic estimates of inflation in the original plans, though this may be difficult if governments do not want to show plans 'going up' very fast. Another possibility is to break down the price assumptions from broader into smaller categories to try and predict future movements more accurately.

A realistic amount in reserve is the main way in which uncertainties involving *both price and quantity* can be accommodated. This may come about through an allowance for public expenditure as a whole from the centre, 'slack' within each programme to allow for a certain amount of overspending, or a combination of both. In recent years there has been a tendency to try and ensure that individual programmes are tightly controlled by providing a larger central reserve rather than allowing slack within each department. This has the advantage that allocations be controlled from the centre with amounts provided only for selected programmes.

Even with reduced uncertainties, it is still quite possible for individual departments or the government as a whole to be in danger of overspending. This can be avoided by a number of means already identified – delaying purchases, changing policies and so on. But there are other methods too. There can be greater rewards for keeping within budget and greater penalties for not doing so. Or a moratorium can be imposed on capital spending or grants. Or the overall total can be made to balance by accelerating sales of assets, assuming any are available for sale and that the government is willing to sell them.

Although the emphasis of the control mechanism is to take action before overspending occurs, the limit may be increased if these are not successful and overspending is clearly inevitable. Alternatively (and very much as a last resort) there may be agreement to overspend.

The problem of control is greatest for the government in the field of local authority expenditure where methods can only be indirect and designed to influence the authorities (often of a different political persuasion) to keep their spending in line with the government's plans. If, in total, they do not, the government is only likely to hold overall public expenditure within the planning total by absorbing the overspend through the Reserve.

Although the purpose of the control mechanism within departments is to take action before any overspending occurs, if this is not successful and overspending becomes inevitable the planning total may have to be increased as a deliberate change of policy.

It is not impossible for an individual department to overspend its vote and cash limit without authority. Unlike private individuals, the government cannot go back on commitments made by departments and departments' cheques cannot therefore 'bounce'. In such a case the department would have to live with the consequences of being regarded as a poor housekeeper. It would for example require an Excess Vote (a form of retrospective Supplementary Vote) from Parliament which would be examined by the Public Accounts Committee. The cash limit breach would mean that the next year's allocation would be affected, since the amount of overspending in one year on cash limited expenditure is deducted from the cash limit in the following year.

What are the political and personal sanctions for overspending? Depending on the reason, there may be some political cost to the Minister involved and the reputations of some officials may also be affected. There will certainly be uncomfortable post-mortem discussions between the Treasury and the department to find the causes of the problem and remedy them if possible. The Public Accounts Committee is likely to examine the department's senior official and to comment unfavourably in a published report to Parliament if they feel that the overspending was avoidable or could have been foreseen in time to have sought a Supplementary Vote. There may also be some indirect sanctions in the form of bad press publicity if the area is politically sensitive or if the reason for the overspending is not considered good enough.

So, like a private individual with the bank manager, departments are wise to exceed their original allocation only with the knowledge, and if possible the agreement, of the Treasury by seeking any necessary increase in cash limit and/or Vote provision via a Supplementary Estimate presented to Parliament at the proper time. In practice, those who do overspend their Votes do not do so without good reason and if this is the case then there is not likely to be any lasting damage to politicians or Civil Servants.

In identifying whether control has been exercised or not, comparisons may be obscured by reclassification. Reclassification is a continuous process of tidying up public finances and, because it often affects many items each year, identifying what has happened is not made any easier. To illustrate the problems, it is worth quoting the full conclusions on changes in classification made by the House of Commons Treasury and Civil Service Select Committee in their analysis of the 1983–84 Public Expenditure White Paper.

The interpretation of the White Paper and comparison with previous plans is hampered by a number of substantial changes in classification.

From 1983–84 the cost of providing accommodation and services has been reclassified from common services (under the Property Services Agency) to departmental programmes. For 1983–84 the sum involved is around £800 million. In principle we regard this change as desirable. It is obviously better that Departments should know the cost of their accommodation rather than have it hidden under the Property Services Agency. But this change, as the commentary on the common services programme makes clear, 'makes it impossible to compare most figures for 1982–83 and earlier with those from 1983–84 onwards'. While Table 4.5 gives some indication of the overall effect of classification changes, no indication is given in the White Paper of how this and other individual changes affect individual programmes: in general terms it means that the expenditure commitments of most Departments will be higher in 1983–84 than in earlier years. This change will affect only the reallocation of expenditure between programmes, not total expenditure.

This is not the case with the second main change – the reduction in the National Insurance surcharge from 2½ to 1½ per cent from April 1983 which will reduce the public sector wage bill. Since the benefit of this change is not meant to accrue to the public sector, the expenditure plans of central government and the external financing limits of the nationalized industries have been adjusted downward. For local authorities, who in 1983–84 will pay the surcharge at the originally intended rate of 2½ per cent, no such adjustment has been made for 1983–84. Downward adjustments have been made however for 1984–85 and 1985–86. The Treasury supplied us with figures which enabled us to make adjustments for these classification changes. *In our view these adjustments should have been more clearly set out in the White Paper so that the independent effects could have been estimated.*

The third major change in classification arises from the allowance for over-spending by local authorities. Since local authorities budgeted to spend £1½ billion more on current expenditure in 1982–83 than allowed in the previous plans (Cmnd 8494) plans for 1983–84 would clearly have been overshot. Provision for 1983–84 has been raised by £1.3 billion, 'most of this increase has not been assigned to services and is in the form of a general addition reflecting the fact that some local authorities will need more time to moderate their expenditure'. (Public Expenditure White Paper, Cmnd 8789, vol.1, para.22.) Figures for programmes with local authority content are likely to be underestimated in the White Paper because this amount has not been allocated between them.

Further classification changes within programmes also affect the meaning of comparisons between years. An important example is the treatment of expenditure on housing benefit in the social security programme. Under the Social Security and Housing Benefits Act 1982 people who previously received help with rent and rates through the supplementary benefit scheme will henceforth receive help from local authorities. The scheme had a partial start in November 1982 and comes fully into operation in April 1983. From these dates, the cost of assistance with rent and rates is excluded from supplementary benefit expenditure and the amount attributable to rent is added to housing benefit expenditure. Unless this is taken into account it could be concluded erroneously that *per capita* expenditure on the unemployed, for example, would fall dramatically in 1983–84.

It is clear from the foregoing discussion that great care must be taken in interpreting the changes in plans for individual programmes, because of the reclassification of or changes in treatment of certain items of expenditure, parts of housing benefit, sickness benefit and so on, which are now included in the revenue side of the accounts as offsets to total government income. When adjustment is made to the planning totals for these classification changes which move expenditure to the revenue side of the account, the planning total for 1983–84 becomes £120,775 million, compared to the previous plan (in Cmnd 8494) of £120,695 million (an additional £80 million of expenditure). Thus although the cash plans show a reduction of £1.1 billion from the last budget this is wholly accounted for by these transfers on to the revenue side. The government's financial position is in no way improved by this kind of change even though the public expenditure figures are thereby reduced.[13]

Table 4.2 Public expenditure as a whole – variations from planning total

	£ billion
1980–81	1.4 overspend
1981–82	0.4 underspend
1982–83	1.2 underspend
1983–84	0.7 overspend
1984–85	3.3 overspend
1985–86	1.5 overspend
1986–87	0.7 overspend

Note: Figures are regularly revised after the end of the year as a result of classification and other changes.

Source: Public Expenditure White Paper, 1987

Control in central government

Leaving aside the reclassification issues, overspending is more common than is generally realized. Table 4.2 gives figures for variations from plan in public spending as a whole in the early 1980s, a time when very tight controls were in force. It can be seen that there were major variations from plan, though the 1984/85 figures are dominated by the effects of the miners' strike. The Chief Secretary acknowledged this to the House of Commons in 1987:

'Given the overall size of the programmes and the inevitable uncertainties, our record has been creditable. In the five years since the introduction of cash planning, the average overrun for the planning total set for the year ahead has been about 0.8 per cent and, but for the coal strike, would have been about half that. So there has been no weakening in the efforts to maintain control.'[14]

The author and Susan Bloomfield pointed to some implications of the overspending:

What is interesting is that this does not seem to have damaged the government's credibility. The focus of attention has been more on priorities and on the overall levels of spending, rather than on underspending or overspending, despite the fact that variations from plan mean that the elaborate system of decisions about priorities has not been carried into effect.[15]

The major areas of overspending are shown in Table 4.3. Those factors which regularly contribute to uncertainty – local authority expenditure, demand-led programmes, unpredictable pay settlements, new

Table 4.3 Average overspends (selected programmes), early to mid 1980s

	£m	% of programme
Social security	804	2.0
Education and Science	793	5.8
Overseas aid and other overseas services	300	11.4
Agriculture, Fisheries and Food	282	13.8
Health and Personal Social Services	201	1.2

Note: Average of 1982–83 to 1985–86. 1985–86 figures affected by reclassifications.

Source: Likierman and Bloomfield, 'Publication Expenditure Control in the 80s – Success or Failure?', London Business School Economic Outlook, vol. 10, no. 9, 1986.

projects, etc. – appear to cause the biggest problems. Cash-limited items as a whole tend to be underspent, since departments prefer if possible to undershoot slightly to make sure that they keep within their total.

5

PUBLIC SPENDING, MANAGEMENT
AND PERFORMANCE

———————

The love of economy is the root of all virtue. (Bernard Shaw, *Maxims for Revolutionists*)

The most important stimulus to controlling government expenditure as a whole in the 1980s was probably the surge in inflation in the 1970s. There were also a number of different influences promoting changes in management in general and performance measurement in particular.

One of the most important of these was the need to try and make the money available for public expenditure go further in view of the continuing problem of reconciling increasing demands for public services with a rate of economic growth too low to finance them. Another was pressure from a government which clearly believed that much of the public sector was inefficient, overstaffed and had a good deal to learn from the private sector. There was an almost evangelical flavour to what might be done. In 1980 Michael Heseltine, then a Minister at the forefront of thinking on management in Whitehall, wrote:

The management ethos must run right through our national life – public and private companies, civil service, nationalized industries, local government and the health service. By management ethos I mean the process of examining what we are doing, setting realistic targets, fitting them to the resources available, and monitoring performance – and then, very important, telling people what the results are so that we can go back to the beginning of the loop and improve from there.[1]

But the climate of managerial change was to be dominated by other considerations. The government had made it clear that cutting public expenditure as a percentage of national income was central to its overall strategy. Part of that strategy involved reducing public sector manpower.

As a result, it was often difficult to disentangle three different policy elements – an interest in efficiency improvement for its own sake; an interest in cutting public spending; a desire to cut the size of the public sector. The resulting ambiguities about government motives were undoubtedly a problem in the introduction and encouragement of managerial change and aroused deep suspicion among some public sector managers. Many felt that the government was impervious to argument and was anti-public sector. Managerial innovations were seen as manifestations of distrust and a thinly veiled way of disguising cuts.

Indeed, as far as public expenditure is concerned, developments in management could, theoretically, be ignored. Tightening or loosening the purse strings could proceed independently of what happens once the money is allocated. In practice, however, pressure to spend will be highly influenced by how well that money is managed. And well-integrated planning and control systems are far more likely to succeed than those where there is no connection between systems for allocation and those for management. So although only selected aspects of the area can be covered, it is worth spending some time understanding the impact of recent management changes and the prospects for their survival.

The main vehicle for promoting changes in the Civil Service was the Financial Management Initiative, or FMI as it soon became known. The main object of the FMI, according to a 1982 White Paper setting it up, was to

... promote in each department an organization and a system in which managers at all levels have

- a clear view of their objectives, and means to assess and, wherever possible, measure, outputs or performance in relation to these objectives

- well-defined responsibility for making the best use of their resources, including a critical scrutiny of output and value for money

- the information (particularly about costs), the training and the access to expert advice that they need to exercise their responsibilities effectively.[2]

This does not mean that the FMI represented the first attempt by the Civil Service to come to grips with management techniques. Well-established sets of procedures were in place within departments, including staff inspection (assessing gradings and work loadings), and internal audit and management services. There was also the in-house training facility of the Civil Service College, established in 1969. But these alone had not satisfied successive governments, and between the 1960s and the early 1980s there were a number of attempts to accelerate the improvement of management in the Civil Service. Indeed the areas identified for improvement in the Plowden Report of 1961, the Fulton Report of 1968, and by Edward Heath (the Prime Minister of the day) in the early 1970s were very similar to those of the initiatives of the 1980s. Even the language used was similar. What distinguished the FMI was that it was carried forward with a far greater degree of political energy and conviction and for a longer period than its predecessors.

The government's effort was initially spearheaded by Sir Derek (later Lord) Rayner. Rayner, one of the Managing Directors (later the Chairman) of Marks and Spencer, was brought in to look at ways of improving efficiency in central government. His name was soon well known through 'Rayner scrutinies'. These were investigations of ways in which specific managerial improvements could be made in government departments and other public bodies. They involved examining a specific policy or activity, questioning all aspects of work normally taken for granted, proposing ways of achieving savings and increasing efficiency and effectiveness, and finally implementing any proposals made. In terms of money saved, the Rayner scrutinies undoubtedly paid their way. By the mid 1980s it was calculated that they had resulted in identifiable savings amounting to several hundred million pounds a year, substantial enough in their own right but only a very small proportion of the totals in each department. Rayner, however, was also deeply concerned with what he called 'lasting reforms' of the way in which civil servants thought about the management of the resources under their control. Many of his ideas were influential in creating the climate for the FMI and some were also incorporated into it.

The government's work was given additional stimulus by parliamentary pressure, particularly from the Treasury and Civil Service Select Committee in their 1982 report on Efficiency and Effectiveness in the Civil Service. The Committee examined internal Civil Service systems and commended one in particular, the MINIS system in the Department of the Environment (DoE), introduced by Michael Heseltine when he was Secretary of State, as a result of a Rayner scrutiny. MINIS sought to give ministers a comprehensive grasp of the activities of the DoE, to take decisions on relative priorities, review progress and the effectiveness of policies and to understand the impact of cuts at a political level. It provided a highly detailed analysis of all the activities in the DoE, their objectives and the means by which their performance could be assessed. The extract from a mid 1980s version of MINIS in Table 5.1 shows how. Concentrating on the administrative rather than the political aspects of the system, the Committee recommended that, as far as was practicable, other departments should introduce similar systems. What appealed to them was the idea that Ministers and civil servants would act more as managers of the resources under their control through the close monitoring of expenditure which MINIS offered.

Within a few years most departments had indeed installed systems of this kind to enable them to have a comprehensive method of performance measurement, cost analysis and internal control. Each department produced systems which varied to some degree from those of others and sought to reflect the particular circumstances of the department's work. The variations were also reflected in the acronyms used, which included MINIM and MAIS for the systems of the Ministry of Agriculture, Fisheries and Food, MAISY for the Cabinet Office and FMIS for the Department of Education and Science.

While MINIS was influential in showing what was possible, it became only a small part of the FMI initiative. The main areas of innovation in the FMI as a whole included:

- making the overall aims and objectives of departments and other public sector organizations more explicit as a basis for setting priorities and formulating plans in financial and non-financial terms.

- increasing delegation and decentralization, making managers responsible for agreeing the detailed objectives and performance measures against which they were held accountable. This involved clearer definitions of managerial responsibility and accountability and included devolving responsibility for budgets within the overall policy framework set out by Ministers. Units of accountability were set up, including budget centres and cost centres, to identify financial responsibility for activities.

- introducing new types of information systems at various levels in the organization to report on both policy and operational activities. Some of these systems were 'top management systems' of the type pioneered by MINIS, designed to provide information to Ministers and civil servants to enable them to manage. The idea was to provide the basis for assessing whether policies in general and targets in

Table 5.1 A MINIS example

MINIS 6 – Planning Directorate (Planning Inspectorate), December 1984

Description of function	April 1984–March 1985 planned performance	Actual salary cost April–Sept. 1983 £k
Casework under the Housing Acts (Mr Barnes)	- maintain ability to deal expertly with a similar level of housing work and maintain expertise in order to cope with any future expansion. - arrange inquiries within shortest possible time of their being requested by Regional Offices keeping average period to within 13 weeks.	77.9
Casework under other legislation (Mr Millington – Water Act cases	- be prepared for increase in water proposals if drought	52.3
Mr Cross – rights of way under the Wildlife and Countryside Act and inquiries under the Highways Acts Mr Roberts – Nature Conservation orders.	- footpath workload uncertain but expect up to 200 inquiries and 100 site visit cases relating to rights of way, including definitive map work. Increase could be equivalent to 300 Inspector weeks.	
Inspectors from all groups undertake these cases, reporting to the ACPIs above) [Estimated proportion attributable to DTp = 47%]	- continue evolving practice and methodology for administrative section dealing with rights of way and consider applicability of procedures elsewhere in PIMS. - be prepared to deal with more nature conservation orders and other work. - be prepared for wide range of other work, e.g. hazardous waste proposals.	

Performance assessment April 1984–September 1984 + envisaged performance October 1984–March 1985	Targeted performance 1985–86 (+ any new functions)	Trend in costs 1985–86 ±
- dealt with 95 housing CPO inquiries between April and September, much the same as in 1983. Expect further 100 cases in rest of year.	- be prepared to deal with 220 housing cases.	+
- average period for arranging inquiries between April and September 12 weeks.	- maintain period for arranging inquiries at 12 weeks.	+
- dealt with inquiries into 11 drought orders between April and September. Further orders expected in rest of year.	- be prepared for at least as many drought orders.	o
- dealt with 35 inquiries and 17 site visit cases relating to rights of way between April and September. Further 60 cases expected in rest of year. Definitive map work slow to start.	- be prepared for 100 inquiries and 60 site visit cases relating to public path orders and 130 inquiries and 50 site visit cases relating to definitive map orders.	+
- rights of way administrative section running smoothly.		o
- dealt with 1 inquiry into nature conservation orders between April and September. 1 further order expected in rest of year.	- be prepared for 3 inquiries into nature conservation orders.	+
- other work included: 95 inquiries under Highways Acts and 25 inquiries under other legislation for DTp; 22 inquiries under Highways Acts and 26 inquiries under other legislation for DoE; and 4 scheduled monument consent appeals under the Ancient Monuments and Archaeological Areas Act 1979.	- be prepared for wide range of other work.	+

particular were being achieved. Other information systems translated overall objectives into more specific aims and targets, into statements giving the costs of activities and on performance against objectives and specific targets.

- in support of these systems, costing activities more accurately and making the costs explicit to managers to enable them to exercise control. Devising suitable performance measures, including those for activities without easily identifiable measures of final output.

- improving the information and control mechanisms for and within agencies spending public funds on the government's behalf, to ensure that the agencies were not out of control and that they kept to planning targets.

- increasing the range of available skills, including the recruitment of more accountants and the greater use of management consultants; increasing the interchange of staff with those working in private sector organizations, to improve the cross-fertilization of ideas.

- improving internal audit procedures and encouraging value-for-money studies to reinforce many of the elements of good managerial practice outlined above.

So the introduction of the FMI was intended to cover much more than financial matters. It became a general term to cover many different initiatives, brought in at different times and by a variety of instigators, covering all kinds of managerial activities. In essence it was a fresh approach to the management of the Civil Service and touched on all aspects of the conditions to make the use of public funds more effective.

In parallel, there were a number of initiatives supporting FMI work to help those involved. The measures included reassessing personnel policies, one part of which was to identify and develop good managers as part of a deliberate succession plan to fill key jobs in the future; emphasizing the importance of management skills in promotion and appointments (not excluding those made at the very top of the Civil Service); reorientating training to reflect the need to improve managerial skills in general and financial skills in particular; identifying means of motivating managers and seeking ways of rewarding merit and developing personal incentives, one of which was the development of performance-related pay.

The overall responsibility for implementing these changes is split between the Office of the Minister for the Civil Service (OMCS, part of the Cabinet Office) and the Treasury. The split reflects problems in finding a suitable mechanism for organizing responsibility for work in this field. The abolition first of the Civil Service Department in 1981 and then of its successor, the Management and Personnel Office, in 1987 meant that increasing numbers of functions have been transferred to the Treasury and the impetus for further change now will have to come from them.

The OMCS covers, among its other responsibilities, Civil Service selection and promotion, management development and training, and the Civil Service College. The Treasury is responsible for pay, conditions of service, manpower and the development of good management practice. Computerization too comes under the Treasury and although technological advances have made it possible to provide information far more cheaply than ever before, implementation of managerial initiatives has been patchy.

Outside the structure of the central departments is the Efficiency Unit. This is organized as another part of the Cabinet Office, but it works independently for the Prime Minister's adviser on efficiency, an indication of the Prime Minister's own interest in carrying the efficiency work forward.

Operating on behalf of Parliament and independently of the government in this field is the National Audit Office (NAO) with its value-for-money (vfm) work. Their work is based on requirements laid down in law and represents a formal appraisal of vfm, normally defined as having three elements:

1 Economy: obtaining inputs of the right quality at the lowest possible cost.
2 Efficiency: producing the greatest useful output from the given level of inputs.
3 Effectiveness: achieving the objective or objectives of the activity.

One of the most important aspects of the work of the NAO is to provide recommendations or suggestions for improved practice, and their work in doing so is described in Chapter 8. But the main emphasis on vfm has increasingly been within government departments, and vfm is an important part of the FMI. In a book on value for money dealing with the public sector as a whole, two experienced consultants were emphatic about the approach to be taken:

It cannot be stressed enough that value for money is not just a collection of techniques. It is above all an attitude of mind, a commitment to good practice on the part of politicians and officials. It is particularly important for management to instill a positive approach towards achieving value for money at all levels, so that the commitment permeates the whole organization. Having said that, value for money cannot be achieved by merely inspiring the organization with the necessary crusading spirit. Management's enthusiasm and drive has to be supported by the right organizational structure and also formalized budgeting, evaluation and monitoring systems.[3]

So while the NAO represents a formal appraisal by 'outsiders', the responsibility for implementation will lie with the department concerned.

Performance measurement and public expenditure

Interest in the whole area of performance measurement in central government, like the interest in management, is of long standing. The Fulton Committee commented that accountable management 'depends on identifying or establishing accountable units within government departments – units where output can be measured against costs or other criteria, and where individuals can be held personally responsible for their performance'.[4]

As a result of the factors stimulating an interest in management in general outlined at the beginning of the chapter, the focus of performance measurement has moved away from a narrow definition of accountability – checking the propriety and legality of public sector activities through the audit mechanism – to a search for wider measures. It has become an important element in vfm work. It has also become of interest in looking at ways in which rewards can be linked to performance through performance-related pay.

It is not easy to define performance in relation to public expenditure. And even if performance is defined, there are still problems in how best to measure it. One means, increasingly developed in recent years, has been to devise performance indicators. These are potentially a means of relating plans to outcomes, justifying the use of resources, assessing the overall effectiveness and efficiency of the activity, providing a basis for calculating rewards and incentives and helping to establish whether value for money has been obtained.

The way in which performance indicators have been developed has varied from one part of the public sector to another and the definitions of what is an indicator have also varied. Common measures used are for staff productivity, efficiency in dealing with a task, cost per unit produced or processed, quality, reliability and speed. Examples given in a National Audit Office report on the FMI[5], taking the three elements of vfm, are

1 Economy: average rent paid for office space by the Property Services Agency in relation to prevailing market rates;
2 Efficiency: average number of claimants dealt with by staff of the Department of Employment;
3 Effectiveness: comparison of the target for the percentage of Corporation Tax returns investigated with that achieved.

Performance indicators are not to be confused with output or activity indicators which measure only one variable, whether in money or non-money terms. Examples of these are

- numbers of miles of motorway built;
- hospital out-patient attendances;
- full-time students in higher education;
- subsidies to Housing Associations.

The idea behind performance indicators is that they should provide management with the information necessary to make decisions, not that they should be constructed simply because the data is available, or for their own sake. As the Chief Secretary to the Treasury put it in introducing a debate on the Public Expenditure White Paper:

'. . . these measures and targets for costs, output and performance are not simply descriptive material produced for the purpose of the White Paper. They are being used by Departments in their day-to-day management and in the year-by-year planning and control of programmes.

I see three main benefits from better measurement and targeting. By relating outputs to the costs involved, managers can make better choices. By setting out in advance what a programme is expected to achieve, by when and at what cost, subsequent review and evaluation is improved. By telling this House and the outside world what has been achieved and how that relates to previous targets, Departments are made more accountable.'[6]

The Minister even went on to commend a positive role for Parliament in this field – certainly a sign of confidence in the product:

'I am grateful to the Treasury and Civil Service Select Committee for the attention it is giving to this subject. It has an important role to play in following through, year by year, the performance of government in achieving their targets. I hope it will encourage other Select Committees to pursue more rigorously these aspects, not only because it is an important development in accountability but also because it focuses directly on Parliament's role of ensuring that taxpayers' money is not only properly but also wisely spent.'

Like other means of measuring performance, indicators need to be consistent with the objectives of the activity being measured. There is also a need for some external check in the development process to ensure that the selection is not biased or based on a self-fulfilling prophecy – discharging patients too early to ensure that there is an 'improvement' in patient throughput, for instance. Managerial commitment can also be damaged if the indicators are used in, or are seen to be part of, what is simply a cost-cutting exercise.

In this field, as in all aspects of management, managerial commitment can also be affected by the way in which schemes are implemented. Christopher Pollitt, commenting on the whole field of performance measuremen, noted:

One lesson seems to be that the general climate in which performance assessment schemes are introduced is extremely important. If they are seen as part of a cost-cutting exercise, or as a top management device for rewarding 'good' and penalizing 'bad' staff, then defensiveness and antagonism may be expected to ensue. Hurried implementation, with scant training, will only reinforce this view.[7]

Norman Flynn pointed to other important considerations

As well as being in line with the organization's objectives, the indicators must be susceptible to managerial influence. Nothing but frustration can result from a set of performance indicators over which a manager can have no control. For example a Skillcentre may have a performance indicator based on the ability of its trainees to obtain employment. Although the manager is able to alter the mix of trades training offered, s/he cannot be held responsible for the state of the local labour market at a particular time.[8]

Even if performance indicators have the right attributes and have been carefully introduced, there are a number of factors to bear in mind in developing and using them. For instance, not all activities can be easily quantified or summarized in terms of a few indicators, though measurement by a set of measures may well be a better reflection of the complexity of operations than using a few or – worse – one alone. Often it is necessary to use intermediate or proxy measures in measuring performance, rather than final outputs. In other words, it may be difficult to measure the objective, so other measures, to which at least some figures can be attached, are used, even though they do not measure what is being sought. An example that can be cited is the programme of building advanced factories in certain parts of the country to be ready for different firms to move into. The benefit being sought is to the economy of the region, but since this is difficult to measure, jobs created (or safeguarded) and the cost per job tend to be used as indicators. Furthermore, it may be difficult to interpret the results because there may be a time lag before there are benefits from a particular policy, and because it may be difficult to separate the impact of policy from other factors.

In spite of these problems, performance indicators are being developed throughout the public sector. The number in the Public Expenditure White Paper, for example, rose enormously. However, many of the indicators in this document, and indeed elsewhere in the public sector, are still concerned with activity rather than performance, and with economy and efficiency rather than effectiveness. Examples and a useful breakdown by Malcolm Levitt[9] of types in a recent Public Expenditure White Paper are given in Table 5.2

The fact that more information on performance is being published is an important development in itself. Finding out what is happening within departments has not always been easy. One, little discussed, issue in the field of performance measurement is how far it is reasonable to assume that information will be published; and if published, accessible; and if accessible, understandable; and if understandable, published at a price which people can afford to pay. There is a need for adequate public information, though this in itself is an ill-defined concept. There is the need to get on with the business of government without having to spend endless time answering questions, as well as the temptation to ensure that as few potential weaknesses as possible are exposed. As Sir Gordon Downey, a former Comptroller and Auditor-General (see Chapter 8) pointed out:

Nobody – particularly government – wants to volunteer the material by which they may be judged and found wanting. Nobody wants to set out clearly in

Table 5.2   Examples of performance measures

---

1. Input volumes
       MOD Front Line Units
       Staff numbers (most departments)

2. Efficiency/Unit costs
       DES   Unit costs in Higher Education
       DE   Gross and net costs per job
       DE   (Unemployment Benefit Service) – Staff: Claimant ratios
                                                 – Costs per payment
       DHSS   Administrative costs as % of benefit expenditure
               Administrative costs per beneficiary

3. Activities/Intermediate output
       MOD   % contracts placed by competition
       DE   Numbers counselled
               Job Centre placings
       DOE   Number of house improvements
               % of homeless households
       HO   Number of offences cleared up
       DHSS   Number of benefits paid

4. 'Quality' indicators
       DE   Unemployment benefits paid within 6 and 12 days
       DHSS   Clearance times and error rates for benefits
               Waiting times spent in local offices

5. Final outputs
       DEn   Value of energy saving achieved
       FCO   Value of additional exports promoted
       DTI   Jobs created

Source: Public Finance Foundation, *Public Domain 1987*, Public Finance Foundation, 1987.

advance what they mean to achieve, and then provide the information on results that show how far they may have fallen short.[10]

Nevertheless, as the FMI has developed there have been reports by some of those participating in implementation on how it has been applied in different contexts. Examples of these are given in Appendices B and C.

Ways of measuring performance

'His promises were, as he then was, mighty;
But his performance, as he is now, nothing.'
                                                (Shakespeare, *Henry VIII*)

Performance, using indicators or other kinds of measures, can be measured in this particular area in a variety of ways. Trends over time is one. Performance against aims, objectives and targets is another. There is also performance compared with that of other bodies.

PERFORMANCE USING TRENDS

Trend information is almost always used in measuring developments over time. The trends may be based on financial information (for example, the cost of a job-creation scheme), or non-financial information (for example, the numbers of police officers). This kind of trend information is not in itself performance measurement. More spending on a job-creation scheme may indicate that the scheme is being inefficiently administered. It may reflect the results of automatic entitlement to benefit. It may be a manifestation of failure of employment creation. It may be more or less than planned. Similarly, changes in the number of police officers may be due to a large variety of factors and may mark neither a good nor a bad performance. Financial trends need special additional care in interpretation – more spending may only be a reflection of changing prices.

The key question with trend information is whether the trend relates to objectives and to plan? Taking the job-creation example, increased spending may reflect success in getting to more people but failure to keep to the limits set. Greater police numbers may reflect success in recruitment and in retaining existing police, but also failure to recruit the numbers planned for and required. Trend information, then, can only sensibly be used for performance measurement if it is taken together with other information.

PERFORMANCE AGAINST AIMS, OBJECTIVES AND TARGETS

An important part of the attempt to make government more efficient and more accountable has been to make public sector bodies state the aims, objectives and targets against which their performance can be measured. Unless they do so, it is very difficult for those who work for them, those who deal with them and the politicians who control them to know and agree on what they are supposed to be doing. And unless they know this, it is very difficult to assess whether the organizations are performing well or not. The distinction between aims, objectives and targets is that:

- *aims* are the purposes for which an organization exists;
- *objectives* are the specific statements of how an aim will be pursued;
- *targets* are more specific still, quantifying what is to be achieved and by when.

Thus the stated aim of a part of the Department of the Environment has been 'to deal with the effects of long-term changes in the economic structure of our cities'. An objective which follows from that particular aim is 'to reclaim and improve derelict land', and one of the targets within the objective is that the London Docklands Development Corporation will 'reclaim and service eighty hectares of land and release land for a further 445 house starts' in one particular year.

While the general idea behind hierarchies of this kind is widely agreed to be sensible, there are difficulties involved. Many of the statements of aims and objectives are very general, both at higher and lower levels of management, and in practice it is hard to know how to measure performance against them. There are also conflicts between different aims and objectives. The dilemma faced by the Ministry of Agriculture, Fisheries and Food in having to safeguard simultaneously the interests of farmers, consumers and conservationists is one such example.

This kind of dilemma illustrates why, despite the fact that much of the terminology of public sector management implicitly assumes that the public sector is much the same as the private sector, there are significant differences in measuring performance against objectives (as indeed there are in the field of performance measurement in general). A factor common to both private and public sectors is that, in assessing performance, much depends on how 'tight' or 'loose' was the target set. But more fundamentally, public sector objectives and aims are often of a very different kind from those in the private sector. They are much more about direction, policy and regulation. The objectives may thus be more difficult to pin down; they may be deliberately obscure as a means of reconciling differing political objectives, consistent politically but not administratively, and framed with the need to leave sufficient freedom of manoeuvre to take account of political uncertainties. All this makes life very difficult for the public sector manager.

Nevertheless, an example of how performance-related targets have been introduced for certain activities as part of the FMI was given by officials of the Lord Chancellor's Department:

In 1984 the department introduced specific performance-related targets in respect of the length of time cases had awaited trial in the Crown Court, and the length of time needed to deal with various items of business in the County Courts.

These areas were selected because they represent key aspects of the work done in the courts and were widely recognized as such; and also because they were able to take advantage of statistical information already collected for other purposes.

Although the targets related to performance in individual court centres they were constructed so as to apply to the whole circuit. Circuit administrators could however set different targets for the individual courts within their circuit targets.

The targets were set in this way for two reasons. Firstly, it allowed management the greatest degree of flexibility to take account of local conditions. Secondly, and more importantly, it explicitly recognized the fact that the circuit administrators are at the apex of the local management organization with clearly defined delegated authority for resources and performance.

The target-setting process comprises in effect a series of bargaining sessions between a Grade 2 officer, who is in charge of the court service and legal administration, and each circuit administrator over the level of resources which can be made available in return for an expected level of performance. The circuits' budgets and performance targets are settled at the same time.

At the beginning of this process in 1984 the relationship between performance and resources was informal. Since then the mechanism has been formalized and become better focused. Improvements to the objectives system will include specific measures of productivity, as well as indicators of the effectiveness of the service.[11]

PERFORMANCE IN RELATION TO OTHER BODIES

Comparison with another organization undertaking the same functions is frequently used in both the public and private sectors to measure performance. In the public sector such comparisons, if they are possible, give useful information as a basis for asking questions of those responsible for organizations which appear to be doing badly and a means of motivating those doing well.

Comparisons can be between

- similar units within an organization, such as schools in the same education authority or hospitals in the same Health District;

- organizations in the same public service, such as Health Districts within the NHS or social service departments in different local authorities;

- organizations in different countries – the Ministry of Defence in the UK compared with its equivalent in another country, or the Metropolitan Police compared with the police force covering another capital city.

Given the difficulties of measuring performance in general in many services, such comparisons are a potentially useful tool for those seeking to improve the performance of public organizations. But any comparisons need to be handled with great care.

Most important of all, the organizations being compared must be reasonably comparable. This means offering the same kind of service. An inner-city police organization will not be directly comparable with one in a rural area, a general hospital with a geriatric hospital, or a road-building programme based largely on building new roads with one concentrating on improving existing ones.

Another factor to consider is any variation in objectives and the degree to which there are constraints on the services being provided. If the objective of a programme is quantity – say, to build 300,000 houses a year – the performance cannot be compared with one where the objective is less specific, involving the upgrading of some houses as well as the building of others.

When making the comparisons, care must also be taken to make sure the figures are calculated on a comparable basis. For example, costs may not include the same items – indirect costs of administration are sometimes included and sometimes not. When comparing organizations across international boundaries, fluctuations in the currencies may well distort trends over time; even taking one year, the relative amounts which can be purchased in each country need to be taken into account.

Finally, care must be taken in interpreting the results. The great danger with comparisons of this sort is that they are used naively or to make political points. Figures on their own cannot explain the myriad variations between different types of authority. Indeed in each of these types of comparison, whether using trends, aims, objectives and targets, or other organizations, the figures can only be a starting-point for more detailed investigation. A commentary showing the reasons for differences is essential.

Public expenditure and the future of the FMI

> Socrates was the first person to do a PAR,* he did it in Athens, going around asking fundamental questions. Athens put him to death, and that's why I don't want to do any more PARs. (Official at the DTI, quoted in Heclo and Wildavsky, op. cit.)

Will the managerial initiatives of the 1980s survive, or will they, in the graphic phrase often used by civil servants, 'run into the sand'? The 'public expenditure dimension' will only be one of many in the answer. Improved management should mean improvements in the planning and control process. But there are those who would argue that a continual preoccupation with economy could yet undermine the whole basis of what the FMI is trying to achieve. Certainly the resolution of this tension will be one of the factors which will determine its future.

The FMI does not appear to have had much direct effect on the public expenditure Survey process within departments. A former DoE civil servant commented:

> Of course, there is a limit as to how far public officials can take the initiative and be entrepreneurial with programme expenditure in the spirit of the FMI. Resource allocations remain firmly the responsibility of Ministers acting within the framework determined by Parliament. Officials remain largely resistant to the suggestion that Ministers should be influenced by officials' thinking except when views are positively requested. As far as programme expenditure vfm is concerned, the jocular comment of one Under-Secretary that, 'if the news is good Ministers do not need to know, and if the news is bad they do not want to know', is possibly not so far from the truth. Ministers have welcomed the FMI initiatives in general but have not conspicuously acted to reallocate resources because of them.
>
> The impact of the FMI on the use of programme resources has been far more modest ... Elsewhere improvements in quantification and identification of vfm *within* programmes has been patchy, and assessment of vfm *between* programmes remains unexplored territory. It seems that for there to be significant improvements in this area greater interest and stimulus must come directly from Ministers.[12]

The Treasury has yet to demonstrate its belief that departments can be trusted. One of the conclusions of a report on devolved budgeting in the Civil Service[13] was quizzically interpreted by Sue Richards:

* Programme Analysis and Review, a technique with similar objectives to parts of the FMI which was tried and then abandoned in the 1970s.

Report: At the moment we see insufficient flavour of objective setting and performance review as the background to resource allocation.

Translation: The Treasury behaves as though the FMI does not exist.[14]

There are wider issues, too, about the role of the centre in relation to initiatives taken by departments. In a report on progress in implementing the FMI, the NAO neatly stated the dilemma without attempting to resolve it:

Although the central departments (the Treasury and the Cabinet Office) took a leading part in indicating the main lines on which the spending departments should seek to develop their management arrangements, they discharged their duties in an essentially advisory manner. They considered that this approach was consistent with the government view ... that the central departments should adopt a stronger and where necessary more prescriptive role in reviewing the effectiveness and efficiency with which management operates. I think this approach to FMI proved sound in the event.

The wide range of business carried out by government departments suggests to me that departments are best placed to devise, within any framework prescribed from the centre, their own detailed management arrangements. In this way managers will recognize change as coming from within and be more ready to accept the new systems and working practices. At the same time the Treasury's responsibilities for the control of public expenditure provide them with a powerful tool to back up the efforts of departments to increase their administrative efficiency and the effectiveness of their programme expenditure, and to question the suitability of any revised management arrangements which appear to fall short of the general level of departmental achievements.[5]

Another important factor in the tension between central control and delegated responsibility is in the field of accountability. Current procedures, whether within departments, to the Treasury or to Parliament, do not yet allow for the mistakes which are almost inevitable in any system of delegated managerial responsibility. The statement by John Fielden that 'Ministers will have to be prepared to let mistakes happen and to accept situations where individual manager's initiatives at lower levels do not always reconcile with the broad policy objectives set at higher levels',[15] goes beyond what would currently be acceptable in practice, and certainly as a constitutional principle. This is one of the main reasons why the degree of delegation has not gone as far as many hoped. Those operating such systems usually find in practice that they have very little control over most of their budget and that their freedom of action has been severely constrained.

As in measuring performance, it is not easy to define what is meant by 'success' in this field, but for the FMI as a whole there is little doubt that much more has been achieved in the 1980s than many had thought possible. Describing changes in the Inland Revenue, one of those responsible for introducing reforms wrote of the process:

> The collective aim was to secure maximum value for money; to ensure the awareness of changing priorities; and to ensure fast adaptation to such changes at all levels.

> The department was very quick to recognize that in order to meet these objectives it would be necessary to involve individual line managers in the planning process. It also foresaw the need to identify individual managers within the department who would be given responsibility for budgets and the authority for controlling costs.

He was sanguine about the results:

> What is certain is that managers are now deeply involved in the financial planning process. They are also being provided regularly with detailed information about the costs of running their own local offices, and are now responsible themselves for budgets and for trying to make the best use of available resources and securing maximum 'value for money'. The groundwork of a major and significant long-term change has, the department believes, been well laid.[16]

So too were the two officials from the Lord Chancellor's Department:

> The impact of the FMI, with its principles of sound management, has presented a new atmosphere in the department which should benefit court user and taxpayer alike, as well as the court staff who now enjoy greater responsibility and enhanced job satisfaction.[11]

A description of developments in the Scottish Office gave some specific examples of what had been done:

> ... the costs of running individual hospitals can now be analysed in a detailed way and cases of market variation identified. The proportion of Health Boards' budgets which is devoted to management costs has been reduced by 10 per cent since 1979.

> Budgetary control was introduced at twelve Scottish prison establishments from 1 April 1985, with unit costing and improved overtime and stock controls.

In the directly controlled tertiary education sector, student:staff ratios in the central institutions have been raised by over 20 per cent since 1979.[17]

A DHSS civil servant in Newcastle felt that the experience factor was particularly important:

I think initially we may have rather oversold the notion that the budgeting system would give Cost Centre Managers flexibility in how they handle their groups, with a greater expectation than was realistic of virement between sub-heads and an ability to use savings to improve working conditions and staffing levels. There is of course, also, suspicion that the next door Cost Centre Manager is not being very rigorous in his budgeting and is concealing resources in his back pocket. I think all of this is probably inevitable in any budgeting system and will diminish considerably as we gain greater experience in the process.[18]

Where now?

Despite the cheerful examples set out above, there is no guarantee that the FMI is secure. The history of several failed managerial initiatives in recent years in the Civil Service would certainly not give grounds for optimism. But there are several elements which could mean that FMI will survive where other initiatives did not. There is the commitment to improved management, which has been given far greater priority than in the past; this undoubtedly has the potential to improve the lot of officials at all levels in the Civil Service. There is the continued ministerial backing which the FMI has enjoyed – the moves to improve management have been pushed further, across a broader front and for longer than anything of this kind before. While political will is not enough in itself to guarantee success, it is at least a good start.

Against this there are concerns about whether the managerial model of the FMI, relying as it does on private sector practice, will successfully translate to the needs of the Civil Service in the long term. Or indeed whether elements transferred from the private sector have been the right ones. The relative weakness of the institutional arrangements for promoting managerial change in the Civil Service has long been a problem. There are also worries about whether there is a continuing commitment by many Civil Servants to improved management; change in systems has not necessarily been accompanied by changes in attitudes and managerial culture. Suspicion about motives for introducing the FMI remain. As the Public Accounts Committee reported:

Notwithstanding Treasury's assurance that there is no crisis of morale in the Civil Service we are concerned that scepticism and mistrust of FMI seems to be widespread among middle and lower management grades. This is all the more worrying given that the Initiative is concerned with a fundamental cultural change in the ways that managers discharge departments' business.[5]

At a more down to earth level there are practical problems to be overcome in implementing the FMI and it is worth giving more detail in one area, vfm, to show what such problems mean in practice.

With vfm it has often proved difficult to reconcile its three elements – economy, efficiency and effectiveness. In education, for example, an attempt to improve efficiency, as measured by a student:teacher ratio, may lead to a decline in effectiveness, measured by exam success. A notable example of the difficulty in reconciling short-term economy with long-term efficiency was the decision in 1981 not to go ahead with a more efficient way of delivering unemployment benefit because of the short-term expenditure involved. But the main conflict has been in reconciling economy and effectiveness. In the case of a conflict, economy has tended to win. Thus the level of service in Department of Health and Social Security offices suffered in the early 1980s because manning levels fell far behind their increased workload.

Nor is value for money easy to quantify. Costs are more easily measurable than benefits, especially for services. And where some aspects of the vfm assessment are more easily quantifiable than others, it is difficult to give adequate weighting to those that are not. Thus it is easier to determine how many students in higher education finished their courses last year than it is to measure the quality of education.

The fact that an activity may be intended to achieve more than one objective may also cause difficulty. A prison service may have the dual tasks of keeping prisoners in custody and of rehabilitating them. It may do well on the first objective, but badly on the second. Does this mean it is effective or ineffective? The answer could be determined if the relative importance of objectives were made clear. But it is politically difficult, and therefore rare, for relative importance to be associated with objectives of public sector activities in this way. Determining vfm therefore often means considering how far the best fit between objectives has been achieved in this complex position.

Despite problems and difficulties, it is hard to believe that the FMI, or elements of it, will not survive in some form. Departments themselves have seen benefits, as the former DoE civil servant noted:

. . . the FMI has stirred up the DoE. It has led to some profound changes in the management structure of the organization and to important reforms, especially in the flow of information and in enhanced awareness of the importance of financial and other resource allocations. These changes have been largely beneficial.[12]

Because of the same problems, it is less clear that the F M I will reach its full potential. How much further things might go will depend to some extent on resolving key issues, a number of which have been outlined above. But above all it will depend on whether Ministers in general, and the Prime Minister in particular, can maintain their commitment and transmit that commitment to their officials.

6

DEVOLVED FINANCIAL RESPONSIBILITY

Introduction

The reluctant obedience of distant provinces generally costs more
than it is worth. (Lord Macaulay, *Historical Essays*)

A large proportion of public expenditure is spent by public bodies with
funds provided for them by central government. Responsibility is passed
to these bodies from central government in a variety of ways. Chapter 3
has already outlined the process by which Scotland, Wales and Northern
Ireland receive funds which are then administered by the relevant
territorial government departments. So while dealing in outline with the
special provisions for health or local government in Scotland, Wales or
Northern Ireland, this chapter deals mainly with the direct allocation
from central government departments to local government, the National
Health Service, government trading funds and quangos (quasi autonomous non-governmental organizations), including nationalized industries.

There are few common factors in the relationship between government
departments and the other public bodies to whom they devolve spending
responsibility. It will be seen that there are major differences in the
statutory relationship these bodies have with central government, and in
the degree of their independence. Constraints may be highly formal in
some cases and subtly informal in others. Many of the bodies dealt with
in this chapter have the power to raise their own funds in whole or in
part. This too has a major impact on their relationship with central
government departments. At a personal level, there are differences in
the way relationships are handled and in the style of management. Often
there are informal relationships which operate in parallel with the more

formal ones. Such relationships vary from the collusive to the highly
acrimonious. In a brief survey of this kind it is not possible to cover all
the details, but it is worth remembering that the relationships may not be
quite as straightforward as they at first appear.

Local authorities

Local authorities are responsible for about a quarter of total public
expenditure, representing about 10 per cent of national income. They employ over two million people. As with central government, their prominent
position in the country's affairs only developed during the twentieth
century as successive governments extended the role of the public sector
as a whole.

WHERE THE MONEY COMES FROM

Central government is the largest single source of local government
revenue in England, Scotland and Wales. (The figures are not easily
comparable to those for Northern Ireland, with its different balance
between services provided by local and central government and a different basis for raising revenue.) But local authorities also have other major
sources of finance which together add up to far more than is provided
by central government.

The largest of these is income from local taxation, currently rates.
Rates are a property tax levied by local authorities. All occupiers (the
word is used in a special sense in this context) of non-agricultural land
and buildings are liable to pay rates, and the nature of the liability is
linked to the rateable value of the property. Rateable values are set by
the Inland Revenue in England and Wales and by the Assessors in
Scotland. They are based on the notional annual rent which the property
might attract. The amount to be raised from rates is set yearly by each
local authority, which must establish how much is needed to provide the
level of services that has been agreed after taking into account the
announcement of central government's contribution.

Another major source is the income from the local authority's own
assets and activities. These include rents for housing owned by the
authority, charges for recreation facilities, such as swimming pools,
income from trading activities (for example, from markets and industrial
waste disposal) and fees for various services provided, such as adult
education and home helps.

In recent years capital receipts have been of increasing importance as

Table 6.1   Local authority income (Great Britain only)

	Current/Revenue %*	Capital %*
Unallocated central government grant	30	—
Specific (education; roads; housing; police, etc.)	10	5
Rates	30	—
Rent, fees, interest	25	—
Borrowing	—	50
Sale of capital assets (i.e. council houses)	—	45
Other	5	—
	100	100

* Rounded, 5 per cent bands.

Source: Byrne, op. cit. (adapted) for 1983.

an additional source of income, arising directly out of government policy to sell local authority housing to its tenants. The local authority may not necessarily be able to spend all the proceeds of such sales.

Borrowing is the final major source of finance. Local authority borrowing is usually through commercial sources, but if local authorities do not borrow in the commercial market, funds from the National Investment and Loans Office – a government-funded but independent body that lends only to local authorities – are available to them. The Office provides about half the finance for local authority capital expenditure.

Table 6.1 gives a breakdown of the relative scale of the major sources of local authorities' income. To those who pay domestic rates, one of the most surprising features of these figures is probably the relatively low proportion of local authority finance – about 30 per cent – which rates provide. The high proportion of funding from central government certainly helps to explain the government's concern to exercise control over local authority expenditure.

SPENDING THE MONEY

Local authorities have a statutory duty to provide many of the services for which they need finance. Table 6.2 provides a breakdown of what local authorities as a whole spend, differentiating between capital and current expenditure. But this pattern will not be mirrored in each authority. There is no such entity as a 'typical' authority. Different types of authority cover different geographical areas, there is discretion on how

Table 6.2 Local authority expenditure, by service category

	% of total	
	Current/Revenue	Capital
Education, libraries, arts, museums, milk and meals	36	8
Environmental services	7	10
Roads, lighting, transport	7	12
Housing (including subsidies and rebates)	17	53
Personal social services	7	2
Police, fire, justice	10	2
Others, including trading	16	13
	100	100

Source: Byrne, op. cit.

they spend some of their funds and there are very disparate local needs which they have to meet. One only has to imagine the difference between an inner-city authority such as Hackney in east London and the relatively prosperous County of Hampshire to see what these differences are likely to mean.

The types of local authority vary from one part of the United Kingdom to another and the services they provide depend on the type of authority involved. Table 6.3 gives a breakdown for Great Britain as a whole. The arrangements for central government financing in Wales are similar to those in England, with the Department of the Environment responsible for grants to Welsh local authorites. In Scotland, however, the allocations are administered through the Secretary of State for Scotland.

The position is different altogether in Northern Ireland, both in structure and approach. While the other parts of the United Kingdom have a two-tier system, in Northern Ireland there is only one tier. This position arises from the breakdown of the established relationship with Westminster in 1972 and the subsequent failure to find a body to administer many central government functions for the province as a whole. As a result, many of the functions performed by local authorities elsewhere in the United Kingdom are carried out by agencies or boards appointed by the Secretary of State and responsible to the relevant Northern Ireland department. So the twenty-six Northern Ireland District Councils are only directly responsible for a limited

Table 6.3 Which local authority provides what? (Great Britain only)

ENGLAND	*Responsible for*:
Metropolitan areas	Education, personal social services, housing,
36 districts	planning, environmental health, leisure services and (via joint boards) transport, police, fire
Non-metropolitan areas	Education, personal social services,
39 counties	transport, police, fire, some planning and leisure services.
296 districts	Housing, planning, environmental health, leisure services
Over 7,000 local (parish and town) councils	Local amenities
London	
Inner London Education Authority*	Education in inner London
32 London boroughs	Housing, social services, leisure, public health, education (outer London boroughs) and (via joint boards) fire, civil defence
WALES	
8 county councils ⎫	Much the same as non-metropolitan
37 district councils ⎭	authorities in England
About 800 community or town councils	Local amenities
SCOTLAND	
9 regions	Overall planning, education, social work, transport, water, police, fire services
53 districts	Housing, local planning
Over 1,200 community councils	Local amenities
3 island areas	All regional and district powers

* Until 1990, thereafter only London boroughs.
Source: Byrne, op. cit. (adapted).

range of services, though they have the right to be represented on certain of the public agencies or boards. This applies, for example, in education, libraries and Health and Personal Social Services. District Councils also have the right to be consulted on issues for which they have no executive responsibility, such as housing and planning.

On the financial relationship between central government and local authorities in Northern Ireland, as Table 2.2 showed, finance for local authorities expenditure is a much smaller proportion of the funds under the control of the Northern Ireland Office than the figures for Wales and Scotland. Furthermore, the dependence on central government grants –

about a quarter – for local authority expenditure on current account is also a much smaller proportion than for the rest of the United Kingdom. The position is different with funds on capital account, where a substantial percentage of the funds are covered by central government grants.

How then does a local authority decide what to spend? Individual authorities differ in their planning and budgeting arrangements, but it is possible to identify certain common factors. The process of drawing up a budget (which separates current and capital items for both income and expenditure) begins up to twelve months before the beginning of the financial year, with the Policy and Resources Committee or the Finance Committee starting to draw up the financial policy guidelines for the committees responsible for providing resources. By the autumn the spending plans and detailed budgets are being drawn up by each of the individual committees. As in the case of central government, their planning baseline is the level of current provision with adjustments to existing and the establishment of new policies. The result then has to be related to the guidelines – effectively the restrictions – initially drawn up. There will then almost inevitably be a great deal of negotiation to fit spending aspirations into the financial policy guidelines.

Although the government gives an indication of some of their assumptions in July, only in November or December are the total amounts announced which central government will make available to finance local authorities. The details of grants may be changed, even shortly before the setting of the rate for the coming financial year. Expenditure plans can only therefore be finalized very late in the planning cycle. Indeed further changes may be required almost up to the last minute before plans are presented to the full council. Decisions about charges – rents, etc. – may be made at the same time, though these can of course be altered later in the financial year.

Balancing financing options is a complex business, particularly in an authority without a party in overall control, but in general the Council's decision on the level of expenditure will determine the level at which the local rate has to be set, since it is rate income which will balance the books between spending plans and the income available from other sources. In practice, however, all decisions are not left so late. There will be a reasonably clear idea at the beginning of the planning cycle about the levels of service to be achieved or the acceptable level of the rate to be levied, and this will have informed the discussions about expenditure. There may even be an attempt to set the level of rate income at the beginning of the cycle as a means of constraining the discussions about expenditure.

Central/local government financial relations

Central government provides finance to local authorities for a variety of reasons. It uses them as the vehicle for delivering certain kinds of services, such as education, which are national in nature but under local control. It has also long been a matter of policy that central government should alleviate the burden of local taxation which is considered to be regressive – that is, which bears more heavily on those who are less well-off. Grants from central government are also sometimes used to make up a deficiency when local authorities are prevented from raising other sources of finance for one reason or another (including restrictions by central government itself). But a fundamental principle which governs the financial relationship between central and local government is the concept of equalization.

Equalization aims to resource a standard level of service throughout the United Kingdom. However, local authorities vary enormously in their needs. Some authorities have low-quality housing stock and high levels of unemployment. Others are relatively prosperous. Some have a high proportion of children of school age, others a high proportion of the elderly. Even without having to meet special circumstances, authorities must spend very different amounts to fulfil their statutory obligations. Such obligations will also depend on whether they are urban or rural areas and whether they cover deprived or prosperous parts of the country. Their ability to raise funds for themselves through rates or other means also varies greatly. In these circumstances, equalization means that some central involvement in local authority finance is inevitable.

The formula for deciding the level of funding for individual local authorities, taking account of the resources available and the needs of each authority, is the Rate Support Grant (RSG). The level of the RSG is set as a result of a series of decisions taken annually, a process which starts with a meeting between central government and local authorities to discuss the overall allocation to be made in the government's plans for total local authority spending for the coming year. The amount under discussion will exclude mandatory payments by the local authorities – that is, those payments which the local authorities are bound to make for services such as student grants.

Once the government's allocation has been made, the government has to decide what proportion of the total it should meet from central funds (the 'aggregate exchequer grant'). About 20 per cent of the aggregate exchequer grant consists of specific grants for such items as police, housing improvements and supplementary grants for transport and National Parks. The remaining amount is the RSG.

The RSG is divided into two main components. One of these is the block grant, which is intended to achieve equalization by reflecting the different needs and resources of authorities by ensuring that each is able, if it wishes to do so, to provide services of a similar standard. A standard rate poundage is assumed by the government for the calculation of the RSG.

The second component is known as the domestic element. This is a form of relief to domestic ratepayers who, as a result, pay a lower rate poundage than industrial and commercial organizations.

The current basis for deciding the level of the RSG is the Local Government Planning and Land Act 1980 and subsequent amending legislation. This act was the result of discussions following the recommendations of the 1976 Layfield Report into local government finance. It was the 1980 act which introduced the concept of the block grant, with the intention of simplifying the previous (even more) complex system for deciding the level of central government funding for local authorities. It placed a limit on the extent to which authorities increasing their expenditure would be entitled to extra grant based on what was called 'the grant-related expenditure assessment'. To combine control with an element of flexibility, local authorities were allowed to spend up to 10 per cent over their allocation.

Since the 1980 act, there have been two major attempts to tighten control over local authority expenditure. Neither was foreseen or recommended by the Layfield Report and they were grafted uncomfortably on to the block grant system. The first attempt was in 1981 and involved the imposition of spending limits; but it was found that these created a dual measurement standard and did not work. As a result, the limits were abandoned after a few years. The second attempt was the 1984 Rates Act which was designed to control local authority income through rate-capping. This act stopped local authorities using income from rates to fund expenditure which was considered excessive by the government. It gave the Secretary of State for the Environment power to limit rate increases for individual authorities (the selective scheme) or across the board (the general scheme). Since its introduction, rate-capping has been applied to about twenty authorities, and there have been very public battles with authorities such as Liverpool which refused for some time to acknowledge the right of central government to impose constraints of this kind. Every year there have been some modifications in the criteria used.

Controls of various kinds have also been exercised for many years over local authority capital expenditure. Again, the basis of the present set of controls is the Local Government Planning and Land Act 1980, although the detailed techniques often vary. Approval is given to each authority for a year at a time, based on a rolling programme which covers a variety of periods, depending on the service. The amounts are known as prescribed expenditure allocations. The allocations are divided into five blocks – housing, education, transport, personal social services and other services – though once the allocations have been made, individual local authorities can vary them, so deciding their own priorities. Additional flexibility is provided by the ability of certain local authorities with unused capital allocations to transfer them to other authorities which need them. Approval for specific projects is generally only required if they have a regional or national significance. Under the act, a local authority can also only use a prescribed proportion of any receipts from sales of housing.

One result of the succession of controls imposed on local authorities has been that the Consultative Councils on Local Government Finance, one for England and one for Wales, which were originally set up to allow the authorities to have some input into the central government budgetary allocation system, have effectively ceased to function. As the gap between what local authorities have actually spent and government allocations has widened, successive Secretaries of State for the Environment have found it necessary to impose more and consult less. The idea of a body which would discuss 'matters of policy affecting local authorities which have major financial implications' has thus come to be largely irrelevant to any real decision-taking.

INTERNAL CONTROL, ACCOUNTABILITY AND AUDIT

It would be a mistake, in the light of all the constraints which central government has sought to exercise over local authorities, to assume that all authorities have proved financially irresponsible or profligate in internal control. Internally, Standing Orders and financial regulations provide the framework for financial control and a local authority Finance or Policy and Resources Committee, in conjunction with the relevant officials, will monitor expenditure profiles during the year.

There is also external audit of their affairs. Until 1982, the District Audit Service (D A S) was responsible for auditing most local authority accounts in England and Wales. Since 1983, the Audit Commission has had the responsibility for appointing auditors for these authorities. The Commission has the right to choose whether the audit should be by the DAS or by private sector accountants approved by the Secretary of State; the private sector has now taken about 30 per cent of local authority audit work.

The Audit Commission itself was established under the Local Government Finance Act 1982 and it was significant that the Act extended the audit function to cover ways of achieving value for money. The Commission has taken a high profile in its general studies in recent years and reports have included such topics as 'Managing the crisis in council housing', 'Towards better management of secondary education' and 'Improving cash-flow management in local government'. These reports have identified ways of making savings by obtaining better value for money. Handbooks on best practice have been produced.

There is a separate external audit system for Scotland, where it is the responsibility of the Commission for Local Authority Accounts. This body has the power to recruit its own staff to do the audit work, but traditionally it appoints a substantial number of private sector accounting firms to do so.

The National Health Service (NHS)

The NHS came into being in 1948 and, although there is a small private health sector, it is overwhelmingly the most important provider of health care in the United Kingdom. Over 10 per cent of all public spending goes on the NHS and it is the country's largest employer.

It is curious to note that at the time when the NHS came into being, it was hoped that (after the initial 'catching-up' on services which previously had to be paid for but which were now available free of charge) the call on NHS funds would decrease. In fact there has been almost continuous growth in government expenditure on the NHS in real terms – that is, adjusted for inflation (though as Chapter 3 showed, what this means is open to dispute). Another major reason is that with the improvement in health standards, there has been a big increase in the number of the elderly. No less than half of total NHS resources are spent on the over-65s and it is estimated that this proportion will continue to rise.

WHERE THE MONEY COMES FROM

Almost all the money to finance the NHS comes from the government. At the local level the NHS gets income from donations, sales of land, voluntary fund-raising, private patients and charges for services to private hospitals. But such sums are relatively small – a few hundred millions compared with the billions spent on the service as a whole. Government accounting conventions treat prescription charges and a proportion of National Insurance charges as NHS income. In practice this 'income' is paid into the central government's general funding pool. Indeed, if these were paid direct, only about 4 per cent of total NHS expenditure would be met by charges and around 12 per cent by the health element of National Insurance.

WHAT THE MONEY IS SPENT ON

As Figure 6.1 shows, expenditure on hospital and community health services dominates the NHS budget. Of this, the bulk of the funds goes towards staff costs, mainly for staff in hospitals. Family practitioners, it should be noted, are separated organizationally. They are self-employed and are therefore funded on a different basis – a division which has some important implications described later in this chapter.

THE FINANCIAL RELATIONSHIP BETWEEN THE DHSS AND THE NHS

Overall responsibility for the NHS in England is borne by the Department of Health and Social Security (DHSS), which also administers the country's social security. There is a great contrast between the decentralized way in which the NHS is administered and the highly centralized social security system. Indeed there are variations in the structure of the NHS in each part of the United Kingdom, so that although provision may be national, organization is not.

In England, the two-tier structure of the NHS, established by the Health Services Act 1980 and implemented in 1982, is organizationally more like a federation than a centralized national service. At the first level, England is divided into regions, and the fourteen Regional Health Authorities (RHAs) are responsible to the DHSS. At the level below come 191 health districts, each with a District Health Authority (DHA). The boundaries of the district are largely determined by the idea of a 'natural community', often based around a district hospital and its catchment area.

The variations in other parts of the United Kingdom include the absence of a regional tier in Scotland, Wales or Northern Ireland. For the provision of services, all have common services agencies. In

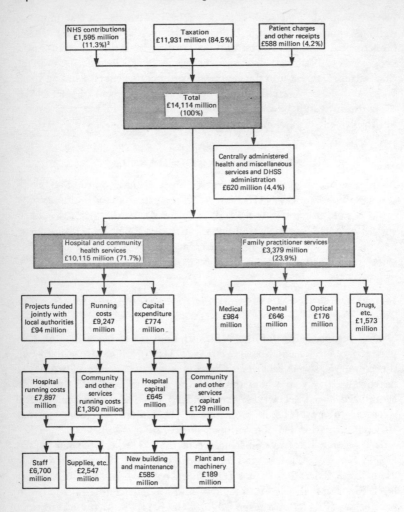

Figure 6.1   *National Health Service funding and expenditure in England,*
1984–85[1]

1. Figures for health authorities and Family Practitioner Committees are derived from their summarized accounts. They are before deduction of direct credits (e.g. receipts from staff for accommodation) and include certain other income and balances as well as funds made available by central government and through patients' charges.
2. Percentage figures given in brackets are based on the total.

Northern Ireland there are also joint Health and Social Services Boards. Responsibility for health services in these three parts of the United Kingdom rests with the three territorial Secretaries of State, and their allocations, as described in Chapter 3, are on population-based formulae. The formulae apply not only to health but also to other programmes and, as Chapter 3 showed, the Secretaries of State have some discretion on priorities between and within individual programmes.

Nor is all health provision at local level controlled by the districts. As already noted, family practitioners are self-employed and under contract to the NHS to provide services. So too are dentists, chemists and opticians. The basis for payment differs between these groups using a variety of criteria, including the number of patients and the types of service provided. The cost to the NHS of these services therefore depends on which services are being paid for, the rate paid for each service and the number of people who choose to use them. This element of discretion by the 'customers' of these NHS services makes it much harder to predict and control costs, unlike the allocations to regions described below, where limits can be set on the amounts provided.

For England, allocation of the bulk of their funds is made by the DHSS to the regions on the basis of principles that have been the subject of a great deal of argument over many years. Just as one of the main principles in the allocation of local government finance is that there should be comparable levels of service throughout the United Kingdom, so one of the major aims of the NHS has been to create equal access to health care. Until the mid 1970s there was a wide variation in the scale of provision between different parts of the country. To achieve greater fairness, the Resource Allocation Working Party (RAWP) was set up by the government in 1975. A year later, the committee recommended that the needs of regions should be assessed on a number of formulae based on factors such as population characteristics, standard mortality ratios and flows of patients across regional boundaries. From these were derived targets for each region.

Since then, the allocation of funds has followed the principle that the worst-off regions receive the largest proportion of annual funding growth in order to achieve equalization over time. The better-off regions are given correspondingly less to bring them down. The annual allocations to regions have been based on the previous year's approved expenditure with an allowance for inflation. To this has been added a percentage growth determined by the funding relative to the RAWP targets.

Included in the revenue (or current) expenditure is provision for the

purchase of furnishings and most equipment. There is a different basis
for the allocation of capital funding. This includes new buildings, plant
and major items of equipment, such as computers and ambulances. A
separate R A W P formula covers about 80 per cent of the sums dis-
tributed. This is based on forecasts of population distribution. No account is taken of age, suitability or condition of the existing buildings or
other capital items, which means that revenue and capital programmes
are not always compatible. Indeed, the policy is to move towards greater
equity in the distribution of capital stock on the basis of relative need in
relation to future population trends rather than on inadequacies in the
present stock. The impact of the formula may, however, be mitigated
for the remaining 20 per cent of capital, which is retained for specific
purposes and in some cases particular hospitals and units.

Financial allocations below the regional level do not continue on the
precise basis of the R A W P formula; in fact there is no requirement that
the funds should then be passed down from region to district on a

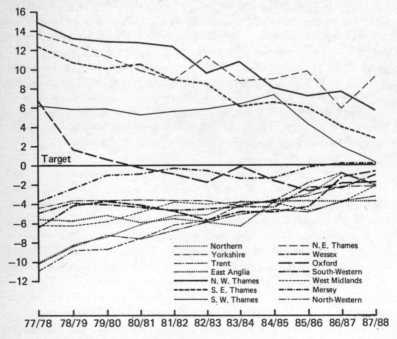

Figure 6.2 *R A W P*
Source: DHSS.

comparable basis. There are a variety of different allocation methods, and the RHAs have discretion over how much they retain, a practice known as 'top-slicing'. The 'top slice' may include provision for their own administration and for regional services such as supplies and procurement. However, some RHAs also keep back reserves for areas of particular need or imbalance.

One group is protected from some of the uncomfortable effects of RAWP. Although they are paid by the district, doctors are employed directly by the NHS. Unlike spending on nurses, therefore, savings cannot be made on doctors' salaries to make up any shortfalls at district level. It is worth noting that this split causes a further problem in any attempt to equalize provision between regions. The distribution of doctors' posts is not covered by the RAWP formula and this tends to undermine RAWP's redistributive effects.

RAWP implicitly assumed that additional funds would be available, so that better-off regions would not be subject to cutbacks. But funding has not grown as fast as had been hoped, and there has been resistance from the better-off regions to cutbacks in the levels of service provided. The London-based regions in particular have lobbied successfully to avoid those cuts in their services which would be necessary under RAWP. Since the government has not been willing to put in the necessary additional resources, the result has been that the objective of achieving equalization has been put back to the mid 1990s, although, as Figure 6.2 shows, progress towards greater equality has certainly been made.

INTERNAL CONTROL, ACCOUNTABILITY AND AUDIT

Accountability for NHS funds does not necessarily mirror the way those funds are allocated. Technically, for England (the rest of the United Kingdom have their own arrangements) district management is responsible to the DHA, whose chairman is appointed by the Secretary of State for Social Services. Regional management is responsible to the RHA, all of whose members are appointed by the Secretary of State. The Secretary of State is responsible to Parliament.

In practice, there are ambiguities in the chain of accountability. The relationship between DHA and RHA is unclear and there are direct links between regional management and the Management Board, set up in 1985 to carry out management functions on behalf of the DHSS. The Management Board is itself responsible to the Secretary of State.

Finally, accountability is complicated by the power of the medical profession in the management of the NHS. What this means in practice is that doctors are able to take decisions based on their professional discretion which may not fit easily with what the district or region is trying to do.

Internal NHS controls have been developed considerably in recent years. This has been the result of the need to conserve resources in an extended period of cash constraint and of pressures to identify costs. Normal budgetary procedures have been supplemented by improved management information systems, including the widespread use of performance indicators. Rayner scrutinies, too, have been extended to the NHS. Appendix C gives a flavour of the results of a scrutiny in the form of a ministerial letter and an extract from the scrutiny to which the letter relates.

As for the formal audit procedures, these operate at three levels. First, the detailed work is undertaken by the internal NHS auditors with responsibility going from the Treasurer at district level to the Regional Treasurer. The work of the internal auditors is complemented by the audit staff of the DHSS, who report to the Regional Health Authority and, if necessary, to the Secretary of State. Finally, the National Audit Office (NAO) certifies the consolidated NHS accounts on the basis of their own examination, taking into account the work already carried out by the DHSS.

Quangos

Quangos, an acronym for quasi autonomous non-governmental organizations, are of three types:

1. Executive bodies which carry out a wide variety of operational and regulatory functions of which the nationalized industries, the Advisory, Conciliation and Arbitration Service (ACAS) and the British Council are some examples.
2. Advisory bodies of various kinds, bringing specialist expertise to bear on public issues. Some, such as the Dangerous Pathogens Advisory Group, are little known outside their field. Others, such as the Royal Fine Arts Commission, are rather better known.
3. Tribunals, such as Rent Tribunals and Industrial Tribunals, which carry out quasi-judicial functions.

It is only the first type of quango which is of particular interest in the context of public expenditure. While quangos of the other two types may be influential, they are not directly involved to any great extent in spending money.

There are a large variety of different financial arrangements between quangos and the government departments from which they draw their funds. In so far as it is possible to generalize, however, there are a number of key variables which determine the degree of control involved. One of these is whether the quangos are given the power to raise fees or charges, and therefore their dependence on public money. The amount of public money which they receive is also important. The less required in total and the smaller the proportion required from public funds, the easier for such a quango to be free of detailed financial control. Thus in the case of the nationalized industries, which often count organizationally as quangos, it was easier for British Gas before privatization to pursue a more independent line than British Rail. While the former was in the position of repaying large amounts to the government, the latter has always received a substantial annual amount from the government.

Another variable in the control mechanism has been the way in which the rules have been laid down. In some cases, only funds as a whole are subject to scrutiny; in others, large capital projects have to be separately justified. Some, however, have detailed control over both capital and current expenditure, while, as the next section makes clear, nationalized industries have their own very particular rules.

Finally, it is worth noting that there are a variety of audit provisions for quangos. Some – the Manpower Services Commission, for example – are audited by the NAO. Others, such as nationalized industries, have accounts which are audited on a very similar basis to those of large private sector commercial organizations. Indeed, in the greater amount of information they make available and their use of inflation adjustments in their accounts, they are in some ways ahead of the private sector. Their accounts are audited by private sector accountants, with the Secretary of State of the government department responsible for the industry (the 'sponsoring' department) having considerable influence on their choice of auditor.

Nationalized Industries

Nationalized industries are a particular form of quango. Despite continuing privatizations, their importance in the economy in general and for public expenditure in particular means that they merit detailed separate consideration from the others. Formally, financial control over the industries is exercised by Parliament and the Minister responsible is answerable to Parliament for all aspects of policy. But in practice it is the direct relationship between government and the particular industry which is crucial.

In general, the relationship between government and the nationalized industries is supposed to be 'at arm's length', but is in practice much more complicated. The industries' statutes stipulate in most cases that there should be ministerial approval for their capital spending programmes, and that they should break even, taking one year with another. These provisions in themselves have not been sufficient to achieve a satisfactory balance between the interests of the government and those of the industries. Various ways of controlling and monitoring have been tried since the Second World War; none has proved satisfactory. The overriding problem has been that successive governments have wanted to intervene in the affairs of the industries. As a result, relations between nationalized industries and the government have usually been strained, and sometimes acrimonious.

The key to control has been the need of many industries for government funds. Although they normally raise the bulk of their revenue from their customers, industries have often required additional financial help for their activities. Unprofitable industries have used the money to fund their losses, profitable ones to finance major capital expenditure programmes to provide for their growth. Such funds come mainly through government loans, or in some cases private sector loans guaranteed by the government. The required sums for a single industry can amount to hundreds or thousands of millions of pounds, so the government is clearly interested in the basis on which the funds are allocated. The current method of doing so is the annual Investment and Financing Review (IFR).

The sequence of the IFR is that each year every industry compiles a projection of its financial requirements for the year ahead and formulates a proposal on how it intends to fund its requirements. This proposal is discussed with the sponsoring department each summer, about nine months before the beginning of the financial year. It may well be modified as a result of the discussions. The sponsoring department then brings the proposal to the Treasury for review about three months later, still some months before the beginning of the financial year. Because the total borrowing of the nationalized industries counts as part of public expenditure, the financing requirements of each industry becomes involved in the Survey process. The results of the whole negotiating procedure to decide what is available for each industry are published in the Autumn Statement in November. An industry then has a maximum limit on the amount of government (or government backed) finance available. This amount, the external financing limit (EFL), covers government subsidies, loans, market and overseas borrowing, and the capital value of newly leased assets. Full details are given in the Public Expenditure White Paper, with a breakdown as shown in Table 6.4 using the Civil Aviation Authority as an example. Note that the profit contribution is shown on a current cost (inflation-adjusted) basis and that depreciation is separately identified.

Sometimes the EFL is negative; that is, the government expects a net repayment of funds (usually loans) during the year. Table 2.3 showed the very different amounts required for various industries in a single year.

Table 6.4   Civil Aviation Authority, external financing limit (EFL)

	£ million	£ million
Capital requirements		
Purchase of fixed assets in the UK	30	
Other	6	35*
FINANCED BY		
Internal funds		
Current cost operating profit	15	
Less interest, dividends and tax	(14)	
Depreciation	19	20
External finance		
Government grants	3	
NLF loans, etc.	21	
Market borrowing, etc.	(9)	15
		35

* Rounded.

Source: Public Expenditure White Paper, 1987

The IFR system is only the latest of many attempts to develop a financial relationship with government acceptable to industries and government alike. But agreement has been elusive. The industries have criticized many aspects of the control mechanism, including:

- the inflexibility of government plans for industries trading in an uncertain commercial environment – a former Chairman of the Post Office once likened it to trying to land a jumbo jet on a postage stamp;

- the concentration on the short term and on a one-year planning cycle when many industries (such as the water industry) have to operate with very long planning horizons;

- the temptation of successive governments to put the burden of financing on the consumer, as in the case of the energy industries.

The industries have long argued that since they are commercial undertakings they should be given much greater freedom to raise capital from the private capital market. This would give them more flexibility in financing projects and a greater level of control over the form of financing. It would also enable them to consider longer time horizons, and meet other, non-cash measures of performance, such as quality of service. But successive governments have feared loss of control of a key item in the planning of public expenditure. They have argued that such a move would deprive the private sector of funds and so have made few concessions to the calls for greater financial independence.

Although the emphasis of the control mechanism has been largely on EFLs, government influence and intervention have been exercised through a combination of several other methods. These have included controls over pricing and investment policy. There are also administrative controls, including performance targets, the requirement to present corporate plans to government, and regular efficiency reviews by the Monopolies and Mergers Commission. The way these other controls are exercised varies depending on the type of control, the financial performance of the industry, and the personalities of the Minister and chairman. Thus pricing may be subject to heavy-handed intervention; performance measures may be largely ignored. Loss-making industries are much more likely to be subject to greater scrutiny than those which are profitable.

The practicalities of control are less straightforward than they may seem. Some chairmen are cajoled, others threatened. In theory, the

Table 6.5   External financing limits in the 1980s: plans and out-turns

	£ billion			
	Requirements	Internal resources	EFLs	Original EFLs
1980–81	6.2	3.0	3.2	2.3
1981–82	7.5	3.9	3.6	2.3
1982–83	6.9	4.8	2.1	2.7
1983–84	6.9	4.6	2.3	2.6
1984–85	4.5	0.7	3.8	1.9
1985–86	5.7	4.0	1.7	1.3
1986–87 [1]	4.2	3.6	0.6 [3]	—
1987–88 [2]	4.5	3.8	0.7	—
1988–89 [2]	4.7	4.3	0.3	—
1989–90 [2]	4.7	4.8	(0.1)	

1. Estimated.
2. Projections.
3. Includes 0.4 for privatized industries.

Source: Public Expenditure White Paper, 1987.

government can take a variety of measures to ensure that industries keep within their limits. But as trading entities, the industries are subject to many factors outside their control. This means that although a nationalized industry has some flexibility in its pricing, its ability to stay within its EFL, as well as to meet other targets, will depend on a combination of economic, political, industrial and other variables. Thus the prices that British Coal can get for its products are affected by those for competing fuels, particularly oil. The quantity it can sell may well be determined by government attitudes to the mining unions. The demand for the output of all energy industries is determined by the weather. Just how much these have caused plans to be upset in the past is shown in Table 6.5, which gives the comparison between plan and out-turn for the nationalized industries as a whole in the early 1980s. In recognition of these uncertainties, the government has often had to modify EFLs originally set.

Other public corporations and trading entities

Nationalized industries form only one group of public corporations. For the purposes of public expenditure control their transactions with central government are classified in a variety of ways, reflecting a different degree of integration into government finances. The treatment of each corporation is decided by the Treasury.

Not included as public corporations are companies which are wholly owned or controlled by the government. Unlike public corporations (which are governed by statute), these companies are effectively private sector organizations, but with the government as the only or majority shareholder. The most prominent in recent years has been Rover. Funds for such companies come through the government department which is responsible for them, and any allocations are therefore part of the normal budgeting process for that department.

Organizations which are trading funds are also grouped with public corporations for statistical and planning purposes. Trading funds are an attempt to give government bodies a commercial framework, with financial targets set by Ministers. Her Majesty's Stationery Office (HMSO), for example, was given loan capital to finance its operations in 1980 and its financial target was to 'produce an operating surplus equivalent to a return on average net assets of 5 per cent after allowing for current cost accounting adjustments, but before payment of interest on long-term borrowing'.

Some general issues

The 1980s have seen a dramatic reappraisal of the borderline between the public and private sectors. The basis of the reappraisal has been part ideological and political, part organizational, administrative and financial. The Conservative government has certainly held fast to the belief that the private sector can generally run most services more efficiently than public bodies and that greater efficiency will go hand-in-hand with demands for less public money. There has also been a distrust of the ability or willingness of public bodies, especially local government, to carry through national policies and to respect financial constraints.

The most dramatic consequence of the reappraisal has probably been the huge privatization programme for nationalized industries, though important issues on the conflict between national and private interests are still involved in the work of the regulatory bodies that have been established to protect the public. With local authorities, the reappraisal has taken the form of questions about the conflict between local and central control, and about whether certain services should be provided by local authorities or by the private sector on a contracted-out basis.

For those services which it is intended should remain in the public sector, there has therefore been an attempt to combine more devolution of decision-making with greater controls over the total amount of money available. This has proved an uncomfortable combination. In the case of those areas of the public sector where there was already an element of devolved decision-making, the need to control public spending has meant increasing pressure by central government to exercise control at a local level. A variety of control mechanisms have been put in place to achieve this, often with drastic consequences, as in the withdrawal of grant from some local authorities.

The result of the proliferation of controls has been a great deal of resentment among many administrators. Appointed and elected local representatives, where involved, have also resented what they have seen as challenges to their independence. Relationships have often then deteriorated. For a few public bodies, this deterioration has at one extreme included open conflict with central government, based on the claim that their local mandate was superior to the national mandate claimed by central government. Central government has been most prominently at loggerheads with a number of local authorities, notably in Liverpool. In 1980 they went much further with Lambeth district health authority and took over the running of the authority. Most of the authorities involved were Labour-controlled, but there were also political rows with some Conservative authorities, such as Oxfordshire County Council.

For many of the resentful public bodies, however, the result of their resentment has been greater sophistication in managing their financial relationship with central government. In some cases this has meant conforming to the letter, but not the spirit, of legislation. In others it has led to more creative accounting (as it is euphemistically called), a practice made easier by the increasing complexity of the control mechanisms. Thus some local authorities have resorted to devices that include the capitalization of revenue expenditure, rescheduling of debt repayments, and sale and leaseback of assets. In some of the more exotic schemes, there have been discussions about leasing back bathroom and kitchen fittings in local authority housing, parking meters, street lamps and even town hall buildings. An article described how

Manchester City Council, for instance, is using this device to raise £14.6m in the 1987–88 financial year. It is selling £200m of properties – including an art gallery and abattoir – to a company owned by the council. The buildings will be leased back under a twenty-year lease, with the first two years rent free.[1]

Central government has responded to such devices with yet more complex mechanisms of control, which in turn have made these public bodies, with the active assistance of financial institutions, even more determined to circumvent central government. Among the strategies listed in the same article describing Manchester's ingenuity were:

- Payments under leasing arrangements come under current spending. So by leasing computers, instead of buying them under a capital programme, councils can provide more equipment while still meeting capital allocations.

- ... a piece of council land is given to a developer on condition he builds the authority a leisure centre on part of the site. The developer gets the remainder of the land for his own schemes and the council gets a new leisure centre without encroaching on its capital allocation.

- Many authorities are taking housing repairs and renewals into their capital programmes, reducing current spending and hence avoiding penalties for overspending.

- Arrangements to repay debt at a fixed interest rate are swapped for variable rate repayments. By gambling on interest rates falling, councils are able to take the profit early – yielding revenue for current spending.

Nevertheless, the initiative has remained with central government and financial power has moved steadily back to the centre. Creative accounting schemes have been blocked and local authorities such as Camden, Greenwich, Southwark and Liverpool are among those who may well have problems in future years in coping with the consequences of their ingenious financial arrangements.

One effect of the problems of the confrontation with local authorities is that it has strengthened the government's determination to change the basis by which local authorities raise finance. Some have always seen rates as the best method of local taxation. There is no such agreement about what should replace it. At the time of writing the government was proposing changes which would radically transform the relationship between central and local government, and provide a completely new system for financing services. There would be three main sources of local authority funding: government grant, a uniform business rate and a community charge. It was proposed that the government grant would be based on a simplified assessment of local need and, unlike the block grant, would be fixed in advance of the year and not related to actual spending by individual authorities. A uniform business rate would replace the non-domestic portion of local rates by a standard rate set nationally. Its introduction would be accompanied by the first revaluation of non-domestic properties since 1973. The community charge would replace the domestic rate on properties by a flat rate payment by each adult in the country, and the proposal is that it will be introduced first in Scotland in 1989 and for most of England and Wales from 1990. The community charge has been criticized as being easy to evade, expensive to collect and likely to favour the rich and the poor at the expense of middle-income groups.

The problems associated with planning in cash, discussed in Chapter 4, also apply to the methods of allocating funds for every type of devolved body. All have an assumption about inflation built into their plans for the coming year. They will therefore be able to buy fewer goods and services if the costs of those goods and services rise faster than the level of inflation which has been assumed, more if they are lower. Here too, cash planning and control has made it more difficult to know what level of services can be delivered.

But as in the case of cash limits, there is more flexibility in the control system than is commonly supposed. In one year alone an analysis[2] of the external financing limits for nationalized industries showed that when there were large numbers of potential overspends, action taken included:

- deferred payments to the next financial period (National Coal Board – now British Coal – and British Telecom);

- earlier/larger price increases than planned (British Telecom);

- reductions in spending (many industries, but most publicly British Gas, British Airways and British Railways Board);

- capital spending cuts (the same three industries);

- increased disposals of assets (British Railways Board and British Airways).

As for internal management and control, in common with other parts of the public sector, devolved bodies have been encouraged to be more sophisticated in this aspect of their operations. The emphasis on value for money, the measurement of performance and the improvements in internal control are all proceeding quickly and will certainly help these bodies to become more efficient. As already outlined in Chapter 5, it is less clear whether some of these methods are wholly suitable for bodies of this kind in the form in which they are being introduced, and in particular how far private sector methods are appropriate for them. There is still much work to be done in finding suitable control mechanisms, bearing in mind the need in each of these sectors to reconcile different measures of control including cash constraints; manpower targets; performance against aims, objectives and targets, and performance indicators. For local authorities, for example, the attempt to graft a system for controlling expenditure on to a system for distributing grant has meant that it is possible for local authorities to have targets but not the means to meet them. Indeed, the overwhelming importance attached to public spending constraints over everything else has been a major source of resentment.

Finally, it is worth noting that the calculation of the formulae for allocating funds is still little understood. The complexities of the R S G, introduced – ironically – to simplify the system as well as to achieve a measure of equality, are legendary. The following extract from a speech in the House of Commons shows why:

'. . . these documents are completely incomprehensible. The rate support grant report on England cost £6. Anyone who pays £6 for it is an idiot, because no one understands it. I do not understand it, nor do other hon. Members, Ministers or anyone else.

'I shall quote some of the indicators that the government used to decide how much help to give local councils. It is unbelievable. I shall read direct from page 51 of the wretched document where an adjustment is made for road maintenance.

'"The sum in the area of the authority of Indicators B5a, B6, B7a and B8 defined above, multiplied by the sum of the following –"

'I hope that you are following this, Mr Deputy Speaker –

'"(i) the annual average number of days of snow lying during 1979–80 to 1982–83 as estimated by the Secretary of State for Transport, multiplied by 9.60745 –"

'Is that clear to everyone?

'"(ii) the annual average number of days of air frost during 1979–80 to 1982–83 as estimated by the Secretary of State for Transport, multiplied by 1.14303."

'Crystal clear.

'On page 50 provision is made for road maintenance for which local authorities are responsible. I shall quote paragraph B9 at length to let people understand the idiocy perpetrated by the government on local authorities. The report says:

'"B9. Usage adjustment factor for road maintenance. The sum in the area of the authority of (i) and (ii) below:

(i) Indicator B5a as defined above, multiplied by 1.0;

(ii) Indicator B7a as defined above, multiplied by 0.3283 –"
'everyone is following this –
'"multiplied by the sum of the following:
(iii) – 1209.35;
(iv) Indicator A1 divided by the sum of Indicators B5a, B6, B7a and B8 as defined above, multiplied by 9.91626."

'Hon. Members are doing their sums; they have the calculators out. Subparagraph (v) is a beauty:
'"... annual average vehicle kilometres on principal roads in built-up areas excluding principal motorways during 1982 and 1983 divided by the length (in kilometres) of principal roads which are subject to a speed restriction not exceeding 40 miles per hour and of principal motorways in the area of that authority as at 1 April 1984, but excluding any such roads or motorways responsibility for which passed to the Secretary of State for Transport from 1 April 1986, all as estimated by the Secretary of State for Transport, multiplied by 0.0007899357 ..."

'I did not intend to take part in this debate, but then I read some of these figures and happened to receive a reply from the Under-Secretary of State for the Environment – the hon. Member for Southampton, Itchen (Mr Chope) – who is sitting there bemused by the figures produced by his department. He cannot understand them. He cannot tell me how that figure of 0.000 and seven other digits has been arrived at. I should like him to say who produced that figure – and give him the sack.'[3]

Good knockabout stuff. The serious aspect is that the complex nature of the system is one of the factors which has undermined the confidence of local government in the RSG. The Audit Commission in 1984 found that even some officers had given up trying to understand or explain it.

7

PARLIAMENT'S ROLE IN PLANNING AND MONITORING

The basis of parliamentary control

> Parliament is a deliberative assembly of one nation with one interest, that of the whole; where not local purposes nor local prejudices ought to guide, but the general good, resulting from the general reason of the whole. (Edmund Burke, Speech to the electors of Bristol)

Its building is one of the world's best known. The clock tower is a symbol as well as an authority. Its members are proud of its history and traditions. It is the mother of Parliaments. Yet while there is grandeur, there is only influence, not executive power, which is wielded in more humble surroundings in the ministries of Whitehall and beyond.

The procedures built up carefully over time mean that some of the technicalities of Parliament's work in the field of public spending are highly complex. Those who need to know about these things should go through the more technical paragraphs of this chapter in detail. Others can skim on first reading and come back later to whatever they find they want or need to know.

Parliament's role in the scrutiny of public expenditure is part of its constitutional position as a counterbalance and check on the power of the Executive (government). The subtle and complex modern forms taken by this role are the result of shifts in the balance of power between the Monarchy, Executive and Parliament which have been going on for many hundreds of years. The decisive move to take power away from the Monarchy and give it to the people, through Parliament, came in the seventeenth century and the predecessor of the Standing Order which sets out the relationship between government and Parliament on financial matters was first passed as a resolution in 1706. However, most of the current formal procedures of financial control, audit and accountability were developed in the nineteenth century.

This formal procedure can be briefly summarized – the terms used will be explained later in the chapter. It begins with the Queen's Speech at the State Opening of Parliament which marks the beginning of the parliamentary session – the parliamentary year normally, and rather confusingly, starts in November, though with the precise date fixed by the government. The Queen, addressing only the Members of the House of Commons, announces that 'Estimates for the public service will be laid before you in due course'. Details of these Estimates are provided to Parliament so that it can grant Supply. The Estimates are considered by the House of Commons and, if approved, are passed to the House of Lords. Assuming that the Lords agree, an Act authorizes the payment from the Consolidated Fund of whatever has been approved (less any sum already authorized by an earlier Vote on Account). Finally, after the end of the year, Parliament has to satisfy itself that the funds have been used for the purposes for which they were approved.

In practice, as this chapter shows, the relative importance of the various procedural stages is very different. Assuming the government has a majority in the House of Commons, there should be no difficulty about obtaining authorization for funds. The strength of the party system ensures that powerful pressure can be exercised on MPs of the majority party to support the party line. Failure to grant Supply would effectively mean a vote of no confidence – something which the government's supporters would hardly vote for unless they had lost confidence in their own leaders.

The House of Lords has almost no role to play in any aspects of financial procedure. As early as 1678, the House of Commons resolved that:

. . . all aids and supplies are the sole gift of the Commons and . . . ought to begin with the Commons, and that it is the undoubted and sole right of the Commons to direct, limit and appoint in such bills the ends, purposes, considerations, conditions, limitations and qualifications of such grants, which ought not to be changed or altered by the House of Lords.

Over the years, the powers of the Lords have become further circumscribed. Following a constitutional crisis when they tried to block the 1909 Budget, they can only delay by one month the process of granting Supply, even if they were unwise enough to want to do so. In practice, this would not only be unlikely but absurd.

The House of Commons, too, is circumscribed in what it can do. Only the government can initiate demands for Parliament to provide money. As the Standing Orders of the House of Commons put it:

> This House will receive no petition for any sum relating to public service or proceed upon any motion for a grant or charge upon the public revenue, whether payable out of the Consolidated Fund or the National Loans Fund or out of money to be provided by Parliament, or for releasing or compounding any sum of money owing to the Crown, unless recommended from the Crown.[1]

So Parliament can only reduce, reject or accept the proposals for expenditure presented to it; it cannot increase the amounts proposed. Nor is the House of Commons concerned with voting the whole of public expenditure, as Figure 7.1 shows, since a number of public sector activities are in any case financed wholly or partly by income which does not come from the central Exchequer, notably money raised by local authorities. Figure 7.1 gives the most significant flows, though one unusual feature about the year shown is that borrowing by public corporations is shown as a flow out. This means that there was a net repayment during that year. If there had been net borrowing, it would have counted as public expenditure.

Despite these limitations, Parliament has considerable potential to influence matters of expenditure, as well as having its constitutional role. For both these reasons it is important to know about its work.

Formal requirements

Unlike the more flexible timetable of the administrative planning and control process described in Chapters 3 and 4, there are a number of specified dates by which certain parliamentary events must have taken place. Thus the Supply Estimates, which give the information required to enable Parliament to vote Supply and provide the government with funds from the Consolidated Fund, must be approved by 5 August, the 'Guillotine Day'. (On the parallel, revenue-raising side, the Finance Bill must complete its passage through the legislature before 6 August so that government has authority to levy taxes.) Before that, indeed before the financial year begins on 1 April, the Vote on Account must have been passed to provide funds while Parliament discusses the full year's Estimates.

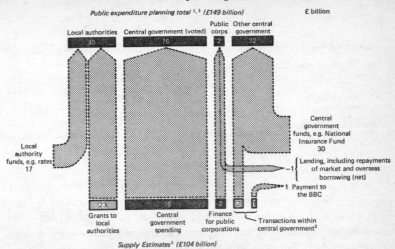

Figure 7.1 *Relationship between public spending plans and the Supply Estimates for 1987–88*

In voting the main Supply Estimates the House of Commons has to vote on the summary total of each Estimate. Since the Vote on Account already exists, the new money voted is described as the 'balance to complete'. This forms the basis of a Supply Resolution which, when it has gone through all the necessary stages, becomes the equivalent of a Consolidated Fund Act although it is, in practice, subsumed in the Appropriation Act described in the next paragraph.

During the year the government will almost inevitably require Parliament to authorize additional funds for some services. Parliament's Standing Orders provide three regular opportunities for this and they are known as Summer Supplementaries (presented in June), Winter Supplementaries (in November) and Spring Supplementaries (in February). Guillotine days for these are 5 August, 6 February and 18 March, and Votes on Supply must not be later than these three dates. All Estimates not set down for detailed consideration on Estimates days, the vast majority in practice, are voted together. The Summer

Supplementaries will go through together with the Main (and any Revised) Estimates to which they are in effect a 'postscript'. The Winter and Spring Supplementaries go through in the same way and lead to their own Consolidated Fund Acts.

As mentioned above, the Summer Consolidated Fund Act is actually presented as the Consolidated Fund (Appropriation) Bill. When enacted it is then known as the Appropriation Act. This is because it not only provides authority to draw money from the Consolidated Fund but also appropriates their money to the separate purposes specified in each Estimate. It does so in respect of Main Estimates and also in respect of all Supplementary Estimates since the last Appropriation Act. Thus the Appropriation Act completes parliamentary authority for the government's expenditure by, in effect, recalling the several authorities to draw on the Consolidated Fund and specifying the purposes against which the amounts are in due course to be set. Each year's expenditure is thus covered by two Appropriation Acts (three if an Excess Vote should become involved – see Chapter 8).

If funds are required at other times during the year they will still have to be obtained through Supplementary Estimates but the procedure for these will not have the benefit, for the government, of the guillotine procedure to give them a smooth passage through the House. Excess Votes are taken with the Spring Supplementaries, following the Public Accounts Committee's reports on them.

A major development in parliamentary scrutiny of Supply Estimates in particular and public expenditure in general in recent years has been the emergence of the departmental Select Committees. As early as the 1880s it was realized that the Estimates were too complex to be checked thoroughly in the forum of a debate which involved the whole House of Commons. As government expenditure grew and government became more and more complex, particularly after the Second World War, it became obvious that there was a need for smaller groups of Members of Parliament to become involved in the detailed process of investigation.

In 1978 a Procedure Committee of the House of Commons therefore recommended the setting-up of departmental Select Committees, one for each government department, to help scrutinize the work of government, including public spending. Until then the Commons had relied on a single group (sub-committees first of the Estimates Committee, then the Expenditure Committee) to do so. The incoming Conservative government of 1979 endorsed these recommendations and the committees were set up under Standing Order 99. A list of them is given in Table 7.1. Their terms of reference are to 'examine the expenditure, administration and policy of the principal government departments and associated public bodies' and they have the power to send for 'persons, papers and records' in order to do so. They are not, however, obliged to look at expenditure proposals, and this chapter makes clear later that some rarely do. As the Table 7.1 shows, Northern Ireland does not have its own departmental Select Committee. This means that the Northern Ireland Estimates have to be considered by the House of Commons as a whole.

The final stage in the formal parliamentary process is audit by the National Audit Office and consideration of Appropriation Accounts and their reports by the Public Accounts Committee. These aspects of parliamentary control are dealt with in detail in Chapter 8.

The process of scrutinizing and authorizing expenditure

The law of triviality. Briefly stated it means that the time spent on any item of the agenda will be in inverse proportion to the sum involved. (C. Northcote Parkinson, *Parkinson's Law*)

The proper officers bring in the estimates. It is taken for granted that they are necessary and frugal. The Members go to dinner and leave the Joint Secretaries of the Treasury to do the rest. (Lord Chesterfield, 1759)

Table 7.2 summarizes Parliament's timetable for public expenditure. It is clear that Parliament is involved at most stages of the process. In any one session, Parliament will be considering at least the next financial year, the current year, the previous year and the year before that. This

Table 7.1 Departmental Select Committees

Agriculture	Home Affairs
Defence	Industry and Trade
Education, Science and Arts	Scottish Affairs
Employment	Social Services
Energy	Transport
Environment	Treasury and Civil Service
Foreign Affairs	Welsh Affairs

Table 7.2 Parliament and public expenditure: a summary timetable [1]

November (-5 [2])	AUTUMN STATEMENT considered by TCSC [3]
December (-4)	Parliamentary debate on Autumn Statement
January (-3)	
February (-2)	PUBLIC EXPENDITURE WHITE PAPER considered by TCSC (but see p. ix)
	Parliamentary debate on public expenditure
March (-1)	
April (1)	(until July)
	Departmental Select Committee consideration of SUPPLY ESTIMATES
	Estimates Day debates
May (2)	
June (3)	
July (4)	REVISED ESTIMATES, SUMMER SUPPLEMENTARY ESTIMATES available for consideration
	Appropriation Act
August (5)	
September (6)	
October (7)	
November (8)	WINTER SUPPLEMENTARY ESTIMATES available for consideration
December (9)	*Consolidated Fund Act*
January (10)	SPRING SUPPLEMENTARY ESTIMATES available for consideration
February (11)	LATE SPRING SUPPLEMENTARY ESTIMATES available for consideration
March (12)	*Consolidated Fund Act*
April ($+1$)	
May ($+2$)	
June ($+3$)	
July ($+4$)	CASH LIMITS WHITE PAPER published
	Appropriation Act
August ($+5$)	
September ($+6$)	
Autumn ($+7$ to $+9$)	APPROPRIATION ACCOUNTS published and available for consideration by PAC [4]
January ($+10$)	
February ($+11$)	STATEMENTS OF EXCESS published
March ($+12$)	
Following year: ($+13$ to $+24$)	Series of TREASURY MINUTES on PAC reports published
	Parliamentary debate on PAC reports

1. Timing may vary.
2. Months before financial year ($-$); after year end ($+$)
3. Treasury and Civil Service Select Committee.
4. Public Accounts Committee.

chapter deals with their work on the current and the next financial year, Chapter 8 with their work on previous years.

In view of the emphasis on scrutiny in the formal role of Parliament, it is ironic that the first action in the first stage of the scrutiny process is to vote a significant proportion of the money required for the coming year without any debate at all. But because of the way in which expenditure is only authorized about four months *after* the beginning of the financial year, this pre-authorization is inevitable. Without Votes on Account, as they are known, the business of government would grind to a halt. So each November the government requests a total of about 45 per cent of the amounts authorized for the previous year through Votes on Account. There is also an emergency arrangement for the government to get urgently needed money in advance of parliamentary authorization through the Contingency Fund. This can be used at any time in the year in anticipation of funds being voted. (Parliament will have to authorize them later, and the 'borrowed' funds will have to be repaid.) The limitation on using the Fund is that total outstanding advances at any one time may not be more than 2 per cent of the total Estimates of the preceding year.

The most important feature in the public expenditure area in the period before the beginning of the financial year is the consideration of information about government spending plans.

The first set of plans is published at the very beginning of the new parliamentary session, when the government issues the Autumn Statement, a recent arrival on the parliamentary scene – it was first published in 1982. The Autumn Statement gives a general summary of economic prospects for the coming year and an outline of planned public expenditure for each department for the next three financial years, reflecting the result of the public expenditure Survey process. It has separate sections on nationalized industries and local authorities.

As soon as the Autumn Statement is published, the Treasury and Civil Service Select Committee set about reviewing it, with a view to producing a report quickly, in December. This report provides much of the raw material for a debate on the Autumn Statement for the House of Commons as a whole which takes place almost immediately after publication of the Select Committee report.

A second, much fuller, set of plans comes a few weeks later with the publication of the Public Expenditure White Paper, which has been produced since 1968 (but see page ix). It gives very detailed plans for the coming year, outline plans for the next two in much greater detail than in the Autumn Statement, and out-turns (the technical term for actual expenditure) for the previous six years.

The Public Expenditure White Paper has become steadily bigger over the years. It includes a good deal of technical analysis, but the bulk of the document is a detailed breakdown of the expenditure programmes of each central government department, and those who want more details of the analysis of government spending set out in Chapter 2 of this book will find it a fascinating read. There is also a breakdown of expenditure on local authorities, nationalized industries and other public corporations. This document too is immediately reviewed by the Treasury and Civil Service Select Committee. Their report is again the raw material of a debate on public expenditure for the House of Commons as a whole.

The Budget, which comes just before the end of one financial year or at the beginning of the next, marks the start of the second phase of parliamentary involvement in the public spending process, and Budget Day sees the publication of the Financial Statement and Budget Report. Since the Budget is primarily concerned with the raising of revenue, most of this document is not focused on expenditure matters. It gives the details of Budget measures in the context of the macro-economic background, including a short-term economic forecast and the government's medium-term financial strategy which outlines economic policy for the next five years. The expenditure element includes details of any revisions to expenditure plans as a result of the Budget, although these figures will not be given in detail. (Note, therefore, that such revisions mean that some of the details of the Public Expenditure White Paper will be inaccurate as a result of Budget measures within a few weeks.)

The Supply Estimates are also published and presented to Parliament on Budget Day, though they used to appear earlier in the calendar year. They cover Great Britain and allocations to Northern Ireland, who have their own detailed Estimates, presented separately after approval by the Northern Ireland Department of Finance and Personnel.

Although Supply Estimates and public expenditure cover different areas (Figure 7.1) they are closely linked. The setting of plans in the Survey forms the basis of what is requested from Parliament and the corresponding financial control information comes from the same base. In the Estimates the departmental programmes are covered by 'Classes', with an additional Class for parliamentary administration and the National Audit Office. If a department has responsibilities in more than one Class, this will be covered by separate Votes so that the basis

Table 7.3 Variation in Vote size (1986–87)

Range	Number of Votes	% of total expenditure
Nil (token Votes)	11	—
Up to £10 million	34	0.1
£10–49 million	39	1.0
£50–100 million	19	1.4
£0.1–0.5 billion	49	11.5
£0.5–1.0 billion	8	6.8
£1.0–5.0 billion	19	37.1
Over £5.0 billion	5	42.1

Source: National Audit Office Report, 1986.

of accountability and control is clear. One set of figures in the Estimates but not the information documents are internal government transactions – payments for services from one government department to another.

The Supply Estimates are divided into twenty Classes, each covering a government department or departments. Each Class has a number of Votes (divisions of Classes used for control purposes) and there are about 180 of these. The subdivisions of Votes are called subheads.

The Supply Estimates are very detailed, with expenditure often broken down into very small amounts. (A sum of £1,000 for educational allowances to the children of Poles who were servicemen in the Second World War was separately identified in the 1987–88 Supply Estimates, though this is an extreme example.) At the Vote level – the Vote being the unit by which Parliament approves expenditure – the differences in the size of Votes are astonishingly wide. For example, for 1987–88 there was a Vote of £939,000 for an art gallery (the Wallace Collection), while the single defence procurement Vote amounted to over £8,700 million. Table 7.3 gives a breakdown of Vote size and shows how over half the Votes account for less than 3 per cent of voted expenditure, while less than 3 per cent of the Votes account for nearly half of voted expenditure.

Figures are provided in the Supply Estimates of out-turn for the previous year, total provision for the current year and the amount provided for the next year. The documents are uncompromisingly statistical, with little or no commentary on the figures. Figure 7.2 gives an extract from one Supply Estimate.

Figure 7.2 *Supply Estimate extract*

1985–86	1986–87		1987–88
Out-turn £'000	Total provision £'000	*Subhead detail*	Provision £'000

Section A: Regional and general industrial support (Development Commission)

| 28,051 | 25,876 | **A1 Development Commission: grant in aid** The Commission promotes the economic and social well being of the rural areas of England, through the building of workshops, small factory units, assistance to small firms, help with housing and support for community activity. The cost of the factories programme is partly offset by an estimated £2,700,000 in receipts retained by the English Industrial Estates Corporation. The total cost to government funds is additionally offset by receipts from charges for services and repayments of loan capital. Table 1 shows the expected use of the grant in aid. This subhead includes £1,000,000 which is not classified as direct public expenditure. | 27,792 |

Section B: Grants to environmental bodies

30,112	37,349	**B1 Sports Council: grant in aid** Covers an annual programme of grants for sports coaching and competitions and for the provision of sporting facilities locally and nationally. Table 2 shows the expected use of the grant in aid.	37,000
22,761	32,118	**B2 Nature Conservancy Council: grant in aid** The Council manages certain nature reserves in Great Britain, advises Ministers and others, and commissions or supports research. Table 3 shows the expected use of the grant in aid.	36,500
15,308	17,790	**B3 Countryside Commission: grant in aid** The Commission promotes conservation of the countryside and assists in provision of informal recreational facilities there. Table 4 shows the expected use of the grant in aid.	19,500
2	3	**B4 Surveys, studies, inquiries, etc: current expenditure** Water: Payments to Anglian Water authority for expenses incurred in connection with the collection of information on rainfall, etc, and payments associated with the Wash estuary storage project.	3

317	327	**B5 Hazardous materials service**	335

Fixed grant towards the cost of the Waste Management Information Bureau and deficit grant towards the cost of the Chemical Emergency Centre, both operated by the United Kingdom Atomic Energy Authority, Harwell, to enable advice and a limited disposal service to be provided for other bodies.

265	175	**B6 The British Board of Agrément: grant in aid**	352

The Board's expenditure on technical assessment and certification of new building materials and products, and its running costs, less expected income from testing fees.

142	285	**B7 National Building Agency**	288

Closure costs of the Agency.

1,538	1,910	**B8 Grants to voluntary bodies**	1,845

Contributions towards expenses incurred mainly by national and regional bodies which assist D O E policies in the environment conservation, co-ordination and urban initiatives fields.

80	85	**B9 Contributions to the Local Authorities' Conditions of Service Advisory Board**	88

Half the cost of operation by L A C S A B of the joint manpower watch to provide information on local authority staff numbers in England and Wales.

547	554	**B10 Keep Britain tidy group**	568

Contribution towards anti-litter activities.

32	57	**B11 Council for Environmental Education**	47

Fixed grant for the Council's staff and accommodation costs.

3,000	2,619	**B12 Grant to the Zoological Society of London**	2,250

Assistance towards operating costs and capital expenditure.

750	1,000	**B13 Contribution to the Fund of the United Nations Environment Programme**	1,000

Fixed contribution representing about 5 per cent of the total contributed by other countries.

Source: Supply Estimates, Class X, Vote 2 (adapted).

Published at the same time is a 'Summary and Guide to the Supply Estimates', which is very helpful to those who want to find their way around the volumes.

In the Budget debate, which follows immediately after the Budget speech, public expenditure is not a major part of the discussion, which centres on tax proposals and macro–economic policy. Indeed the debate tends to broaden out to cover government policy as a whole. Macro-economic policy is also the dominant theme of the report on the Budget of the Treasury and Civil Service Select Committee.

Between the Budget and the end of July, however, comes the most intensive period of Parliamentary scrutiny of the government's expenditure proposals set out in the Supply Estimates. These, not the Public Expenditure White Paper, contain the information for formal parliamentary authorization. It may be helpful, therefore, to make a clear distinction between the two kinds of documents which Parliament considers, reflecting the two parallel elements of government expenditure planning and the request for funds.

Information documents give Parliament the necessary information to enable it to understand the government's public expenditure plans as a whole. They are statements of government policy, not requests for funds. They are nevertheless of great interest to those who want to know about government spending policy or who want to influence future spending priorities. They include:

the Autumn Statement;

the Public Expenditure White Paper (but see page ix);

the Financial Statement and Budget Report.

Authorization documents cover the field of parliamentary Supply and are the means by which Parliament authorizes government expenditure. They include:

Supply Estimates;

Revised Estimates;

Supplementary Estimates.

Returning to the parliamentary timetable, Revised and Summer Supplementary Estimates have to be dealt with at the same time as the Supply Estimates. They come so soon after the beginning of the financial year because the original spending plans are fixed many months before the main Supply Estimates are presented to Parliament, having been submitted by departments to the Treasury in late November or early December and approved by Treasury Ministers in January. Since Parliament is not in session for three months in the summer, leaving them until November would be to wait too long to announce any adjustments.

Supplementary Estimates, which are a normal part of the public expenditure process, not the result of inefficiency or irregularities, can only be submitted with the approval of the Treasury and may be the result of one or more of a number of factors:

- new policies requiring more money than was provided in the main Supply Estimates;

- more money required for services, such as social security, which are determined by demand, and where demand is greater than forecast;

- to meet a shortfall in Appropriations-in-aid (receipts authorized to offset expenditure);

- to get parliamentary authority to change the use to which money is put within a Vote;

- to get parliamentary authority to use additional receipts to meet additional expenditure within the same Vote.

In the last two cases a token amount (£1,000) will be presented for authorization to alert Parliament to the fact that there is a change, but not one that requires more funds. Another change which requires no additional funds is the use of savings on one subhead to meet excess spending on another within the same Vote. This is known as 'virement' and can be authorized by the Treasury, acting on behalf of Parliament, if no significant change is involved.

The three-month summer break is usually also responsible for the need to consider Revised Estimates. These are submitted, with the approval of the Treasury,

- to reduce the provision on a Vote;

- to vary the terms of a Vote for which a main Supply Estimate has been presented but without a net increase in the Vote;

- to transfer provision between Votes without any net increase in the funds being sought.

In this case the original Estimate will simply be withdrawn before it is voted and only the Revised Estimate will lead to provision in the Appropriation Act.

All the departmental Select Committees have the opportunity to review and report on the main Supply Estimates and any Revised or Supplementary Estimates for the departments whose affairs they monitor. These will include any other public bodies sponsored by those departments. In choosing which to consider, the committee chairman or members may suggest topics, and pressure groups or advisers may be influential. But most often it will be the Committee Clerk – the House of Commons official responsible for servicing the committee – who will take the lead in suggesting areas for consideration. Among the main criteria for selecting subjects are:

- to seek explanations of unusual changes in expenditure;

- to go back to issues which were examined before but which are still unresolved;

- to examine areas where changes in policy or other conditions require a reassessment of the amounts provided.

Although the process of scrutiny has the Supply Estimates as the focus of the committees' attention, they are not obliged to consider them. If they do, it may well be only to consider a small fraction of the total requested. Indeed they have preferred to concentrate on the Public Expenditure White Paper if they looked at expenditure matters at all (see page ix). Certainly the proportion of the Estimates and Supplementary Estimates which are examined varies enormously, as does the proportion which these sums represent of the Vote and Class total. In some cases, it is a sum amounting to less than 1 per cent of the Vote. In others, the whole Class is considered. Committees may even ignore the Estimates altogether and concentrate exclusively on the White Paper.

Standing Orders of the House of Commons require seven clear days between the presentation of an Estimate and the vote on it by Parliament. In practice, and by internal arrangement, departmental Select Committees have a minimum of fourteen days to consider Supply, but they usually need longer. Committees are under severe time pressure to consider and approve Estimates because of the congested timetables of the government and the House of Commons itself.

On public expenditure, as in all their inquiries, departmental Select Committees can use their powers to call for papers and summon witnesses. The Minister is ultimately responsible to Parliament for policy and officials for the execution of that policy. Nevertheless, in this context the committees will usually ask officials rather than Ministers to give evidence, since they are more in touch with day-to-day matters. Only occasionally are Ministers specifically asked to attend. Independent experts or representatives of important groups are also sometimes asked to give evidence, as the extended quotation from Ian Marsh, quoted below, illustrates.

There are limits to what departmental Select Committees are likely to get out of officials. The government's 'Memorandum of Guidance for

Officials appearing before Select Committees' gives civil servants the right to withhold information such as advice offered to Ministers and information passed between Ministers and departments. Officials are also generally highly circumspect in their replies. The career of a civil servant is unlikely to be greatly advanced by giving a lot away at such hearings, thereby helping M Ps to embarrass Ministers. The following exchange, after a reply by a Treasury official to a question on interest rates from a member of the Treasury and Civil Service Select Committee, shows what officials know, but rarely say:

MR BUDGEN: 'Mr Odling-Smee, do you regard yourself as having said anything new?'
MR ODLING-SMEE: 'I hope not.'[2]

In his book, *Policy-Making in a Three-Party System*, Ian Marsh has given this analysis of one year's scrutiny by those departmental Select Committees which examined the Estimates:

The seven departmental committees approached their estimates reviews in different ways. For example the Defence Committee took extensive evidence from the Secretary of State about the government's re-equipment plans soon after the Falklands conflict. The Secretary of State's evidence provided the most detailed public account of the government's intentions. He provided tentative indications of the budgetary implications of this programme. The committee formed no judgement about this evidence. However, it subsequently undertook a series of inquiries into the lessons of the Falklands exercise, including equipment procurement and performance. The Education Committee used the estimates hearing to gain an overview of policy developments. Committee questions related to other inquiries it was pursuing concurrently on specific issues (e.g. school meals). They also covered issues on which it was contemplating inquiries or which were of current public concern (e.g. closure of village schools). Similarly, the full Foreign Affairs Committee took extensive evidence from the Secretary of State but reached no conclusions. Estimates inquiries typically involved two or three evidence sessions.

Reports were compiled within approximately two to three weeks of the hearings.

Only two of these inquiries included evidence from interest groups. The Overseas Development Sub-Committee in its hearings on support for voluntary agencies took evidence from some voluntary groups about the impact of proposed funding cuts. The Social Services Committee provides a pertinent example of the use of interest group evidence to check information supplied by departments. The committee took evidence concerning the use of departmental indicators at the area level. The groups concerned represented responsible officers – the

Association of Directors of Social Security. They testified, contrary to the department's claim, that the indicators were not being used for local planning.

The Industry and Trade Committee held hearings on five nationalized industries. It adopted a common approach. Evidence was taken from senior executives of the industry, from unions, departments and sometimes the relevant Ministers of State. The inquiries were relatively short. In the case of the Post Office, British Shipbuilders, British Steel and Rolls-Royce, formal reports were tabled. In the case of British Leyland, the inquiry took the form of evidence hearings only. The purpose of these hearings was to enable senior management to report progress in meeting particular targets or to explain why performance had failed to meet expectations.

The British Steel Corporation hearings reflect the committee's approach. The committee took evidence in November from a BSC group and in December from the Secretary of State. BSC was represented by its Chairman, Deputy Chairman and three functional managing directors. Questions covered the current state of negotiations with the United States on BSC's alleged dumping, the effect of non-tariff barriers on BSC's export prospects, its severance payments and plant closure programme, its internal arrangements for planning and reasons for its failure to reach forecast production and market share figures. The committee's short report expressed its concern about several of these issues. The primary result of the inquiries was to bring up-to-date information into the public domain. In its inquiry into the Post Office the committee took evidence from the unions, the various users' committees, and private groups pressing for the right to compete for some services on which the Post Office continued to hold a monopoly. The British Shipbuilders inquiry took evidence from management, the Department of Industry, the TUC, the Confederation of Shipbuilding and Engineering Unions, the Engineers and Managers Association, and the Shipbuilding and Allied Industries Management Association. There were three evidence sessions over a six-week period. The report subsequently took four months to finalize.

Finally, in its hearings on the MSC corporate plan the Employment Committee illustrates how systems of functional and parliamentary representation can be bridged. Evidence sessions with the Chairman of the Commission show committee alertness to the danger of a corporatist consensus emerging on the Commission at the expense of the public interest. Committee questioning explored the frequency with which the 'public' representatives acquiesced in an arrangement congenial to union and employer representatives, but not congenial to other groups or to the public. The committee probed how the Commission informed itself about the attitudes of other interests. The committee also sought information on the Commission's relations with the Department of Education and local government. It explored differences between the Commission's and ministers' projections for unemployment. The cross-examination of the

Chairman addresses these points in the context of Commission recommendations and proposals. His defence is available for scrutiny on the public record.[3]

Since 1983, Parliament has provided three Estimates Days in each session when reports on Supply Estimates or Supplementary Estimates can be debated by the House of Commons as a whole. The subjects to be debated are selected by the Liaison Committee, which is made up of the chairmen of the Select Committees. They tend to choose subjects where there is a wider public interest or where there is some general policy issue involved. Table 7.4 gives a selection of some of the subjects covered in Estimates Days debates.

In the case of Northern Ireland, which has no departmental Select Committee of its own to report on Northern Ireland affairs, there are normally three debates each year on Northern Ireland Estimates and Supplementary Estimates. Their separate detailed Supply Estimates are theoretically debated by the House of Commons as a whole, though in practice the debates are only likely to be attended by those Members of Parliament interested in Northern Ireland.

In the last half of the financial year, between the time when Parliament reassembles after their summer recess (holidays) and the end of the financial year in March, a day is set aside to consider the European Communities Budget. Otherwise there are the Winter, Spring and late Spring Supplementary Estimates to deal with so far as the current year is concerned. Departmental Select Committees' consideration of these is patchy. Some committees do not consider them at all; others do so very systematically. Nor do the committees pay much attention to the statement published with the Winter Supplementaries showing spending for the half-year for each Vote, though this could provide the opportunity for involvement in the control process if they wished to take it.

Table 7.4 Examples of Estimates and Supplementary Estimates considered by departmental Select Committees

	Select Committees	*Report debated*
Dog and game licences	Environment	No
Payments to the coal industry	Energy	Yes
Trade with China	Trade and Industry	Yes
NHS voluntary redundancies	Social Services	No
H.M. Customs and Excise	Treasury and Civil Service	No
Support for overseas students	Foreign Affairs	No

Not all departmental Select Committee reports require a response from the government, but for those that do, a reply is given within two months – or within six with the committee's consent. Committees have to rely on the strength of their arguments to persuade the government to change policy and there are a variety of ways in which government responses are couched, with subtle variations between each. Only rarely are reports 'accepted' or 'rejected' explicitly. The gradations include:

Acceptance
- with a time-scale for implementation;
- without a time-scale for implementation;
- in principle;
- in principle, but rejection in practice.

Neutrality
- providing facts and figures;
- thanks for agreeing to existing policy;
- noting the committee's view.

Rejection
- for reasons other than those given by the committee;
- repeating the reasons given in evidence;
- outright.

Whatever the response, the government is always courteous to the committee, with thanks for the work undertaken, even if it rejects every recommendation outright. Yet even a wholly negative response may not be the end of the story. As one Select Committee quietly pointed out, citing Concorde as an example, 'Non-acceptance may not be the last word. Government policy may change eventually, as result of a Committee report.'[4]

The hearings of departmental Select Committees and the debates on subjects chosen by the Liaison Committee for Estimates Days are not the only opportunities which MPs have to question the government on its expenditure plans. MPs can ask written or oral questions at any time, ask for an emergency debate (if the matter is significant and urgent enough), raise issues when the business of the House for the following week is announced, and use debates on any related subject including those on the Autumn Statement, Public Expenditure White Paper or the Budget. The Opposition is also allocated nineteen days a year on which to select the subject for debate, and they can use this opportunity to discuss expenditure in general or particularly contentious items.

Issues in parliamentary expenditure control

> The problem is that MPs' ultimate objective is to affect or influence the government. They want to be seen to be doing something. (Select Committee official)

> MPs are lazy, busy people. (MP)[5]

At the beginning of the twentieth century, Sir Sidney Low had made a comment which would have been regarded as just as topical in the 1980s:

> In practice the control of the House is largely inoperative; first because of the feverish scuffle against time, which forbids deliberate and prolonged examination of detail; and secondly, because a serious attempt to refuse a Vote, or alter an item that is on account, can usually be foiled by setting the party machinery to work.
>
> The province of private members in regard to finance is limited to criticism, and there are special reasons why such criticisms should be ineffective. The details are often highly technical, and most members are ignorant of the complicated questions which arise in connection with the financial and departmental measures presented to them.[6]

There has been a great deal of discussion in recent years about whether parliamentary expenditure control is effective and whether the recent reforms have been a success. Part of the difficulty in answering these questions lies in the different interpretations about what is meant by 'control'. In its modern use, it does not mean stopping the government from spending. The last period in which control was exercised in this sense was in the period from 1858 to 1872, when Estimates were voted down on seventeen separate occasions (though in 1919 it was decided that the Lord Chancellor did not need two bathrooms). Control here means informed appraisal, careful scrutiny and the provision of material for public comment, though these are processes whose effectiveness is difficult to assess.

Whatever the definition, it is acknowledged that full-scale House of Commons debates are not a very satisfactory forum for exercising control. The strength of the party system means that such debates have to be regarded as votes of confidence in the government. Even if the matter is relatively trivial, once it becomes a party issue MPs will hesitate to go against their party Whip. Nor are the large and complex figures involved in any discussion of public spending really suitable for detailed dissection in the often heated atmosphere of a House of Commons debate.

These are some of the reasons why the setting-up of departmental Select Committees has been seen as so important in establishing a workable method of control or at least influence, and why their attempts to establish a non-party approach based on agreed reports is a central part of that approach.

An assessment of the system after a few years can record some successes. There is far more detailed scrutiny of the Estimates than before departmental Select Committees were introduced. The reports on Estimates and the Estimates Days debates have certainly yielded a considerable amount of interesting information. Some of the recommendations have been accepted by the government. Some committee reports have also provided an important contribution to the public debate about a subject, particularly if the issue has been picked up by the media. Committees also perform a useful role in encouraging departments to improve procedures. Finally, although the effect is difficult to measure, their reports may well influence future expenditure decisions; in some cases there is now some thought about how committees might react.

But in terms of the initial aspirations that the reforms would represent a shift in the balance of power from Whitehall to Westminster, the departmental Select Committee structure and associated procedural changes have not had such a far-reaching influence. Even the hope that, as the 1978 Procedure Select Committee put it, 'the new Committees will concentrate much of their attention on consideration of the Estimates and other expenditure projections'[7] has not been fulfilled, and three years later the Select Committee on Procedure (Supply) watered this down to a recommendation that 'committees should allot some time each session to the examination of their departmental Estimates, but that the amount of time and depth of such scrutiny should be a matter for each committee to determine.'[8]

In practice this has often meant very little time. Committees have been considering the Estimates on average for around only 5 per cent of their evidence-taking sessions. Some of the main reasons have been:

- the lack of political appeal in the detail of public spending matters has meant that coverage has not been as rigorous or systematic as had been hoped. This is explained away as time pressure, but time spent, after all, only reflects where priorities lie.

- that Committees are involved at too late a stage of the decision-taking process. They are unable to influence policy on the documents they are considering, which reflect decisions already taken, commitments already entered into and announcements already made.

- constitutional arrangements. Since only the Crown can propose expenditure, it is difficult for MPs to feel that they are 'doing something'.

- that committees do not have the resources to undertake very thorough investigations of detailed expenditure matters, and the timetable puts them under very heavy pressure to complete their investigations too quickly to do a proper job.

- motivation. There are few debates on Select Committee reports on the floor of the House in this area. Those that do take place are rarely well attended because of the complexity of the subject-matter and the feeling of many Members of Parliament that these are relatively technical matters.

- lack of encouragement; few major recommendations have been accepted by the government. Even those on relatively minor matters which have been accepted have rarely had a time-scale for implementation attached to acceptance in principle.

- that it is probably unrealistic to assume that party politics can be avoided altogether. A major issue, once it comes to the floor of the House of Commons, will usually be regarded as a vote of confidence. Parliament's role is therefore bound to be limited.

- the fact that departmental Select Committees comprise MPs of all parties. This may itself give rise to some problems in contentious areas. If the subject-matter is uncontentious, the committee may well be able to reach an agreed report without concessions. In more contentious areas there may have to be bargaining about the final text or a watering-down of the impact of the report to avoid the committee splitting on party lines. This puts the committees under pressure to choose areas which are less likely to produce dissent among their members.

A number of suggestions have been put forward to re-kindle the earlier flames of hope for a stronger parliamentary role. The timing of debates was the subject of one set of recommendations of the Treasury and Civil Service Select Committee, which recommended that the 'Public

Expenditure White Paper debate should be deferred until late May or early June. This would enable the House to influence spending decisions at the beginning of the following Public Expenditure Survey round, as well as commenting on decisions already taken.'[9] It would also allow the Committees more time to study the Estimates. (See page ix.)

While not agreeing to hold the debate so late, the government at least conceded that there was a problem and the need to allow more time for the Treasury and Civil Service Select Committee to prepare its report. And Peter Rees, speaking as an ex-Chief Secretary, commented:

'It is disappointing to those of us who are in the Chamber this evening and who are concerned about, if not dedicated to public expenditure, that so few hon. Members attend these debates. That may be due to what they see as aridity of the subject. However, they are wrong.

'I share common ground with my right hon. friend the Member for Worthing, in saying that that may be due to the timing of the debate, which almost invariably occurs in what I would describe as the low season, in the run-up to the Budget.'[10]

Providing better information is an area of possible improvement. In commenting on the current 'entry barriers' to understanding, Peter Jackson set out the importance of removing them:

Unless Parliament breaks down these entry barriers to informed debate, power will continue to reside with the executive, with professional bureaucratic groups and with interest groups outside of Parliament. To the extent that the present system is perpetuated, democracy will be weakened.[11]

The quality of financial information presented to Parliament in the early 1980s has steadily improved. But there are still problems in the lack of clarity about the needs of users. These are not only Members of Parliament, but for any one area of public expenditure could well include users ranging from the expert to those who know very little. For most areas there is still too great a concentration on inputs, rather than on what is achieved for the money spent.

The Procedure Select Committee which examined financial arrangements in 1983 also highlighted problems in controlling government borrowing and long-term expenditure. They noted that there was a lack of information relating to levels of service provided and on targets, and commented that the detailed information provided with Estimates was often not what departmental Select Committees required. They recommended that both the Treasury and Civil Service Select Committee and the Public Accounts Committee should investigate financial information available in the House with a view to possible improvements.

The Treasury and Civil Service Select Committee did so in 1984, using a report by the author and Peter Vass[12] as the basis for their inquiry, and recommended[13] that the existing set of documents should be replaced by information more appropriate to the needs of Parliament. Their recommendations included the introduction of a new set of departmental annual reports and the replacement of the Financial Statement and Budget Report by a new Budget document giving a better overview of income and expenditure. (See also page ix.)

The Public Accounts Committee, following a report from the National Audit Office,[14] looked at this matter in 1986[15] and also recommended annual departmental reports, while raising the possibility of producing them after the end of the financial year rather than at the beginning.

In rejecting these proposals, the government indicated that 'the Treasury should continue to edit and publish a core of information on departmental spending plans and performance',[16] but that it was up to departments to consider what else they should publish. The distinction between information issued by the Treasury and information published by departments indicates the importance attached by the Treasury to ensuring that it keeps control of publication of the key information.

Even with improved information, realistically it is unlikely that Parliament will exercise more than a limited form of control over public spending. Anne Robinson, after analyzing the record of departmental Select Committees in the 1979–83 Parliament, divided the committees into three categories. Though some committees were in more than one category, she found that far more were 'unashamed filters for the demands of special interests' than 'balancing committees' – balancing demands for extra spending against control of costs and value for money. A few were 'non-financial', with little interest in such matters. She commented: 'If MPs are not, at heart, interested in the control and scrutiny of public expenditure, then all the procedural changes in the world will hardly encourage them to change their attitudes.'[17]

The record of the 1983–87 Parliament shows that such conclusions drawn after only a short experience of the new arrangements may be pessimistic, but if the reality has not met aspirations, at least, in their attitudes, it appears that United Kingdom MPs are not alone. Earlier in the same analysis, Anne Robinson noted: 'The reluctance of British MPs to play the part of scrutineers of the government's spending plans and their penchant for regarding expenditure as a mere by-product of policy puts them in line with their counterparts in other legislatures.'[18]

Certainly Parliament can bring matters to the attention of the public and may have some influence on priorities. But the crucial spending decisions still take place in the political back-rooms and in the deals Ministers strike with each other in the Survey process. This situation may not be satisfactory for supporters of open government and of a stronger role for Parliament. If a stronger role does emerge, departmental Select Committees are likely to be the engine pushing it forward.

8

AUDIT AND THE NATIONAL AUDIT OFFICE

Thrift should be the guiding principle of our government expenditure. (Mao Tse-tung)

'If no one knows what you're doing, then no one knows what you're doing wrong.' (*Yes Minister*, BBC)

The audit process is the essential final stage in the public expenditure cycle. There are a number of stages after the end of the financial year which involve checking that no more than the amounts authorized have been spent. In addition, there is an increasing emphasis on value for money (vfm) audit. (Because of the amount of technical detail, this chapter should be read selectively by those not concerned with the detail, but who want to get an overview of audit and public spending.)

Audit of central government departments is undertaken both internally and externally. The internal audit process is an independent service to departmental management. Its objectives, spelt out by the government's internal audit manual, are to

(a) review and appraise the soundness, adequacy and application of accounting, financial and other controls;

(b) ascertain the extent of compliance with established policies and procedures;

(c) ascertain the extent to which the department's assets and interests are properly controlled and safeguarded from losses of all kinds;

(d) ascertain that the accounting and other data developed within the department is reliable as a basis for the production of the Appropriation, White Paper and other accounts;

(e) ascertain the integrity and reliability of financial and other data provided to management including that in connection with the decision-making process.[1]

Routine internal audit matters will not normally go to the departmental

Accounting Officer – the official responsible for the accounts of the department. He or she will receive reports on contentious issues and will be responsible for follow-up action where required. One difficult aspect of any internal audit is to ensure that there is sufficient independence to allow the staff to make unbiased judgements on what may sometimes be very sensitive matters, including criticisms of senior staff. For this reason, the function has to be a separate entity within the department.

Despite recent moves to improve recruitment and professional standards, the nature of what is skilled and important but routine work means that it is often difficult to staff the internal audit function fully. So while the internal auditors are supposed to cover all the operations, staff and services of a department, in practice shortage of staff may mean that this is not always possible. As the perceived importance of vfm work grows, however, recruitment may improve.

While the internal audit encourages good housekeeping, the external audit process tends to play a much greater role in the lives of senior departmental officials. Central to this process is the National Audit Office (NAO), which came into existence in 1984 through the National Audit Act 1983. Under the act, the NAO took over the functions of the Exchequer and Audit Department which had existed since 1866 but also gave the NAO new official responsibilities in the field of vfm. The NAO was created not as a government department but as an independent body responsible to Parliament. It covers all parts of the United Kingdom except almost all matters concerning Northern Ireland, which has its own similar arrangements.

The Comptroller and Auditor-General (C and AG) is responsible for the work of the NAO. He personally approves all reports, which are then issued in his name. His full title is the magnificent-sounding 'Comptroller-General of the Receipt and Issue of Her Majesty's Exchequer and Auditor-General of Public Accounts'. The origins of this office can be traced back to at least 1314, and it has existed in some form ever since. The C and AG is an officer of the House of Commons, and is quite independent of the government. His independence also extends to the selection, examination and reporting of vfm studies where, although he is responsible to Parliament, he is free to make his own choices and draw his own conclusions.

The C and AG is appointed by the Queen on the advice of the Prime Minister and the Chairman of the Public Accounts Committee (PAC) and can only be removed from office by the Queen after an address from both Houses of Parliament. He is responsible for appointing staff at the NAO and for deciding their remuneration, numbers and organization. To ensure the highest degree of independence, payment of the C and AG's salary and pension is made direct from the Consolidated Fund and does not therefore require annual approval by Parliament through the Supply procedure.

As his title suggests, the role of the C and AG is divided between two areas of responsibility. As Comptroller, he checks that there is parliamentary authority for the issue of public funds to government departments and other public bodies. Payments out of the Consolidated Fund and the National Loans Fund can be made only on the authority of the Treasury, countersigned by the C and AG. As Auditor-General he is required, by the 1866 and 1921 Exchequer and Audit Departments Act, to satisfy himself that the sums granted by Parliament to a particular body have been used for their intended purpose, and that the Appropriation Accounts produced by each body properly present the transactions during the year. He must report on these matters to Parliament, which means in practice the PAC. The 1983 act formally extended his role by giving him the statutory right to examine the economy, efficiency and effectiveness of the use of resources of those bodies to which he has access. Such work had previously been carried out on a non-statutory basis with the encouragement of the PAC.

Much of the routine work of the NAO is in the auditing aspect of the C and AG's role. About 1,000 people have to complete audits of 500 public bodies each year, as well as thirty to forty vfm audits of the kind mentioned in Chapter 5. In recent years it has been policy that all auditing staff should be graduates and that they should be qualified as, or be training to be, members of the Chartered Institute of Public Finance and Accountancy. The staff are divided among the twenty or so divisions, each one dealing with a separate department, or group of related departments. The hierarchy is shown in Figure 8.1.

The top management team is responsible for the NAO's policy and work programme, while the Directors and Deputy Directors are responsible for overall planning and management, performance of audit and other divisions. The Audit Managers, the next tier down, are in charge of audit sections, with responsibility for individual accounts and for the conduct of vfm audits through the audit teams.

Since the prime focus of the NAO's work is accountability to Parliament, all reports are presented to them and also published. These reports are of two kinds. First are the certificates and reports of audit work published a few months after the end of the financial year, which

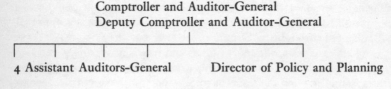

Figure 8.1 *National Audit Office organization and responsibilities*

Comptroller and Auditor-General
Deputy Comptroller and Auditor-General

4 Assistant Auditors-General   Director of Policy and Planning

*Divisions**

24 Directors and 28 Deputy Directors
110 Audit Managers
Senior Auditors
Auditors
Assistant Auditors

* Also support divisions covering audit guidance, personnel recruitment and training.

form part of the Appropriation Accounts. (Appropriation Accounts are published in the autumn after the end of the financial year; they give, by Class and Vote, details of the amounts expended compared with the sum granted by Parliament, together with very brief explanations of the difference between estimated and actual expenditure, including details of estimated and actual receipts used to offset expenditure.)

Second, there are other reports published throughout the year which deal with the results of the NAO's examination of economy, efficiency and effectiveness. On publication, such reports are usually reported in the Press, most prominently if there is an element of potential public scandal involved. It is the job of the PAC to consider them formally, take evidence as necessary, and report its conclusions to Parliament.

The PAC is a Select Committee with up to fifteen members which dates back to 1861. By convention its chairman is an Opposition Member of Parliament, normally with some Treasury experience. The PAC has to consider the Appropriation and other accounts presented to the House of Commons. The committee meets twice a week when the House is in session and follows the practice of other Select Committees in conducting matters on non-party political lines, avoiding debate over matters of party controversy. This is made easier since – unlike other Select Committees – the PAC concentrates on the implementation of policy, not the policy itself.

The PAC has wide-ranging powers to look into any of the accounts submitted by government departments and public bodies and any reports submitted by the C and AG. In practice it concentrates in its work on C and AG reports and, because of pressure of time, rarely examines the original accounts. In its examination of items raised in the C and AG's reports, the PAC almost invariably asks for oral and/or written evidence from the Accounting Officer of the government department concerned. The Accounting Officer, usually the Permanent Secretary, is accountable for the way in which that department has used the funds voted to it for the year. While each C and AG's report will rarely involve more than one two-hour meeting, an appearance in front of the PAC is a difficult time for an Accounting Officer. The questioning, which may be fierce, will be designed to explore the significance of any issue raised by the C and AG, the causes of any weakness in control or poor vfm, and the scope for improvement. The Accounting Officer may well be on the defensive about the department's handling of the programme or project concerned, or about an element of his or her judgement.

The verbatim record of the proceedings of these meetings, together with the PAC report on findings and any recommendations for changes in procedures or action, are presented to Parliament and published. As already indicated, thirty to forty of these reports are normally submitted in each parliamentary session.

The government's response to the findings of the PAC comes in a published Treasury Minute which explains how it intends to follow up the committee's suggestions. The government responds to several reports in each Treasury Minute and about ten are published each session. The PAC may respond to the Minute if they are not satisfied with the government response, taking further evidence and reporting again as necessary, though in practice this is infrequent. In a yearly debate, a selection of the PAC's reports, together with the government's responses, are debated by the House.

Apart from reporting directly to Parliament, a number of public bodies prepare separate reports on their activities. Some have to be produced, for example the Annual Report of the Law Commission, and the Health and Safety Commission Annual Report. Others, such as the Ordnance Survey Annual Report and the commentary on the Scotland programme, are produced because the bodies concerned want to do so. Some (the annual reports and accounts of nationalized industries) are addressed to the Minister, some (the Statement on the Defence Estimates) to Parliament, while some (the Property Services Agency

Annual Report) do not have a specified target audience. Most of the reports serve more than one function, providing information for employees and the public, and where applicable, customers. They are also regarded as important public relations documents.

Finally, it is worth noting the arrangements for the accountability of the NAO itself which is to the Public Accounts Commission, created by the National Audit Act 1983. It is a statutory body and consists of nine Members of Parliament, including the Leader of the House and the Chairman of the PAC, the latter being particularly useful as a source of information about the work programme of the NAO when considering its budget. This is one of the Commission's functions. The other two are to appoint an Accounting Officer for the NAO Appropriation Accounts and to appoint an external auditor for those accounts. The Commission will examine the C and AG as head of the NAO and the budget for the NAO itself. It will then present its findings to Parliament for approval.

In the first few years of its existence, the Commission has reviewed matters such as salaries, numbers and accommodation, and taken a general view of the work and impact of the NAO. Since it has a relatively light workload, the Commission meets infrequently.

The details of audit work

By statute there are a number of accounts which the C and AG must audit. The results of the audit must be reported to the House of Commons. These accounts are:

1. The transactions of the Consolidated Fund (covering much government revenue and expenditure) and the National Loans Fund (covering most government borrowing and lending).
2. All Appropriation Accounts other than those of the NAO itself. The C and AG must audit and certify each Vote and report on any expenditure by the department outside the terms of what has been voted.
3. Departmental Trading Accounts and Funds. The 1921 Exchequer and Audit Departments Act first provided, as required by the Treasury, for the production of income and expenditure accounts and a balance sheet, where it was felt that commercial accounting was more appropriate than the cash basis normally used within government. This principle was taken further in the Government

Trading Funds Act 1973, which allowed certain bodies to be financed through Trading Funds. Trading Funds include some well-known manufacturing or trading operations, such as the Royal Mint and HMSO (Her Majesty's Stationery Office).

4. Other accounts. A number of specific accounts – for example the National Insurance Fund – have been brought under the C and AG's scrutiny by various statutes.

There are also those accounts which the C and AG is required to examine, but not certify separately. These include the Revenue Accounts of bodies which pay their income into the Consolidated Fund – the Inland Revenue and Customs and Excise are two of these. The requirement for examination but not certification also applies to departmental store accounts. As the name implies, these are the records of the store accounting systems kept in organizations such as the Ministry of Defence.

In addition, the C and AG audits:

1. Public bodies mainly financed by government grants. These include such organizations as the Arts Council, the English and Welsh Tourist Boards and the Sports Council.
2. Some international bodies to which the United Kingdom contributes. These include United Nations agencies such as the World Health Organization, which are audited, not on behalf of Parliament, but for the governing boards of the bodies involved.
3. The use of government funds for particular purposes – for example, the unprofitable rural lines of British Rail which are funded through the 'Public Service Obligation'. The NAO will not necessarily be involved in the normal audit of such an organization which, in the case of British Rail, is carried out by a commercial auditing firm.

It is also worth mentioning that there are a very large number of public bodies to which the C and AG has rights of access for vfm and other investigations – universities, for instance – but for which he is not the appointed auditor.

While it is true that in many ways the work of the NAO on certification audits is very similar to that carried out in private sector audits, certain statutory duties are laid upon the C and AG. This often makes the audit wider in scope than what is carried out in the private sector. The C and AG must not only confirm that the figures in the accounts are materially accurate and properly disclosed, but must also satisfy himself that they conform to parliamentary authority and any requirements laid down by the Treasury. He must further check that:

- the funds have been used for the purposes which Parliament intended;
- no more than the sum appropriated has been used;
- the sum has been used only in the financial year for which it was appropriated;
- payments made and receipts collected are complete and in line with statute and other regulations;
- any amount remaining at the end of the financial year is returned to the Consolidated Fund.

The result of the certification audit is the following form of statement, signed by the C and A G at the bottom of each account:

I certify that I have examined the above Account in accordance with the Exchequer and Audit Departments Acts 1866 and 1921. In my opinion the sums expended have been applied for the purposes authorized by Parliament and the Account properly presents the expenditure and receipts of Class —, Vote — for the year ended —.

However, if there are matters about which the C and A G is not satisfied or on which he wishes to comment, the wording will vary accordingly. Appendix D shows examples for three DHSS Votes.

A separate procedure is required for Excess Votes. As Chapter 7 explained, if a government department or other public body overspends in a financial year, the excess has to be voted by Parliament. To get the extra money, any department which has overspent and missed the opportunity to request extra funds through a Supplementary Estimate has to put in a request via the Treasury called a 'Statement of Excesses'. The House of Commons through the P A C will not grant this extra money until the accounts of the department have been audited by the N A O and the C and A G has reported the reasons for overspending or for the shortfalls in receipts. The P A C will consider his report before confirming to the House that it has no objections to the extra funds, but may well comment on procedures and make suggestions for improvements. For the financial year 1985–86, for example, critical comments were made on two of the eight Excess Votes. Statements of Excess are approved with the next Spring Supplementaries in the Spring Consolidated Fund Act and are appropriated in the Summer.

Value for money

Of major importance in the balance of NAO work is the value-for-money (vfm) audit. A great deal of the NAO's work is now devoted to assuring Parliament that the funds it grants are being used in a cost-effective way. The NAO examines all three aspects of vfm. Repeating the definition given in Chapter 5, these are:

1. Economy: obtaining inputs of the right quality at the lowest possible cost.
2. Efficiency: producing the greatest useful output from the given level of inputs.
3. Effectiveness: achieving the objective or objectives of the activity.

The choice of areas to be investigated through a vfm audit lies entirely with the C and A G. He can consider resource use by any body for which he is the appointed auditor, to which he is given access by law or where he has agreement for the purpose. To help the C and A G in his planning of vfm investigations, the NAO draws on what is called a 'general survey' carried out by the divisions responsible for each audited body. The purpose of these surveys is to provide an understanding of the organization and the environment in which it operates. They will evaluate this information and draw conclusions about the risks to vfm. Areas of potential risk are noted as items for possible inquiry and a programme is drawn up.

From this work, strategic plans are drawn up, noting the investigations which are felt to be desirable over the next couple of years. It is these plans which are the basis of the annual discussion between NAO Divisional Directors and Senior management. The priorities for deciding which studies to undertake include the size of the expenditure or resources involved, appropriate cycles of coverage, the likely level of parliamentary interest, political sensitivity and the risk to vfm.

Following discussions between the Divisional Directors and Senior management, the C and A G will make whatever changes he thinks are necessary and give the plans his approval. The approved plans become the central operational programme, forming the basis of the NAO's vfm work for the coming two years and guidance for the three years after that.

To ensure the efficient use of NAO staff in general survey work and other vfm analysis a system of 'marking' has been introduced, which provides a continual update on surveys by the NAO staff working in government departments. The staff examine many aspects of an organization's working, including internal memos and minutes, Treasury correspondence and so on, always on the lookout for problems with vfm. This continual review means that a fresh general survey need only be carried out every four or five years.

Vfm studies are designed to bring Parliament's attention to any areas of potential improvement, including staffing, control, and assessment procedures. Following publication the headlines in the papers are often suitably lurid: 'Public watchdog lashes overspending', 'Too many nurses in the wrong job', etc. etc., but the intention is straightforwardly to point out to the audited bodies ways in which systems might be improved. Recent studies have pointed to the possibility of saving £75 million on improved Health Service purchasing (economy); possible savings of £1.5 billion on Royal Air Force equipment maintenance (efficiency); and weaknesses in the roads programme (effectiveness). In some cases it is too late to take action, though lessons can still be learned for the future. A report on the redundancy compensation scheme for university staff found that many of those who received compensation were those who could probably find jobs elsewhere, leaving the universities with the problem of an age imbalance in the remaining faculty. Table 8.1 lists a number of reports – the basis of the selection being to demonstrate the range of subjects covered. The table also shows that some reports deal with a much broader canvas, with increasing interest in processes and systems. Financial reporting to Parliament, mentioned in Chapter 7, is one of these. Among others dealing with broader issues but not included were review of the Rayner scrutiny programme and the process of referring nationalized industries to the Monopolies and Mergers Commission.

The following extracts give a flavour of some conclusions and recommendations drawn from a number of NAO reports.

Department of the Environment: The urban programme

... the NAO could not satisfy itself from DoE records that appraisal and monitoring by the Department was adequate for it to be certain that the authorities gave sufficient attention to strategies for dealing with local problems, to the assessment of priorities for action, and to efficiency and cost-effectiveness of projects against quantified and targeted, or, as appropriate, qualitative but well-defined, objectives.[2]

Table 8.1 Reports by the Comptroller and Auditor-General: some examples [1]

Property Services Agency: 'Defence Works in the Falkland Islands' (HC[2] 31, Session 1984–85).

Home Office: 'Control of Broadcast Receiving Licence Revenue' (HC 223, Session 1984–85).

Department of Health and Social Security: 'Arrangements for Delivering Social Security Benefits' (HC 235, Session 1984–85).

Ministry of Defence: 'Profit Formula for Non-Competitive Government Contracts' (HC 243, Session 1984–85).

Department of the Environment: 'The Urban Programme' (HC 513, Session 1984–85).

Lord Chancellor's Department: 'Provision of Legal Aid in England and Wales' (HC 182, 1985–86).

'Value-for-Money Developments in the National Health Service' (HC 212, Session 1985–86).

Departments of Energy, Transport, and Trade and Industry: 'Effectiveness of Government Financial Controls over the Nationalized Industries' (HC 253, Session 1985–86).

'Financial Control and Accountability of the Metropolitan Police' (HC 347, Session 1985–86).

Ministry of Defence: 'Management of Work at Research Establishments' (HC 462, Session 1985–86).

'Financial Reporting to Parliament' (HC 576, Session 1985–86).

1. Selected to show the range of reports.
2. House of Commons paper.

Department of the Environment: Local authority capital expenditure

The government's primary objective in introducing the new arrangements from 1981–82 was to enable it to exercise more effective control over the total amount of local authority capital expenditure within each year. But to make the arrangements more acceptable to the local authorities the government agreed to the incorporation in the legislation of a number of elements of flexibility which were likely to reduce that control. The following comments seek to take proper account of the degree of compromise which is thus inherent in the present arrangements . . .

Whether measured by the out-turn against the provisions in the government's Expenditure Plans, or against the Cash Limits based on them, the arrangements have not in practice fulfilled their primary purpose of controlling total local authority capital spending.[3]

Department of Transport: Expenditure on motorways and trunk roads

(a) There was little evidence that individual schemes were ranked for priority and allocated funds so as to maximize expected economic benefits and to meet the most urgent strategic needs. Matters appeared to depend instead on the pace at which schemes happened to clear the different stages of the public objection and approval procedures, on the availability of funds, and on the management of DTp regional workloads.

(b) The limited use made of economic assessments in fixing priorities was shown by the removal in 1980 from the forward programme of fifty-six schemes where the economic benefits were unknown; and the reinstatement of nineteen of those schemes two and a half years later still without any detailed economic evaluation.

(c) This 1980 exercise also deferred five major schemes which, as subsequently developed, proved to have high economic benefits and replaced them with twenty-six bypass or improvement schemes for which detailed economic assessments were not available. DTp explained that, to minimize abortive work, it was not their usual practice to carry out economic assessments before schemes were included in the programme.

(d) The growing importance of environmental considerations is generally increasing the non-quantifiable elements of scheme assessments.

(e) DTp are planning to start in 1985–86 and 1986–87 schemes, costing in total £48 million, which show negative economic returns.

(f) Arrangements introduced in 1981 for the monitoring and comparison of traffic flows were often ignored by regional offices; and DTp were not receiving and following up the information needed to test original appraisals and design and planning assumptions. NAO examination suggested that in a third of schemes the traffic using the road was 20 per cent or more above or below the level forecast.[4]

Foreign and Commonwealth Office: Financial control and accountability of BBC External Services

... notwithstanding External Services' high reputation for professional broadcasting skills and editorial quality, it was not clear to NAO that the present level of output, distribution across target audiences, and operational priorities have been fully reconsidered against rising costs to ensure that today External Services represent the most effective use of the limited resources available.[5]

Department of Employment and Manpower Services Commission: Adult training strategy

(a) MSC training under the Adult Training Strategy, supported by a public information campaign, promises to be significantly more cost-effective than the Training Opportunities Scheme, and to reach a wider range of trainees. Nevertheless, there is still scope for achieving better value for money in some respects, for example by continuing to reduce additional costs resulting from providing an agreed level of custom for skillcentre courses and by reducing the proportion of 'deadweight' in some schemes. NAO recognize however that the benefits of reducing deadweight have to be balanced against the cost of any more complex rules or greater screening effort which may be needed to achieve this.

(b) Area Offices' lack of comprehensive information about local skill needs and available training courses, and the absence of an inventory of skills possessed by the workforce and the unemployed, hinders the matching of MSC-sponsored training to the genuine residual needs of industry and commerce. But more practical experience is needed to establish how sophisticated an intelligence system would ultimately be worthwhile.

(c) A nationally recognized framework of competence-based qualifications would be a valuable aid to the effective working of the labour and training markets, and the setting-up of the National Council for Vocational Qualifications is an important step in this direction.[6]

Ministry of Defence: Service movements

... the NAO considers that the developing financial, budgetary and management information systems which support both individual Service operations and MOD policy committees do not yet provide a sufficient base for ensuring that value for money is achieved.[7]

Value-for-money developments in the National Health Service

There is, without doubt, a great deal of work under way at both departmental and local level to improve vfm within the NHS and I support all the measures currently in operation. The revised management structure introduced as a result of the NHS Management Inquiry places responsibility for the systematic search for vfm squarely on general managers at all levels within the NHS. However, with this devolving of responsibility through the general management function down to unit level comes the need to establish and maintain effective lines of accountability. Health authorities and DHSS need to ensure that the framework of accountability and review procedures now introduced continues to develop in such a way as to focus sharp attention on the achievement of vfm at local level and to prevent cuts in services being presented as real savings. The first round of cost-improvement programmes has produced a significant step forward in the search for efficiency in the hospital service. It has, however, also demonstrated the need for further improvements in both the procedures and their application by health authorities if the potential for achieving even greater vfm in the provision of services to patients in the NHS is to be realized.[8]

In the years immediately following the 1983 act, the resources of the NAO were split roughly two-thirds on certification audit work and one third on vfm. However, the C and AG has been gradually moving towards a fifty–fifty split. The prospects of achieving this level of vfm work have been helped by the 1983 Act which provided authority for reports produced by the NAO to be presented to Parliament separately from the year-end Appropriation Accounts of the body being audited. This has meant the C and AG is now able to plan the year's work so as to create a steady flow of work and useful information to the PAC.

Reporting

Beyond the basic statutory certification of accounts and reports, the C and AG has considerable discretionary powers when it comes to deciding whether, when and what to report to Parliament. He may include anything he feels is relevant to his inquiries, though in practice classified information is avoided. It is then up to the PAC to decide whether, and how, to pursue the matters raised.

1. He must report on almost all the accounts he is required to audit and in particular he must report on any qualifications which he makes in certifying such accounts, including excess votes.
2. He must report on his examination of certain accounts which he is not required to certify, for example revenue accounts.

Apart from statutory requirements, in the main areas on which the C and AG is statutorily required to report to Parliament his decision on whether to report and what to include will be based on a number of considerations. These include the resources and risks involved, how important the matter is perceived to be, whether Parliament is already aware of the issues, how far-reaching the weaknesses are, and to what extent the department involved has tried to remedy the problems. On this last point, the NAO will always discuss its findings with the Accounting Officer of the department to see how far the matters about which they are concerned can be cleared up without the need for a formal report. If a report is still considered necessary, its wording will be agreed with the department concerned. It will also generally include the Accounting Officer's views and responses on the issues raised.

The reason for discussion with the body being audited before the report goes to Parliament and is published is to ensure that the facts are fairly presented. But this practice has led to criticisms that the C and A G's reports are bland and lacking in teeth, since the body being audited will naturally try to ensure that its position is put in the best possible light. This suspicion will inevitably remain as long as there is the requirement to agree a report's wording with the Accounting Officer, although the process specifically provides for different views of the department and the C and A G to be made clear. Furthermore, purple prose and extreme phrasing are not the way to generate useful discussion or effective action. Of course, in the last part of the process there is nothing to stop the P A C from being as outspoken as it likes. In practice it can be very outspoken indeed, as shown by examples of extracts from the summaries of two reports from a recent Parliamentary session. The first is on the control of major developments in the use of information technology in the Inland Revenue:

We are dismayed that after eleven years of development and three years after our predecessors had been assured that the project was under control, I R decided to replace the Accounts Office computer-based systems and then proceeded to repeat their previous basic mistakes in the design and control of I C S. We shall be requiring assurances that these lessons are well and truly learned.[9]

And on the review of the objectives and achievements of the Forestry Commission the P A C concluded:

Generally we found that across many of the Commission's activities there was insufficient assurance on the extent and quantification of the benefits achieved or how far these were commensurate with the resources used to achieve them. We are concerned that there appears to have been no fundamental re-examination since 1972 of the information needed and available to support many of the policy and operational decisions being made.[10]

P A C reports can be highly influential, particularly since, unlike departmental Select Committee reports, they reflect administrative practice (how things are done) rather than policy. The government is much less likely to be defensive on such recommendations; indeed if there is clear evidence of problems identified by the C and A G, the government itself would have every incentive to accept what the P A C suggests. However, some issues may be as politically sensitive as those covered by departmental Select Committees and in these cases the government may give the recommendations equally short shrift ... of course in their usual courteous terms.

The parliamentary debate on the P A C reports and the government responses marks the end of the public expenditure cycle. In all, it will have taken about five years from the time the figures first appeared as year 3 of the Survey. Thus the first indications of plans for the financial year 1989–90 will have appeared first in November 1986. The debate on any P A C reports arising out of those accounts will be held during 1991.

There is one territorial variation in these arrangements. While the N A O covers England, Wales and Scotland, it does not cover Northern Ireland. Northern Ireland has its own C and A G and the hundred or so staff of his department (the Northern Ireland Audit Department) perform basically the same tasks as the staff of the N A O.

Limitations and prospects

Despite the powers and the wide-ranging brief of the C and A G, there are limitations on what he and the N A O can do. The Private Member's Bill which eventually, in an amended form, became the National Audit Act 1983 sought to give the C and A G the power 'to follow public money wherever it goes'. But this right was not granted by the Act. Most controversially, the C and A G is not entitled to examine the books of nationalized industries or local government, despite the large amounts of government money involved.

There are boundaries and other limitations to his duties:

1. He may not formally disallow expenditure by a department. It is his duty only to examine and report on whether or not payments made are compatible with the relevant Votes approved by Parliament.
2. He may not pass judgement on questions of legality.
3. He may not examine questions of maladministration where members of the public are concerned. These matters must be brought to the attention of the Parliamentary Commissioner for Administration (Ombudsman).

4. He must not report to anyone except Parliament, other than for the World Health Organization and other United Nations agencies where reporting is to the governing bodies which commissioned the reports.

5. Perhaps most important, the C and A G is not entitled to question the merits of policy objectives. His duty lies in establishing whether the objectives are being pursued economically and efficiently, how far they are being achieved and having their intended effects, not whether they are the right objectives.

What, then, are the prospects for the development of the work of the NAO in the light of the experience of working with the 1983 Act? John Glynn has commented on some of the general problems for those involved in this area:

> At present the auditing profession cannot deliver fully on its VFM mandates. This is partially due to the fact that the auditor's role is evolving in response to changing public needs and expectations. He is a third party intermediary in a broadly defined accountability relationship between, on the one hand, government and management, and on the other hand, politicians and the public at large ... The major inhibiting factor ... is the lack of a political will to reform the general framework of financial management, and to define more clearly the scope of programme objectives.[11]

There is no question that the NAO has greatly broadened its scope and penetration in the last few years, a process helped by the significant expansion in numbers of its staff. It is well respected inside Parliament and its work for the PAC is seen as useful and important. But as the NAO itself acknowledges, there are problems in gaining recognition for its work outside Parliament, and in recruiting and maintaining the calibre of staff it needs.

To overcome these problems, the work of the NAO has been brought more into the public eye. In particular, considerable effort has gone into ensuring Press coverage of its reports, and presentation is being improved to make the contents more accessible to a wider audience. On staffing, salaries are being improved and greater recruitment efforts are being made. It remains to be seen whether these will be enough to give the NAO the kind of impact which the 1983 Act envisaged and which the NAO itself seeks.

APPENDIX A   INVESTMENT APPRAISAL

In the private sector, investment appraisal is a well-established practice for looking at investment opportunities. In the public sector, it is about looking at the consequences of any proposal to commit resources. This may well involve decisions very similar to those in the private sector about whether new investment should take place, or whether there should be replacement investment. But investment appraisal can also involve discussing the process – when and how investment takes place, whether existing assets should be held or disposed of, how assets should be used and which of a number of expenditure options should be taken up.

There are various types of appraisal, ranging from the commercial (Should we computerize these tasks now done manually? Should we upgrade the computers we currently use?) to the comparison of costs and benefits (What return might be expected from upgrading this road?) and comparisons of cost-effectiveness (Which of these policy options might be expected to do the job most effectively within the available budget?).

In comparison with the private sector, the problems in undertaking an appraisal are often very difficult. Consider, for example, this comment by a former Chairman of Unilever from a British Council annual report:

> To one coming from the business world it can be frustrating that the tangible yardstick of profit and loss or return on investment can be applied to so little of our work of cultural diplomacy. But consider the effects for Britain of not making this investment: of allowing, for example, the number of bright young students who train in Britain and who will be tomorrow's leaders to decline; of reducing the number of artistic events which are evidence that Britain is still intellectually lively and innovative; of not capitalizing on our priceless asset, the English language; of reducing our efforts to promote partnerships in scientific and technical research.[1]

So calculations of return are often not on straightforward commercial criteria (what exactly *is* the return from an aircraft-carrier or a prison?). Comparisons between projects often involve political and other imponderables which do not fit into a tidy framework, as when expenditure on kidney machines is compared with expenditure on brain-scanners.

This does not mean that investment appraisal is impossible. In many cases it is relatively easy. One such calculation is of the consequences of moving to a new building with a lower rent but with some initial costs to upgrade it, compared with staying put in a building with a higher rent. Another is whether or not to hire more Inland Revenue staff to prevent fraud. In other cases approximations to a rate of return can be given, as when the value to the country of better health or better roads is calculated using stated assumptions about the possible benefits. This technique, known as cost-benefit analysis, has to be used with care, and its limitations have to be understood, since there is a danger that more weight will be put on the results than are justified by the assumptions. Thus the benefits from a new road will obviously be heavily influenced by the key assumption about the value of time saved to those who will use it. The National Audit Office gave another example on road evaluation in reporting on the calculation of environmental benefits:

In 1977 the Advisory Committee on Trunk Road Assessment examined the methods used by DTp in deciding which roads to build. It confirmed that the system of cost-benefit analysis (COBA) used to assess the economic benefits of new road schemes was sound, but criticized DTp for not developing a system of appraisal which would also give sufficient weight to environmental benefits.

DTp have since made some progress in developing such a system. This is, however, based on broad descriptions of environmental impact, such as the number of homes affected by noise; it does not attempt the admittedly difficult task of seeking to quantify environmental benefits in monetary terms. DTp considered that their current practice was in line with the Advisory Committee's recommendation. In contrast therefore with the arrangements which enable a quantified comparison to be made between new road schemes justified on economic grounds, comparisons involving schemes justified wholly or partly on environmental or other non-economic grounds have to rely on subjective judgements.[2]

In the standard work on investment appraisal in the public sector issued by the Treasury,[3] the sequence of an appraisal is given as follows:

1. Define the objectives.
2. Consider the options (one of which is probably to do nothing).

3. Identify the costs and benefits of each option adjusted for inflation, including capital and running costs, and identify costs and benefits which affect other parts of the economy.
4. Discount (see below) those costs and benefits which can be valued in money terms.
5. Weigh up the uncertainties. This in practice means looking at the factors which could significantly affect the results.
6. Assess other factors, such as political aspects, feasibility and prior commitments.
7. Present the results, making clear the basis of the calculation to give the preferred option and how this compares with the alternatives.

Stage 4 of the Treasury's list refers to discounting, the most important technique in investment appraisal, usually known by the acronym DCF (Discounted Cash Flow). DCF is a procedure for recognizing the time value of money – £1 received today is worth more than the same sum received at a future date, even without inflation. So in comparing the costs and benefits which arise over the lifetime of a project, a discount rate is used to adjust those costs and benefits in relation to the time-scale in which they are incurred or received. By this means different projects can be compared. The discount rate used in the public sector is known as the Test Discount Rate (TDR).

In incorporating DCF as the standard method of calculation, the public sector follows standard private sector practice. Payback (the number of years required to recoup the cost of a project) and the internal rate of return (the discount rate at which discounted benefits equal discounted costs) are two other techniques widely used in the private sector. The Treasury does not recommend either as suitable for the public sector, because both put excessive weight on the returns which come in the early years of a project. So, for example, with payback a project which repays the cash outlay through savings in three years but has no further savings might be (wrongly) preferred to one which repays them in four years but has a stream of further savings for many years thereafter.

While DCF is a key element in the process of appraisal, there are important stages in preparing a proposal before the process starts. These include the definition of objectives as well as the identification of options and related costs and benefits. If these can be identified, the appraisal process is relatively straightforward. Unfortunately there are problems with each of these stages. Most arise because of the imprecision of the whole business. Objectives may not be clearly defined. The uncertainties may involve a huge range of options. The costs and benefits may not be easily valued, or indeed evaluable at all in money terms.

Other factors which may be involved include wholly political ones which outweigh all other considerations. These factors mean that the process of investment appraisal is usually less precise than those who are looking for rational choices might like. Economic uncertainties and political horse-trading may make what can be a highly sophisticated set of calculations appear to be worthless.

Faced with such pressures, with the difficulties of measuring inputs and outputs, with pressure of work and the need to 'get things done', it is easy to become cynical about appraisal of this kind. But while the limitations of investment appraisal in the public sector are obvious enough, having to set out the calculations can be a valuable discipline in its own right, often exposing additional possibilities. It is more likely that elected members will develop a 'gut feeling' for a rational solution if they at least have an opportunity of taking relevant factors into account.

APPENDIX B   CASE STUDIES IN MEASURING PERFORMANCE

1. Key output indicators and vfm targets for 1987–88 (direct Department of Transport responsibility)
2. Department of Employment: Measures for policy work
3. H.M. Customs and Excise: VAT

Table A.1 Key output indicators and VFM targets for 1987–88 (direct Department of Transport responsibility)

Programme/Indicator	Units	1985-86 Out-turn	1986-87 Target	1986-87 Forecast	1987-88 Target	
I. DVLD						
Output: Drivers transactions	millions	9.6	9.7	9.7	10.0	
Vehicles transactions	millions	56.6	57.5	57.5	60.0	
VED cases reviewed	thousands	315	320	340	355	
Efficiency: Drivers system unit cost	£/transactions (1985–86 prices)	1.58		1.54	1.51	
Vehicles system unit cost		1.40		1.38	1.34	
Effectiveness: Drivers system turn-round	% transactions turned round/days	90%/10 days	90%/8 days	90%/8 days	90%/8 days for 3q of year	
Vehicles system turn-round		70%/10 days			90%/7 days for 1q of year	
VED yield/cost ratio		2.6	over 2.0	c3.0 2.9		
II. Main fee-earning businesses (See Note 1)						
(a) DTT						
Output: L-Test fee-earning periods	thousands	2,083	2,239	2,220	2,175	
HGV/PSV-test fee-earning periods	thousands	[58]	55	55	63	See Note 2
Efficiency: L-Test unit cost	£/period	13.14	13.61	13.44	14.55	See Note 3
HGV/PSV unit cost	£/period	[38.57]	39.92	39.21	41.66	See Note 2
Effectiveness: L-Test queue length	weeks	15	11	13	11	
HGV/PSV queue length	weeks	8	4	4	4	See Note 4
(b) Vehicle Inspectorate						
Output: PSV inspection visits	numbers	3,633	2,279	4,033	3,837	See Note 5
HGV inspection visits	numbers	25,645	38,866	29,992	35,646	
HGV axles tested	thousands	1,939	—	1,977	1,977	

Programme/Indicator	Units	1985–86 Out-turn	1986–87 Target	1986–87 Forecast	1987–88 Target	
Efficiency: Work units/examiner	numbers	1,290	1,304	1,258	1,314	
HGV test unit cost	£/axle inspected	8.10	—	8.05	(8.53)	See Note 6
PSV test unit cost	£/vehicle	26.04	—	23.54	(23.64)	See Note 7
(c) *TAOs* (excl. enforcement work)						
Output: Driving tests booked	thousands	2,199	1,958	2,265	2,009	
Goods 'O' licences: issued	numbers	35,538	35,500	35,200	37,400	
HGV driver licences: issued	thousands	365	365.5	366.1	353.0	
Efficiency: Booking service unit cost	£/booking	1.62	1.94	1.71	1.79	
Goods 'O' licence unit cost	£/licence	90.83	101.08	96.82	99.73	
HGV driver licence unit cost	£/licence	4.67	5.54	5.76	5.47	
III. Highways (See Note 8)						
(a) *National Roads*						
Output: New starts	miles	63	110	112	188	
Completions	miles	130	75	87	92	
Renewals: M-way	equiv. route-miles single carriageway	70	80	80+	80	
Trunk	equiv. miles	145	185	185+	190+	
VFM: Benefit/cost ratio (excl. M25)		1.5	1.5	1.5	1.5	
Contract cost over-runs	% reduction	—	16%/3 years	3% (£3m)	16%/3 years	
Lane rental schemes	numbers	12	15	22	30	See Note 9
IV. MARINE						
(a) *SGO*	Indicators to be decided in light of 1986–87 Rayner report on marine survey service					

(b) HMCG

Output:	Incidents recorded	numbers	5,477	—	nya	nya
	Persons assisted	numbers	9,711	—	nya	nya
	Lives lost	numbers	155	—	nya	nya
V. Research						
VFM:	Contracts let by competitive tender	% of total	31%	40%	45%	50%

NOTES

1. Targets for VCA and IRFO have been agreed but are not included in this table.
2. HGV and PSV tests were standardized in 1986–87 so that earlier figures are not fully comparable.
3. L-test unit cost target for 1987–88 assumes 3.3% loss of fee-earning periods due to weather.
4. Average queue length at end of period.
5. The target figures are related to an objective of achieving an average of one inspection per operator every five years. However, greater attention is being given to PSV operators at present in support of de-regulation policy.
6. This unit cost is an element of DTT's L-test unit cost.
7. This unit cost excludes technical and enforcement costs.
8. Improved output measures and better means of presenting VFM figures covering a wider range of highways activities will be explored in the context of the Highways Business Plan.
9. Saving is spread over life of contract, so attribution to individual years is uncertain.

nya = not yet available.
Figures in brackets for 1987–88 target = target not yet agreed.
Source: Department of Transport Departmental Plan, 1987–88.

2. Department of Employment: Measures for policy work

1. This case study describes the problems of attempting to develop output and performance indicators for policy work. It was produced by the Survey Unit (now the Management Services Unit), after consultation with other departments, as part of a wider exercise to explore and publicize ways of using performance indicators, undertaken in the department during 1983–84.

2. Measures for policy branches are clearly more difficult than for many other parts of the department. Rather than give a suggested outline of what indicators may or may not be suitable for one section, which may not provide general conclusions applicable to other branches, the general problems of assessing work which in the main passes up to Ministers is discussed.

3. Much policy work can be divided into two main types for which the tasks are primarily either:

(a)   One-off tasks such as drafting a Bill, a White Paper or providing policy advice, for which the workload cannot be meaningfully assessed without detailed examination of the subject-matter based on experienced judgement.

or

(b)   Case-work, briefing, ministerial or public correspondence and PQs, etc. for which at least the work can be counted. (The question of whether the numbers can be meaningful is discussed later.) Most branches already log some of this work, mainly to ensure that none goes astray, but some use the log to control response times or to allocate work.

EFFECTIVENESS

4. For work of either of the above two types, one might ask what effect it has, in relation to set objectives, on employment or the state of industrial relations, for example. In practice the effects of work of type (a) seem more susceptible to such assessment, using for example statistical surveys on other research to monitor what, say, a piece of legislation has achieved; though it may be impossible to identify the specific contribution to the effects made by the policy branch. It is equally important to use such information to monitor the effects of existing policies and this should help policy-formulation generally. The quality of such

monitoring in following up the effects of policies will often itself be a key aspect of the performance of policy-makers, particularly in terms of longer-term objectives. Much might be gained by sharpening standards and setting precise criteria for the quality (e.g. timeliness and accuracy) of information and analysis of the operation of policies, though assessments of how well it is used will usually involve considerable judgement.

5. For internal management purposes, it may often only be possible to make assessments in terms of intermediate qualities of work such as smooth running of the team and how Ministers regard it. Some aspects of quality of the work are discussed later. The best that will often be possible is for the branch to plan specific tasks to be achieved and then later to compare achievement with plan, making separate judgements on the quality of these achievements.

EFFICIENCY INDICATORS

6. Indicators of efficiency appear to be possible only for work of type (b) (if at all). Even if some efficiency indicators were possible for work of type (a), there would in any case clearly be difficulties in assessing trends or in making comparisons between branches.

7. For work of type (b), where quantifiable case-loads account for a substantial proportion of staff time, it may be possible to derive average unit times (and hence unit costs) for each item, provided reasonable estimates of staff time spent on each item are available. This could be done by timing a selection of items or by getting staff to complete work-diaries over a period. This would provide a benchmark against which future workloads might be assessed. Essentially volumes for each item of work could be weighted according to the estimated unit times to give an indicator of the overall workload or 'required' staff time (and costs) to compare with actual staff (and costs).* This would provide a broad indicator of productivity. Particular care would be needed by management in interpreting such figures, taking account of the quality of work and also the views of staff: e.g. on special circumstances or any changes in the nature of the work; but despite the difficulties of predicting future workloads, these could be of some help in budgeting and in adjusting staffing levels when required.

* If staff also perform other unquantifiable tasks it would be necessary to obtain regular estimates of the proportions of time spent on the main activities by keeping approximate records.

8. It cannot be presumed that because work can be counted this approach would necessarily be suitable. The main differences between the work of a policy section and other operational sections where the above technique can be expected to be more useful are:

(a) the times required for each item are usually more variable;
(b) the quality of the work is often less tangible, though often more important than quantities;
(c) the deadlines set are often short and have to be met.

9. (b) and (c) are important but need not inhibit the use of figures along the lines of the above, provided they are interpreted sensibly taking an overall view of performance. However the variation in times to deal with particular items is crucial in determining whether or not such figures would be sufficiently accurate to be useful. This cannot be assessed without some data on the times and ranges of times taken to deal with specific items. Experiments in performance indicators now being conducted in the department may help to indicate what might be possible more generally, but it is too early yet to draw conclusions.

ANALYSIS OF INPUT

10. The internal effectiveness and efficiency of policy branches depend critically on one resource – staff, but frequently how staff spread their time over the various activities is not known, planned or controlled. Typical activities for a policy branch include:

(a) assistance in policy formulation;
(b) parliamentary and public business;
(c) managing/monitoring operational work;
(d) planning;
(e) research and gathering information;
(f) representation (e.g. on committees, or at international bodies);
(g) internal administration (communication training, budgeting).

Even where the outputs from each of these activities cannot be quantified, improved performance might be achieved from improved information about how much staff resource is consumed by each activity. The most appropriate analysis of activities may of course vary from section to section.

Quality of output

11. Some of the main problems are in assessing the quality of service for Ministers and the use made of material provided. As far as the reliability of information or the quality of advice are concerned, there are clearly difficulties. For example one cannot gauge the quality depending on whether Ministers are pleased with the advice given. In principle rated judgements by Ministers on such aspects as presentation, length, coverage and relevance of information might be possible, though such judgements in themselves would be of little value without some indication of any particular points of concern.

12. The essential requirement is for management to be aware of the standards required by Ministers (who should also be aware of any implications for costs). As well as noting praise or problems on re-drafts as they occur, the opportunity can be taken occasionally to obtain views on the general quality of work through Private Office or from Ministers in discussion. In the light of this feedback, it is then primarily a matter for management to set required standards for the quality of work and budget accordingly. This of course means making some assessment of the quality of work in terms of the required standards which will usually be a matter of judgement.

13. A further important aspect of quality is timeliness. Response times or backlogs of items such as letters from the public can be monitored; but such indicators would hardly be worth collecting for work with fixed deadlines which are invariably met (often by staff putting in extra time when necessary) unless significant problems occur.

14. In policy work and in other fields such as research or specialist advice where it may be difficult to measure performance, it may still be possible to make cogent assessments and motivate managers and staff to improve performance, for example by using the annual reporting system. Consistent with corporate objectives, it may be possible to set targets for improvement of specific aspects which need priority, e.g. the development of better management practice, efficiency in the use of resources or creativity in overcoming obstacles, etc. The expectation of what is to be achieved could be made clear at the outset, and favourable assessments for particular aspects of personal performance at the end of the year could depend on specific evidence (not necessarily quantified) as to whether improvements had been made, e.g. in coming forward with and pursuing practical options for more efficient methods of meeting ministerial objectives, or even in improving the criteria for assessing

whether such objectives are achieved. This approach may help to assess performance more systematically, but more importantly may help to stimulate actual improvements in performance even if those improvements cannot be quantified.

CONCLUSIONS

15. There may be some scope for using performance indicators for policy work, though where they do apply they are likely to be limited to aspects such as timeliness and broad indicators of efficiency, which may require a considerable amount of judgement in interpretation. The reliability of any efficiency indicators based on quantifiable workloads depends on the quantities involved and the variations in the times per item. Some experiments being undertaken may help to indicate what is or is not possible more generally, and how useful such indicators can be expected to be.

16. There are no doubt some small policy sections for which there are few if any performance indicators applicable, though much might be gained from simply listing achievements, or tasks performed compared with tasks planned, or details of improvements made, together with corresponding estimates of costs and better information on how staff spend their time on the various activities. This may at least help in setting priorities and organizing work or in questioning the way things are done. Questions about what work would be done if resources were reduced may also lead to ideas for improved efficiency, or for concentrating efforts on the most important tasks. Moreover, even sections which cannot do much in the way of monitoring performance of the resources they consume directly will be interested in using indicators if they are concerned with monitoring performance elsewhere (e.g. in considering the effectiveness of special employment measures) or with assessing the effectiveness of legislation, especially when they have implications for future programme expenditure or other costs. Much might be achieved by setting standards for the quality of monitoring of policies e.g. in terms of the type of information required to fill any gaps of knowledge.

17. In policy sections, and in other similar areas, assessments of personal performance on specific aspects of work which merit particular attention may help to stimulate improvements in the performance of those sections overall.

March 1984

Source: Lewis, op. cit., 1986

3. H.M. Customs and Excise: VAT

1. This case study describes how Customs and Excise have tackled the problem of tailoring output and performance information to meet the different needs of different levels of management.

2. The department's major 'businesses' are VAT, Customs, Excise and Administration. The department has a regionalized structure. There are twenty one Collections (e.g. South Wales and the Borders) headed at Assistant-Secretary level, covering the whole of the United Kingdom, and a Headquarters. The Collections have operational responsibility for carrying out HQ policies to fulfil the aims of the Board of H.M. Customs and Excise.

3. The department had voted expenditure of some £340 million in 1984–85. The bulk was pay and running costs of about 25,000 staff. There is no programme expenditure.

4. The department's FMI work focuses on four interlinked elements: planning, measurement of achievement, accounting, budgeting and costing, and management information. The general approach has been to build on the best elements of present systems so as to develop procedures and information that meet the needs of managers at all levels.

5. Management planning is being developed at three levels. The Board's Plan sets out the broad aims, objectives and general and specific priorities of the department. Collection Plans set out the objectives and priorities for individual areas of work consistent with the requirements of the Board's Plan. Operational Unit Plans set out specific targets designed to meet the requirements of the Collection Plans.

6. Through this structured planning system aims, objectives and responsibilities will be better defined and achievement will be monitored, measured and reviewed more consistently. The intention is to ensure that resources will be controlled and concentrated on those activities which senior management consider important. When achievement does not conform to plan it will be possible to take timely corrective action.

7. Not all activities need necessarily be covered in the plans in a particular year, though all need to be identified in preparing plans. Areas of greatest concern will be included each year. Activities not specifically covered in the plans should continue to be performed to an acceptable standard.

MANAGEMENT INFORMATION AND MEASUREMENT OF ACHIEVEMENT IN VAT

8. The initial work on management planning was undertaken in VAT, so examination of management information and existing measures of achievement took place first in this area of the department's work. VAT is a self-assessed tax, in general falling on final consumer's expenditure. In the financial year 1984–85 the net tax collected was £18,535 million. About 12,500 Customs and Excise staff are involved in VAT work and approximately 8,200 of these are in 87 local VAT offices (LVOs). They deal with about 1.45 million traders. Administrative costs are mainly related to the registration and deregistration of traders, collection and repayment of tax, enforcement and control.

9. The aim is to ensure that the necessary information is provided to managers to enable them to fulfil their responsibilities and to make best use of their resources. The information should:

- be relevant to management decisions;
- highlight areas for management concern;
- be timely and in a suitable form;
- be cost effective to produce.

10. Performance measures and targets are necessary to monitor actual performance and are prerequisites for formal and reviewable management planning.

11. At present managers appear to receive a lot of information merely because it is available, and screening to limit the information to what is essential has been inhibited by computer system operations. It is for this reason that the initial approach to measurement of achievement was to have detailed discussions with three pilot Collections and also HQ VAT divisions to identify their major decision areas and management concerns. The team then listed all existing measures used by management and all information sources and examined the individual measures to establish which would:

- be suitable for a core system to serve all levels of management;
- be suitable for local use;
- may be discarded.

AN EXAMPLE: VAT CONTROL

12. Control visits take place on trader's premises when an L VO official calls to see the trader, the trader's activities, and the business records and accounts to check from all available evidence that the tax has been properly accounted for.

13. VAT control visits were the subject of a previous case study. This described how computers assist the planning of visits by listing those traders due for a control visit. In drawing up these lists priorities are based mainly on compliance of the individual traders business. Final decisions about visits to traders are, however, taken by L VO management.

14. Significant decision areas and related management concerns therefore include:

- organization of control work: management is concerned that demand-led functions are accomplished with greater effectiveness and that time spent at the L VO and travelling is reduced so as to increase the resources devoted to revenue-yielding work;
- selection of visits: management is concerned that traders are visited with proper regard for revenue risk, to improve cost-effectiveness and to preserve preventive effects;
- performance on visits: management is concerned to maximize additional revenue gained from discovered misdeclarations, to improve the identification of risk factors, to minimize abortive visits, to increase expertise and motivation of staff and to preserve the acceptability of the tax.

(This list is not exhaustive.)

15. The primary output measures include:

- number of control visit sessions (i.e. $\frac{1}{2}$ days)
- number of control visits
- number of under and over declarations of tax identified
- value of under and over declarations of tax discovered

the primary inputs are:

- mandays on VAT Control
- mandays on VAT

16. Effectiveness ratios can be constructed relating actual outputs to target outputs. For example:

$$\frac{\text{actual number of control visit sessions}}{\text{target number of control visit sessions}}$$

Other output ratios that are needed for measurement of achievement are the incidence of underdeclarations and the mean value of underdeclaration per session:

$$-\frac{\text{number of underdeclarations}}{\text{number of control visit sessions}}$$

$$-\frac{\text{value of underdeclarations}}{\text{number of control visit sessions}}$$

17. Economy ratios can be constructed by relating actual inputs to target inputs. For example:

$$-\frac{\text{actual mandays on VAT control}}{\text{target mandays on VAT control}}$$

18. Indicators of efficiency can be constructed by relating outputs to inputs. For example:

$$-\frac{\text{value of underdeclarations}}{\text{mandays on VAT control}}$$

$$-\frac{\text{value of underdeclarations}}{\text{mandays on all VAT work}}$$

19. All these items of information and ratios are needed by managers at all levels (aggregated where appropriate) and will be included in a core system of management information.

20. There are some types of information (collected on an on-going basis or by sampling exercises) that would be suitable for inclusion only at a local level. Examples include the number of abortive visits per manday and the number and duration of telephone inquiries at an LVO. This information is important at the local level of management but is not needed centrally except to answer an *ad hoc* query. In this case a sample of local data would probably be sufficient.

21. The examples given illustrate that any one decision area needs a number of measures of achievement to adequately describe performance. Conversely any one measure of achievement can contribute to more than one decision area.

FURTHER WORK

22. The next phase of the work on measurement of achievement will involve:

- identification of areas not well served by measures at present and suggestions for possible indicators in these areas;
- preparation of a user requirement for VAT management information in consultation with various levels of management. This includes design of work returns, report formats and decisions on frequency of reporting;
- decision area and management concern analysis for the other 'businesses' of the department (i.e. Customs, Excise and Administration);
- listing existing management information and measures of achievement in these 'businesses'.

The final phase will involve preparation of user requirements for the other 'businesses' and the design of supporting management reports.

CONCLUSIONS

23. The case study illustrates how an organization with a fair amount of output and performance information has approached the task of organizing this information into a form which meets the various needs of management. In VAT an analysis of management concerns and needs, generated by a formal planning system, has led to a classification into core information required by all, local information for local management and data that can be dropped.

May 1984
Revised January 1986

Source: Lewis, op. cit., 1986

APPENDIX C   CASE STUDY: CATERING IN THE NHS

DEPARTMENT OF HEALTH AND SOCIAL SECURITY

From the Parliamentary Under Secretary of State for Health

To: Chairmen of RHAs
      Chairmen of DHAs
      Chairmen of London Postgraduate SHAs   26 Feburary 1985

Dear Chairman:
I attach a copy of the Scrutiny Report 'The Cost of Catering in the NHS' which was prepared by officers of South East Thames RHA and submitted by Sir Peter Baldwin. Would you please set in hand immediate consideration of how the Report's recommendations can be applied to improve the quality and cost effectiveness of catering services provided by your Authority.

In particular, Ministers would like management action on:

i.   *Catering performance reviews* – all authorities which are not already doing so should institute catering performance reviews. Wessex have developed an approach which other authorities may find useful.

ii. *Reduction of food waste* – authorities should set targets for waste reduction of at least five per cent of total food costs in a year.

iii. *Cost control for staff meals* – authorities should review cafeteria prices and cost control procedures to ensure that contributions to overheads are in line with those recommended in HC(67)10 and

that cost separation is scrupulously carried out as set out in
HC(82)18.

iv. *Energy control and conservation* – authorities should apply the recommendations of DHSS Engineering Data Sheet ECi (September 1980) for metering services to kitchens, timed control of kitchen
equipment and ventilation, improving equipment insulation, regular
equipment maintenance and sensible operating practice.

All districts are asked to report to their Regions on the action they have
taken and the savings they expect to achieve. Regions are asked to
summarise District reports and send these summaries to the Department
to accompany their cost improvement programmes, by December. SHAs
should report direct to the Department by that date.

Section 9 of the Scrutiny Report recommends the employment of
Regional Catering Advisers. This will be something for each Region to
consider in the light of its overall management structure, and Ministers
do not consider it necessary to be prescriptive. What is important is for
each Region and District to ensure that they have effective management
and advisory arrangements for their catering services. It is essential that
unit catering managers work to properly drawn up catering policies and
can obtain professional advice and guidance when they need it.

Section 10.8 of the Report draws attention to the need for more study
of the implications of modern food production technology for NHS
catering. The Department is considering urgently how best to carry this
forward.

Finally, Section 10.1 of the Report suggests changing the present
basis of subsidy for staff meals. Health authorities are invited to
comment if they wish on the present national policy for subsidising staff
meals and on the Report's recommendations in this field. This is a
matter which Ministers will be considering in the light of consultation.
The Management and Staff Sides of the Ancillary Staffs and General
Whitley Councils are being asked for their views.

Yrs. sincerely,
John Patten

(AUTHOR'S NOTE. Extract from the section of the Scrutiny Report dealing with the reduction of food waste. This gives an idea of the detail which can be involved in a report of this kind.)

Food waste – where it occurs and how to reduce it

I. PURCHASE AND STORAGE AND ISSUE

1.1   If detailed specifications do not exist suppliers can deliver foods of poor quality – meat with excessive fat or bone, vegetables which are bruised or damaged for example – and an undue proportion cannot be used.

1.2   Care should be taken to check goods on arrival not only for quality, but also to ensure that the quantity ordered is in fact delivered.

1.3   Many foodstuffs deteriorate if they are not properly stored. The stores must therefore be suitable for the items they are to house and stores staff must be trained to look after foods, and take account of shelf life, stock rotation, etc.

1.4   Opportunities for loss and pilferage exist wherever goods are delivered, stored and issued and appropriate safeguards are needed to ensure security.

1.5   Care must be taken in selecting the most suitable system of issuing goods (such as by requisition or top up) and also in determining the most appropriate unit of quantity. Regular checks are needed that issues match needs, and that goods are not being hoarded.

2. FOOD PREPARATION AND COOKING

2.1   Bad working practices, both in preparing and cooking food, can lead to waste. Staff need to be trained and supervised to ensure foods are trimmed and prepared to obtain maximum yield; it may be more economic to buy prepared foods – meat and vegetables for example – and avoid the waste in time and material of preparatory work.

2.2   Standard recipes and cooking procedures need to be followed to ensure the most economic use of materials. Every opportunity should be taken to maximize food utilization. Meat and fish trimmings should not be discarded but used in stock or pies for example.

2.3   The kitchen must be properly equipped and regularly maintained; if an item has a control – say a thermostat – it must be in working order.

3. FOOD SERVICE

3.1 Food will be wasted at the point of consumption for many reasons, but there will be normally three underlying causes – too much food has been delivered, or the food is unsuitable for the customer, or the food is of poor quality.

3.2 The supply of excessive food is probably the largest cause of waste. Bulk service systems are inherently more wasteful than plated ones, and it is often impracticable to weigh all food to ensure the right amounts are provided. The sizes may be too large for some groups of patients such as children or old people.

3.3 All too often there is inadequate communication between wards and kitchens, with the former failing to inform the kitchen of a death, or a discharge, so the kitchen supplies too many portions. Again, the wards may order extras 'just in case' unexpected admissions might occur. Ordering is often done a day before the meals are needed, and this militates against matching supply with need.

3.4 Poor communication can often mean that unsuitable food is delivered; if no one tells the kitchen the patient is a Moslem or a vegetarian then it can't ensure an appropriate dish is delivered. Diet needs, too, may be overlooked. It is not unknown for ward staff to make the selection for the patient and thus a dish which the patient does not like may be inadvertently ordered.

3.5 Inevitably, there will be occasions when the food is of poor quality, or has been badly cooked, or has been spoiled, or is badly presented. The most commonly voiced criticism of meals sent to wards is that they have been allowed to get cold. Central kitchens may supply items which, however good the delivery system, will deteriorate en route – toast, scrambled or boiled eggs for example. This all leads to one result – the food is unappetizing and the patients reject it.

3.6 Waste also occurs in staff restaurants particularly when the predicted demand is inaccurate and too many portions are supplied. If the items are delivered in too large batches, some portions will stand too long and deteriorate.

APPENDIX D
EXAMPLES OF 'QUALIFIED' AUDIT REPORTS

APPROPRIATION ACCOUNTS
(VOLUME 8: CLASSES XI–XII), 1985–86
REPORT OF THE COMPTROLLER AND
AUDITOR-GENERAL
Class XII, Vote 1: Pension and Disability
Benefits (Non-Contributory)
Class XII, Vote 2: Supplementary Benefits
Class XII, Vote 3: Family Benefits

Social Security payments: Estimated and statistical accounting

1. In 1985–86 expenditure on non–contributory benefits charged to Class XII, Votes 1 to 3 amounted to £14,258 million. Contributory benefits paid from the National Insurance Fund amounted to £22,309 million, making a total of £36,567 million. As recorded in notes to these accounts and accounts for earlier years, DHSS consider that it would be uneconomic to keep detailed accounting records of expenditure on over 30 benefits involved. They therefore employ estimates and statistical analysis methods to apportion part of the total benefit expenditure between the National Insurance Fund and the Votes and to make further allocations between the Vote subheads concerned. Such an approach was accepted by the Committee of Public Accounts in their 26th Report of

Session 1979–80. DHSS indicate in a note to each account the extent to which they have apportioned expenditure in this way. Nevertheless it is possible for the use of such methods to result in significant misallocations of the payments made.

2. Additional notes to Class XII, Votes 1 and 2, 1985–86, record that as there is some evidence of inconsistencies between statistical information from different sources, the apportionment of the total expenditure, though not the total expenditure itself, is subject to a higher margin of uncertainty than usual. Further work is being carried out by DHSS to reconcile the data and adjustments to the 1985–86 figures may therefore have to be made in subsequent accounts.

3. In view of the circumstances described in paragraphs 1 and 2 above, I am unable to give an unqualified certificate to these accounts.

CLASS XII, VOTE 2: SUPPLEMENTARY BENEFITS

Excess of expenditure over grant

4. The Account shows expenditure of £312,981,786 (4.3 per cent) in excess of the gross Estimate, which, as increased by a Supplementary Estimate presented in November 1985 (HC 9 of 1985–86) and a Revised Supplementary Estimate in February 1986 (HC 249 of 1985–86), amounted to £7,319,000,000. There were surplus receipts of classes authorised to be used as Appropriations-in-Aid of £3,214,339. It is proposed to ask Parliament to authorise these surplus receipts to be appropriated in aid towards meeting the excess, leaving a sum of £309,767,447.12 to be voted as a further supply grant.

5. Excess expenditure was incurred on subhead A1, Supplementary pensions, etc, where the provision of £944 million was overspent by £133.3 million (14.1 per cent), and on subhead A2, Supplementary allowances, etc, where the provision of £6,375 million was overspent by £179.7 million (2.8 per cent). DHSS informed me that in-year monitoring of expenditure must rest on forecasts based on expenditure trends in previous months because accounts of amounts paid by encashment agencies are not available until several weeks after the event. An error in a new forecasting system, which meant that forecasts of supplementary allowance paid to the unemployed were £130 million too low, was

detected too late to seek supplementary provision. In addition, actual expenditure in the final months of the financial year, details of which were not available until after the end of the year, was higher than forecast. Explanation for this discrepancy will not be available until relevant statistical information has been analysed. The Department also informed me that re-apportionment, under the procedure referred to in paragraphs 1 and 2 above, of certain order book and girocheque expenditure to take account of statistical data received after the end of the financial year increased the estimated amounts of expenditure on benefits charged to the Account, with a corresponding decrease in the charge to the National Insurance Fund.

REFERENCES

(Full publication details of books here referred to in a shortened form can be found in the Bibliography)

Chapter 1

1. Public Expenditure White Paper, 1986, p. 403.
2. Pliatzky, *Getting and Spending*, p. 161.
3. Hansard, 6 December 1984, col. 541.
4. Hansard, 6 December 1984, col. 525.
5. Barnett, *Inside the Treasury*, pp. 124–5.
6. House of Commons Social Services Select Committee, 'Public Expenditure on the Social Services. Minutes of Evidence. Department of Health and Social Security', Session 1982–83, HC 321, p. 3.
7. Adolf Wagner, *Finanzwissenschaft*, Leipzig, 1890.
8. Peacock and Wiseman, *The Growth of Public Expenditure in the United Kingdom*.
9. W. J. Baumol, 'Macroeconomics of Unbalanced Growth', *American Economic Review*, 242 (1967), pp. 415–26.
10. J. M. Buchanan and G. Tullock, *The Calculus of Consent*, University of Michigan Press, Ann Arbor, 1962.

Chapter 2

1. Rose, *Ministers and Ministries*, p. 243.
2. Public Expenditure White Paper, 1988.

Chapter 3

1. Pliatzky, *Getting and Spending*, p. 53.
2. Hansard, 20 February 1986, col. 507.
3. Hansard, 6 December 1984, col. 588.
4. Heald and Rose, *The Public Expenditure Process: Learning by Doing*.

5. Bruce-Gardyne, *Ministers and Mandarins*, pp. 203–8.
6. Barnett, *Inside the Treasury*, pp. 103, 155.
7. Young and Sloman, *But Chancellor*, p. 24.
8. ibid., p. 108.
9. ibid., p. 44.
10. ibid., p. 113.
11. Hansard, 20 February 1986, col. 502.
12. Second Report, Session 1986–87, HC 27, p. x.
13. Hood and Wright, *Big Government in Hard Times*, p. 213.
14. Barnett, op. cit., p. 99.
15. Barnett, op. cit., p. 190.
16. Second Report, Session 1986–87, HC 27, p. x.
17. D. Tarschys, 'Curbing Public Expenditure: Current Trends', *Journal of Public Policy*, vol. 5, No. 1, 1985, pp. 42–3.
18. D. Wass, *Government and the Governed*, Routledge & Kegan Paul, 1984, pp. 13–14.
19. Hennessey, *Cabinet*, p. 45.
20. House of Commons Treasury and Civil Service Select Committee, First Report, Session 1984–85, HC 44 and vii.
21. Young and Sloman, op. cit., p. 56.
22. Barnett, op. cit., pp. 154–5.
23. S. Jenkins, 'The "Star Chamber", PESC and the Cabinet', *Political Quarterly*, vol. 56, No. 2, 1985, p. 115.
24. Public Finance Foundation, *Collective Decision-making in Government*, p. 29.
25. Hansard, 6 December 1984, col. 624.
26. Hansard, 6 December 1984, col. 588.
27. Public Finance Foundation, op. cit., p. 26.

Chapter 4

1. Hansard, 17 December 1986, cols. 1266–7.
2. Heclo and Wildavsky, *The Private Government of Public Money*, pp. xxiv, xv.
3. Economic Progress Report 139, H.M. Treasury, November 1981.
4. Armstrong *et al.*, *Budgetary Reform in the United Kingdom*, para. 3.4.
5. White Paper, 'Cash Limits on Public Expenditure', Cmnd 6440, 1976.
6. Pliatzky, *Getting and Spending*, pp. 145–6.
7. Third Report, Session 1986–87, HC 153, p. vii.
8. L. Pliatzky, 'Have Volumes Gone Underground? An Interim Report on Cash Planning', *Public Administration*, vol. 61, no. 3, pp. 325–6.

9. T. Ward, 'PESC in Crisis', *Policy and Politics*, vol. 11, no. 2, 1983, p. 169.
10. Pliatzky, op. cit., p. 143.
11. Bruce-Gardyne, *Ministers and Mandarins*, p. 208.
12. 1985.
13. Third Report, Session 1982–83, HC 204, pp. xvi–xvii.
14. Hansard, 18 February 1987, col. 932.
15. A. Likierman and S. Bloomfield, 'Squaring the Circle', *Policy and Politics*, vol. 14, no. 3, 1986, p. 305.

Chapter 5

1. M. Heseltine, 'Ministers and Management in Whitehall', *Management Services in Government*, No. 35, 1980.
2. 'Government Observations on Third Report, Treasury and Civil Service Select Committee, Session 1981–82', Cmnd 8618, 1982.
3. Butt and Palmer, *Value for Money in the Public Sector*, p. 22.
4. Fulton Committee, 'Report on the Civil Service', vol. 1, Cmnd 3638, 1968.
5. 'The Financial Management Initiative', HC 588, 1986.
6. Hansard, 18 February 1987, col. 931.
7. C. Pollitt, 'Beyond the Managerial Model. The case for broadening performance assessment in government and the public services', *Financial Accountability and Management*, Autumn 1986, p. 168.
8. N. Flynn, 'Performance Measurement in Public Sector Services', *Policy and Politics*, vol. 14, no. 3, 1986, pp. 401–2.
9. Public Finance Foundation, *Public Domain 1987*, Public Finance Foundation, 1987.
10. G. Downey, 'Public Accountability: Fact or Myth', *Public Money*, June 1986.
11. D. Watts and B. Preston, 'Implementing the FMI in the Court Service', *Public Finance and Accountancy*, 1 January 1987.
12. M. Whitbread, in Gretton and Harrison (eds.), *Reshaping the Public Sector*.
13. H.M. Treasury, 'Multi-departmental Review of Budgeting', Phase 1, Central Report, 1985; Final Central Report, 1986.
14. S. Richards, in Gretton and Harrison, op. cit.
15. J. Fielden, 'Financial Management and Public Spending', in *Public Finance Foundation Discussion Paper No. 3*, 1985.
16. P. Willingham, 'The Inland Revenue's Response to the FMI', *Public Finance and Accountancy*, 17 October 1986.
17. A. Walker, 'Building on a Firm Foundation', *Public Finance and Accountancy*, 20 June 1986.
18. S. F. Thorpe-Tracey, 'The Financial Management Initiative in Practice:

Newcastle Central Office', *Public Administration*, vol. 65, no. 3, Autumn 1987.

Chapter 6

1. *Financial Times*, 26 July 1987.
2. S. Lewis and A. Harrison, 'Cash Planning in the Public Sector: Theory, Practice and Learning by Doing', *Public Money*, March 1985.
3. Hansard, 25 March 1987, cols. 482–3 (Mr W. Hamilton).

Chapter 7

1. Standing Order No. 46.
2. Third Report, Session 1985–86, HC 192, p. 3.
3. Marsh, *Policy-Making in a Three-Party System*, pp. 50–52.
4. Liaison Committee, First Report, Session 1982–83, HC 92.
5. Quoted in Likierman and Vass, *The Structure and Form of Government Expenditure Reports*.
6. S. Low, *The Governance of England*, Allen & Unwin, 1904, p. 90.
7. First Report, Session 1977–78, HC 588.
8. First Report, Session 1980–81, HC 118, p. xviii.
9. Third Report, Session 1985–86, HC 192, p. vi.
10. Hansard, 18 February 1987, col. 960.
11. 'Fiscal Crisis and Parliamentary Democracy', in *British Politics in Perspective*, ed. R. L. Borthwick and J. E. Spence, Leicester University Press, 1984, p. 161.
12. Likierman and Vass, op. cit.
13. Second Report, Session 1984–85, HC 110.
14. 'Financial Reporting to Parliament', HC 576, 1986.
15. Eighth Report, Session 1986–87, HC 98.
16. Treasury Minute Cm 177, 1987, p. 2.
17. A. Robinson, 'The Financial Work of the New Select Committees', in Drewry (ed.), *The New Select Committees*, p. 318.
18. ibid., p. 308.

Chapter 8

1. Government internal audit manual, H.M. Treasury, 1983.
2. Session 1984–85, HC 513.
3. Session 1985–86, HC 395.
4. Session 1984–85, HC 571.
5. Session 1986–87, HC 44.

References 211

6. Session 1986–87, HC 149.
7. Session 1985–86, HC 441.
8. Session 1985–86, HC 212.
9. Fourteenth Report, Session 1986–87, HC 262, p. x.
10. Twelfth Report, Session 1986–87, HC 185, p. ix.
11. Glynn, *Public Sector Accounting and Financial Control*, pp. 119–20.

Appendix A

1. British Council Report, 1985–86, p. 7.
2. Department of Transport, 'Expenditure on Motorways and Trunk Roads', HC 571, p. 8.
3. H.M. Treasury, 'Investment Appraisal in the Public Sector: a technical guide for government departments', 1984.

BIBLIOGRAPHY

Journal and other articles; parliamentary and official publications

This book covers matters within the scope of several subject-disciplines, including economics, politics, public administration and accountancy. It is also concerned with what is very much a topical subject, where there are frequent policy changes and developments of ideas by the government, in Parliament and among academics. There are therefore a very large number of professional and academic journals where material on the public spending process might appear. Moreover, in each parliamentary session there is fresh, relevant evidence from officials and Ministers to Select Committees, and additional contributions in debate on the floor of the House of Commons.

Bearing in mind the wide scope of the subject and its evolving nature, this Bibliography lists only books. Articles and parliamentary material are included in the References when extracts have been quoted in the text. But to keep up to date with developments, it is well worth looking at the latest edition of the Public Expenditure White Paper (but see page ix), Autumn Statement, and Financial Statement and Budget Report, published, as are all official documents, by Her Majesty's Stationery Office. The most recent reports of the House of Commons Treasury and Civil Service Select Committee on the Public Expenditure White Paper and the Autumn Statement will provide a good indication of current preoccupations (both technical and political). The House of Commons debates on the two documents give a reminder of the limitations of the role of Parliament. For a flavour of the scrutiny process, the reports of other departmental Select Committees on expenditure matters are also well worth looking at, as are recent reports of the Public Accounts Committee.

Among journals publishing articles on public expenditure matters are *Financial Accountability and Management, Parliamentary Affairs, Policy and Politics, Political Quarterly, Political Studies, Public Administration, Public Finance and Accountancy* and *Public Money* (now *Public Money and Management*). The Public

Finance Foundation also produces very useful material in this area in the form of books, pamphlets and other publications. With all these sources it is worth looking through recent issues to keep abreast of developments.

Books

ARMSTRONG *et al.* (1980), *Budgetary Reform in the UK*, Report of a Committee chaired by Lord Armstrong, Oxford University Press for the Institute of Fiscal Studies.

BARNETT, J. (1982), *Inside the Treasury*, André Deutsch.

BEARD, G. C. (1985), *Government Finance and Accounts*, Civil Service College.

BOURN, J. (1979), *Management in Central and Local Government*, Pitman.

BRIDGES, LORD (1964), *The Treasury*, George Allen & Unwin.

BROWN, C. V., and JACKSON, P. (1986), *Public Sector Economics*, 3rd ed., Martin Robertson.

BROWNING, P. (1986), *The Treasury and Economic Policy, 1964–85*, Longmans.

BRUCE-GARDYNE, J. (1986), *Ministers and Mandarins*, Sidgwick & Jackson.

BUTT, H., and PALMER, B. (1985), *Value for Money in the Public Sector*, Blackwell, Oxford.

BYRNE, T. (1986), *Local Government in Britain*, Penguin.

CABINET OFFICE and H.M. TREASURY (1985), *Government Accounting*, HMSO.

CARTER, C. (1984), *The Purposes of Government Expenditure*, Institute of Policy Studies.

CENTRAL STATISTICAL OFFICE (1985), *United Kingdom National Accounts: Sources and Methods*, HMSO.

CENTRAL STATISTICAL OFFICE (1986), *Guide to Official Statistics*, HMSO.

CIVIL SERVICE COLLEGE (1983), *Developments in Financial Management in Central Government*, Note of a Civil Service College Seminar.

COCKLE, P. (1985), *Public Expenditure Policy*, Macmillan.

CURWEN, P. J. (1986), *Public Enterprise: A Modern Approach*, Wheatsheaf.

DIAMOND, J. (1975), *Public Expenditure in Practice*, Allen & Unwin.

DREWRY, G. (ed.) (1985), *The New Select Committees*, Clarendon Press, Oxford.

ENGLEFIELD, D. (1985), *Whitehall and Westminister*, Longman.

ERSKINE, MAY (1983), *Parliamentary Practice: The Law, Privileges, Proceedings and Usage of Parliament*, 20th ed., C. Gordon (ed.), Butterworths.

FLEGMANN, V. (1986), *Public Expenditure and the Select Committees of the Commons*, Gower.

FORTE, F., and PEACOCK, A. T. (1975), *Public Expenditure and Government Growth*, Blackwell, Oxford.

GLYNN, J. J. (1985), *Value for Money Auditing in the Public Sector*, Prentice-

Hall in association with the Institute of Chartered Accountants in England and Wales.

GLYNN, J. J. (1987), *Public Sector Financial Control and Accounting*, Blackwell, Oxford.

GRETTON, J., and HARRISON, A. (eds.) (1987), *Reshaping the Public Sector*, Policy Journals.

HAM, A. (1981), *Treasury Rules*, Quartet.

HEALD, D. (1983), *Public Expenditure*, Martin Robertson.

HEALD, D., and ROSE, R. (eds.) (1987), *The Public Expenditure Process: Learning by Doing*, Public Finance Foundation.

HECLO, H., and WILDAVSKY, A. (1981), *The Private Government of Public Money*, Macmillan.

HENLEY, D., HOLTHAM, C., LIKIERMAN, A., and PERRIN, J. (1986), *Public Sector Accounting and Financial Control*, 2nd edn., Van Nostrand.

HENNESSEY, P. (1986), *Cabinet*, Blackwell, Oxford.

HESELTINE, M. (1987), *Where there's a will*, Hutchinson.

HILL, D. (ed.) (1984), *Parliamentary Select Committees in Action*, Strathclyde Papers on Government and Politics No. 24.

H.M. GOVERNMENT (1976), *Cash Limits on Public Expenditure*, Cmnd 6440, HMSO.

H.M. GOVERNMENT (1980), *Report on Non-Departmental Bodies*, Cmnd 7797, HMSO.

H.M. GOVERNMENT (1982), *Efficiency and Effectiveness in the Civil Service*, Cmnd 8618, HMSO.

H.M. TREASURY (1977), *Supply and Financial Procedures of the House of Commons*, H.M. Treasury.

H.M. TREASURY (1986), *The Management of Public Spending*, HMSO.

H.M. TREASURY (annual), *Supply Estimates, Summary and Guide, HMSO*.

HOOD, C., and WRIGHT, M. (eds.) (1981), *Big Government in Hard Times*, Martin Robertson.

HOPWOOD, A., and TOMPKINS, C. (1984), *Issues in Public Sector Accounting*, Phillip Allen.

JOHNSON, N. (1966), *Parliament and Administration: The Estimates Committee 1945–65*, Allen & Unwin.

LEVITT, M. S. (ed.) (1987), *New Priorities in Public Spending*, Gower.

LEVITT, M. S., and JOYCE, M. A. S. (1987), *The Growth and Efficiency of Public Spending*, Cambridge University Press.

LEVITT, R., and WALL, A. (1984), *The Reorganized Health Service*, 3rd ed., Croom Helm.

LEWIS, S. (ed.) (1986), *Output and Performance Measurement in Central Government: Progress in Departments*, H.M. Treasury.

LIKIERMAN, A. (1981), *Cash Limits and External Financing Limits*, Civil Service College Handbook No. 22, HMSO.

LIKIERMAN, A., and VASS, P. (1984), *The Structure and Form of Government Expenditure Reports*, Association of Certified Accountants Educational Trust.

LYNN, J., and JAY, A. (eds.) (1981), *The Complete Yes Minister*, BBC Publications.

MACKINTOSH, D. (1984), *The Government and Politics of Britain*, 6th ed., Hutchinson.

MADGEWICK, P., and ROSE, R. (eds.) (1982), *The Territorial Dimension in United Kingdom Politics*, Macmillan.

MARSH, I. (1986), *Policy-Making in a Three-Party System*, Methuen.

NATIONAL AUDIT OFFICE (1986), *Financial Reporting to Parliament*, HC 576, HMSO.

NISKANEN, W. (1971), *Bureaucracy and Representative Government*, Aldine, Chicago.

ORGANIZATION FOR ECONOMIC CO-OPERATION AND DEVELOPMENT (1985), 'The Role of the Public Sector', *Economic Studies No. 41*, Organization for Economic Co-operation and Development.

PEACOCK, A., and WISEMAN, J. (1967), *The Growth of Public Expenditure in the United Kingdom*, rev. ed., Allen & Unwin.

PEAT MARWICK MITCHELL & CO. (1984), *Financial Management in the Public Sector*.

PLIATZKY, L. (1982), *Getting and Spending*, Blackwell, Oxford.

PREST, A. R., and COPPOCK, D. J. (1984), *The UK Economy*, 10th ed., Weidenfeld & Nicolson.

PUBLIC FINANCE FOUNDATION (1985), *Collective Decision-making in Government*, Public Finance Foundation.

PUBLIC FINANCE FOUNDATION (1986), *Collective Decision-making on Public Expenditure*, Public Finance Foundation.

PUNNETT, R. M. (1980), *British Government and Politics*, 4th ed., Heinemann.

ROBINSON, A. (1978), *Parliament and Public Spending*, Heinemann.

ROSE, R. (1982), *Understanding the United Kingdom: the Territorial Dimension in Government*, Longman.

ROSE, R. (1984), *Understanding Big Government*, Sage.

ROSE, R. (1987), *Ministers and Ministries*, Oxford University Press.

SILK, P. (1987), *How Parliament Works*, Longman.

THOMPSON, G. (1979), *The Growth of the Government Sector*, Open University Press.

WALSHE, G. (1987), *Planning Public Spending*, Macmillan.

WRIGHT, M. (ed.) (1980), *Public Spending Decisions*, Allen & Unwin.

YOUNG, H., and SLOMAN, A. (1984), *But Chancellor*, BBC Publications.

ACRONYMS

ACAS	Advisory, Conciliation and Arbitration Service
APEX	Analysis of Public Expenditure System
BBC	British Broadcasting Corporation
BSC	British Steel Corporation
C and AG	Comptroller and Auditor-General
CSO	Central Statistical Office
DAS	District Audit Service
DE	Department of Employment
DEn	Department of Energy
DHA	District Health Authority
DHSS	Department of Health and Social Security
DoE	Department of the Environment
DTI	Department of Trade and Industry
DTp	Department of Transport
EFL	External Financing Limit
FCO	Foreign and Commonwealth Office
FIS	Financial Information System
FMI	Financial Management Initiative
FSBR	Financial Statement and Budget Report
GDP	Gross Domestic Product
GNP	Gross National Product
HMSO	Her Majesty's Stationery Office
HPSS	Health and Personal Social Services
IFR	Investment and Financing Review
MAFF	Ministry of Agriculture, Fisheries and Food
MINIS	Management Information System for Ministers
MP	Member of Parliament
MPO	Management and Personnel Office
MOD	Ministry of Defence

MSC	Manpower Services Commission
NAO	National Audit Office
NATO	North Atlantic Treaty Organization
NHS	National Health Service
NLF	National Loans Fund
ODA	Overseas Development Administration
OECD	Organization for Economic Co-operation and Development
OMCS	Office of the Minister for the Civil Service
PAC	Public Accounts Committee
PESC	Public Expenditure Survey Committee
PEWP	Public Expenditure White Paper
PQ	Parliamentary Question
RAWP	Regional Allocation Working Party
RHA	Regional Health Authority
RPE	Relative Price Effect
RSG	Rate Support Grant
SHA	Special Health Authority
VAT	Value Added Tax
vfm	value for money

SELECTED GLOSSARY

Accounting Officer

An officer appointed, normally by the Treasury in compliance with Section 22 of the Exchequer and Audit Department Act 1866, to sign the Appropriation Accounts, and any other accounts within his responsibility. The principal witness on behalf of the department before the Committee of Public Accounts to deal with questions arising from those accounts or reports by the C and AG on matters for which he is accountable.

Appropriation Accounts

An end-of-year account of government departments' spending of monies voted by Parliament which compares the Supply Estimate (down to subhead level, but not below) with actual payments made and receipts brought to account, and explains any substantial differences. An Appropriation Account is prepared for each Vote, audited, and submitted to Parliament.

Appropriation Act

The statute which authorizes issues from the Consolidated Fund, and appropriates all money granted by Parliament to some distinct use.

Appropriation in Aid

Receipts which, with the authority of Parliament, are used to finance some of the gross expenditure on a Vote.

Block Grant

The sum available for distribution to local authorities after deducting from Rate Support Grant (q.v.) money paid as domestic rate relief grant.

Capital Expenditure

Expenditure on new construction, land, and extensions of and alterations to existing buildings and the purchase of any other fixed assets (e.g. machinery and plant) – including vehicles – having an expected working life of more than one year. Also includes stocks, grants for capital purposes, and lending.

Cash Limit

A planned limit on the amount of cash the government proposes to spend or authorize on certain services over a period of one financial year.

Cash Terms

The cost of inputs at the price levels current during the year in which spending is incurred.

Central Government

Parliament, government departments and the Northern Ireland departments, extra-departmental government funds (the largest of which is the National Insurance Fund) and a substantial number of other bodies which are wholly or partly financed from government funds and which do not undertake commercial-type activities as a major part of their work. The National Health Service is by far the largest. In addition there are a small number of trading organizations, whose current expenditure is excluded from public expenditure, but subsidies to them are included.

Class

A group of Votes which broadly correspond to the voted expenditure element of one of the main programmes in the Public Expenditure Survey (PES).

Consolidated Fund

The government's main account with the Bank of England. The larger part of central government expenditure is financed from this fund and the government's tax revenues and other current receipts are paid into it.

Contingencies Fund

A fund which can be used for urgent expenditure in anticipation of provision by Parliament becoming available. It is administered by the Treasury under strict rules agreed with Parliament. Drawings on the Fund must be repaid when Parliament has voted the additional sums required.

Cost Terms

Expenditure in cash terms, adjusted for changes in an index of prices in the economy as a whole. An index often used is the GDP deflator.

Current Expenditure

Current expenditure on goods and services includes direct expenditure by central and local government on providing services (e.g. health or education), but the operating costs of general government trading bodies (e.g. local transport undertakings) are not included. Current expenditure on goods and services is measured net of charges made for certain goods and services. By longstanding convention, notional allowances from non-trading capital consumption (the 'using-up' of schools, hospitals, roads, etc.) are omitted. Virtually all defence spending, on buildings as well as on equipment, is treated as current expenditure on goods and services in conformity with international accounting conventions.

External Financing Limits

(a) A form of cash limit for a nationalized industry.
(b) A means of controlling the amount of finance (grants and borrowing) which an industry can raise in any financial year from external sources.

Financial Information System

A computerized system used by the Treasury to monitor information about the flow of voted and some other expenditure.

Financial Statement and Budget Report

The report presented to the House of Commons by the Chancellor of the Exchequer at the time of the Budget, giving details of the economic background to the Budget, and of public sector transactions.

Financial Year

The year from 1 April to 31 March.

General Government

The central government and local authorities sectors consolidated.

Gross Domestic Product

The value of the goods and services produced by United Kingdom residents, including taxes on expenditure on both home-produced and imported goods and services, and the effect of subsidies. No deduction is made for depreciation of existing assets. (Gross *national* product includes the income of United Kingdom residents from economic activity abroad and property held abroad, less the corresponding income in the United Kingdom of non-residents.)

National Loans Fund

The government's account with the Bank of England through which all government borrowing transactions (including payment of debt interest) and most lending transactions are handled.

Nationalized Industries

An industry owned or controlled by the government.

Out-turn

Expenditure actually incurred.

Parliamentary Session

The parliamentary year, usually starting in early November.

Planning Total

The aggregate used by the government for public expenditure control purposes. It excludes general government gross debt interest but includes the external finance of most public corporations.

Private Sector

Industrial and commercial companies, financial institutions and the personal sector.

Programme

Public expenditure analysed by the purpose of the spending.

Public Corporations

Publicly owned trading bodies with a substantial degree of financial independence – including the powers to borrow and to maintain reserves from central government and local authorities. They include nationalized industries and other bodies.

Public Expenditure

Expenditure by the public sector comprising current and capital expenditure of central government and local authorities and borrowing by public corporations.

Public Expenditure Survey Committee (PESC)

An interdepartmental coordinating committee of officials, chaired by the Treasury, to consider public expenditure matters. Often used as a synonym for Survey (q.v.).

Public Sector

Central government, local authorities and public corporations (including nationalized industries).

Rate Support Grant

The unhypothecated grant from central government to supplement local authorities' own finances, so that each authority can provide the services for which it is responsible to similar standards while charging a similar rate in the pound to its ratepayers. In addition, specific grants are made for certain services.

Relative Price Effect

The phenomenon of wages paid by the public sector changing at different rates to the rate of general price increase in the economy as a whole, thereby affecting the relative costs both from programme to programme and between public services and the economy generally.

Reserve

An amount, unallocated at first, within the total of public expenditure for a given year which is intended to cover unforeseen items of expenditure and items which cannot be properly quantified when plans are published.

Running Costs

Departmental running costs include the gross costs of the administration of central government, including the pay of civil servants, plus the pay of those members of the armed forces engaged in headquarters and support activities and all costs of accommodation, travel, training, etc.

Subhead

Expenditure within a Vote which is separately identified in Estimates and the Appropriation Account.

Supplementary Estimate

A request to Parliament during the course of the financial year to obtain additional money either for a new service or to make good inadequacies for existing services.

Supply Estimate

A statement, presented to the House of Commons, of the estimated expenditure of a department during a financial year, with a request for the necessary funds to be voted.

Survey

The annual review of public expenditure plans undertaken by the government.

Trading Fund

A specific form of trading concern which is a government department but is treated as a public corporation for statistical and planning purposes.

Virement

Transfer of savings on one subhead to meet excess expenditure on another subhead within the same Vote.

Volume Terms

Expenditure in cash terms adjusted for changes in price of each input.

Vote

An individual Supply Estimate.

Votes on Account

Monies granted by Parliament to carry on public services from 1 April of the following financial year until Parliament has approved that year's money by means of the Appropriation Act, which authorizes the issue of the amount required for the full year.

INDEX

Page references in italics indicate Figures; those in bold type, Tables.